INDISTINGUISHABLE FROM MAGIC

CATHERYNNE M. VALENTE

mad
norwegian
press

Published by Mad Norwegian Press (www.madnorwegian.com).
Editor-in-Chief: Lars Pearson.
Cover art: Amy Houser.
Jacket & interior design: Matt Dirkx and Christa Dickson.
ISBN: 978-1935234135
Printed in Illinois. First Printing: March 2014.

Also available from Mad Norwegian Press...

Chicks Dig Time Lords: A Celebration of Doctor Who by the Women Who Love It,
edited by Lynne M Thomas and Tara O'Shea
2011 Hugo Award Winner, Best Related Work

*Chicks Unravel Time: Women Journey Through Every Season
of Doctor Who,* edited by Deborah Stanish and LM Myles
2013 Hugo Award Nominee, Best Related Work

*Chicks Dig Comics: A Celebration of Comic Books
by the Women Who Love Them,*
edited by Lynne M Thomas and Sigrid Ellis
2013 Hugo Award Nominee, Best Related Work

*Whedonistas: A Celebration of the Worlds of Joss Whedon by the Women
Who Love Them,* edited by Lynne M. Thomas and Deborah Stanish

*Queers Dig Time Lords: A Celebration of Doctor Who
by the LGBTQ Fans Who Love It,*
edited by Sigrid Ellis and Michael Damian Thomas

Space Helmet for a Cow: An Unlikely 50-Year History of Doctor Who
by Paul Kirkley (forthcoming)

AHistory: An Unauthorized History of the Doctor Who Universe [3rd Edition]
by Lance Parkin and Lars Pearson

*Running Through Corridors: Rob and Toby's Marathon Watch
of Doctor Who* (Vol. 1: The 60s) by Robert Shearman and Toby Hadoke

*Wanting to Believe: A Critical Guide to The X-Files, Millennium
and The Lone Gunmen* by Robert Shearman

Redeemed: The Unauthorized Guide to Angel (ebook only)
by Lars Pearson and Christa Dickson

Dusted: The Unauthorized Guide to Buffy the Vampire Slayer (ebook only)
by Lawrence Miles, Lars Pearson and Christa Dickson

Table of Contents

Table of Contents

Mars Needs Women: Gender, Race and Storytelling

Indistinguishable from Magic:
Fairy Tales, Myth and the Future

Life on Earth: An Amateur's Guide

Scholar, Poet, Mermaid, Witch

This is all about stories. Remember that, and you'll be fine.

The first time I met Catherynne Valente, it was late at night. She was bright and vivacious, a midnight autumn girl in her element, and I hated her instantly. I snarled and scowled and slunk away to bed, convinced on some deep and indelible level that I had met my nemesis.

The first time Cat Valente met me - because I don't believe everyone meets at the same time; sometimes one party is asleep, or unaware, or having such a bad day that they no longer see anyone outside the structure of their own skin - it was early morning. I was perky and enthusiastic, a midday autumn girl in my element, and from the way she reacted, I'd be willing to bet that her initial reaction was a lot like my own.

With most people, that would be where the story ended. Catherynne Valente, as you will quickly come to learn (if you don't already know - she isn't a secret to be hoarded, but a story to be shared, as all the best stories are), is not most people. We met each other for first time on a train speeding under the San Francisco Bay, and the details of that story belong somewhere entirely other than here, except to say that there is power in threes, and power in differences, but most of all, there is power in stories.

Cat is a story. She is also a storyteller - and this is not a contradiction. Many stories tell themselves. She is a poet and a poem, wrapped up in the same star-and-moon-tanned palimpsest skin. She contains many contradictions. She's the serious mermaid explaining to you why trading fins for feet was a feminist action, and why the sacrifice of a voice is sometimes a simple thing, because there are so many kinds of voices, child; the sea witch left you fingers, left you figures, left you everything you'll ever need to make this tale your own. She's the laughing gingerbread witch standing by the chicken coop, feathers in her hair on a promise on her lips that you may or may not want to hear, because promises are prophecies, in their own way, in their own time. She is her own once upon a time, and her own happy ending, and those are two of the best things in the world to be.

But no story happens in total isolation. Cat is a product of her time, an academic who cut her teeth on Chaucer and Homer and other, stranger sources, who can quote *Under Milk Wood* without any preparation or provocation. She thinks in organized lines, citing her references, coaxing her footnotes into careful positions, like she's planning a school pageant and inviting the entire world. She is also a wild pop culture creature, a scholar of *Buffy the Vampire Slayer* and modern monsters, who is almost as likely to begin gleefully declaiming lines from *Final Destination* and *Jason X*. Her compositions are wildly overgrown gardens, sprouting sentences like brambles that bear the sweet fruit of words you've never heard before, but already understand. She is completely linear; there is nothing of the linear about her. This is her contradiction, and she wears it so well that most people never even realize her secret.

Cat Valente does not exist. She can't: she's too unreasonable. A poet and storyteller living in a house on an island in Maine, surrounded by tall, thin trees like the tines of a comb, defended by two vast dogs from different sides of the world, attended by two equally vast cats, one striped like the shadows in the wood, the other black and white as day and night? A mermaid in denim and lace, with a map written across her shoulders, who can discuss video games and anchorites in the same breath - and will, if you give her half a chance and a quarter of an excuse? No. She can't be real. We must have invented her for some reason, spinning her out of wholecloth and nettles...

But that does her a disservice, and does us one as well. Catherynne Valente is flesh and blood and bone, as real as Tuesday morning and as fleeting as a seiche in the shadow of a storm. She's very real, and very much as contradictory as she sounds.

When Cat concentrates, she looks like she will devour the world. When Cat smiles, she looks like she's just discovered the secret truth behind everything she's ever wanted to know, and is about to share it all with you. I would walk a hundred miles to make her laugh. She has been there for me when I was scared, or sick, or alone, and I know that if I called her tonight and told her I was any of those things, she would come. She's that kind of person, and that kind of friend, and that's so much more than any fiction, don't you think? Catherynne Valente exists because she needs to, because she is as complicated and complete as anything, and the world deserves as many complicated, complete people as it can get.

"But Seanan," you may say at this point, "what does this have to do with the book in my hands? You haven't mentioned Pluto, you haven't told me what I'm about to read, you've just said a lot of weird stuff about mermaids and stories and Cat Valente - and I know she wrote the book, her name is on the cover."

Ah, but you see, I've been talking about the book from the start. Didn't I warn you that this was all going to be about stories?

What you are holding is not a book of fiction. If you had somehow come to the conclusion that it was, I dearly hope that you have not paid for it yet, because you will be happier if you put it down, pause for a moment, and then pick it up again, saying to yourself, "This is not a book of fiction." You should come to this table with a clear mind and an eager heart. No, this is something much stranger, and in some ways more dangerous:

This is a book of stories about the way the world actually is.

It's about connecting with other people, despite the difficulty of finding a way to do it. It's about being insecure, about being frightened, about being outside and wanting a way in. It's also a book about finding all the ways you could ever want, about stepping into the party in your goose feather gown and your slippers of glass, and knowing that you can *own* that shit. It's about navigating both the world as it is and the world as it ought to be. And yes, there's a lot in here about stories. How to write them, how not to write them, how to find your voice and how to sell it to the sea witch, if that's what it takes to make you happy. Stories are the key to everything. Stories about stories may well be the most powerful kind.

Most of all, this is a book about - and by - Catherynne Valente. Your soul gets bared in a very special way when you tell the truth about the world as it is, rather than spinning a safe and sheltering once upon a time. When you read these pages, you will be meeting pieces of Cat. Maybe you'll meet them at night, and maybe you'll meet them in the morning, and maybe you'll meet them on a train passing underneath the sea, but however you meet them, I hope you will be kind to them, and let them be kind to you in turn.

The best stories always ache to be shared. We want to pass them around, once we have them; we want to whisper "look, look" and encourage others to experience them the way that we did.

This is the story of my friend.

Please share it with me.

Seanan McGuire
January 2014

Seanan McGuire lives and writes on the western coast of North America, where she tries not to be bitten by anything that will kill her, as death would interfere with her deadlines. She shares her home with three abnormally large blue cats and a distressing assortment of creepy dolls, and writes an improbable number of books on an annual basis. When not writing or placating the cats, Seanan enjoys travel, visiting Disney Parks, and lurking in haunted corn mazes, where she regularly frightens the masked dude with the chainsaw.

Pluto is Not a Planet

Pop Culture and Genre

Let's Go to Work

These days, it's almost a Cartesian axiom: I am a geeky postmodern girl, therefore I love *Buffy the Vampire Slayer*.

Of course I loved *Buffy*. She's only a couple of years younger than I am (depending on the continuity) and she had this whole high school experience that I had, too, though with fewer vampires. Not *none* - no one gets through life without falling under the spell of someone who just needs you to feed themselves. No one gets out of this fully sanginated. But I had a close knit circle that frayed as age and culture clash took hold, a feeling of standing on the brink of something, of trying so hard to hold onto everything, always, in the terribly bright California sun. I have always been baffled at people's attachment to *Sex in the City*, the endless are you a Carrie or a Miranda - but I was so terribly attached, and I can tell you without shame that I was a Willow, and for awhile, in the long, dreamlike desert between the end of college and the beginning of life, I had demons, and I had trials, and I had *Buffy*.

But for all that, I am not here to talk to you about that show. The fact is, I was just off the bubble of being able to watch the show in high school, with a high schooler's concerns and fears. *Buffy* was always cloaked in this strange golden nostalgia for a youth I almost but didn't quite have, for battles that seemed easy to call, easy to pick out the big bads, easy to root for the blonde in the middle of all those storms. *Buffy*, even when she goes to college, is a show for the young, the being educated, not the 20-something soul cast ashore on the crags of jobs and partners and compromises and the endless bleeding out of adult life. I love Buffy - but I'm not her. She was Chosen, she was special, no matter where she went and who she became when the camera was off, she was always that beautiful paladin girl standing in the light, with a mission and power that she only ever really lost for one episode.

Instead, I want to talk about *Angel*.

Not the character. I never cared much for him - his story was always one of masculinity misused and misruled, a person who could never wholly be a person, older than most of the others, but naive and broad-chested and thick-skulled as any child learning how to be a man. I want to talk about the show, which was also about all those things, so terribly, terribly concerned with masculinity, in an explicit way few other television shows really are, the male animus played out in Wesley, Angel, Lorne, Spike. But sometime around Season Four, *Angel* finally hit on a metaphor as powerful as High School is Hell had been for *Buffy*. It wasn't as easy a metaphor, but for those of us watching as lost 20-somethings, it hit home with a kind of echoing din.

Can you work for the devil and still be righteous?

The most obvious iteration of this idea arrived in the form of Wolfram and Hart, and Our Heroes taking the reigns of that wicked corporation to change it from the inside - as all corrupted folk once intended. I don't think we were ever meant to believe they could; it's only that the classic Faustian bargain requires believing you can control the worse side of your own nature and that of the infernal machines, that you can keep your soul and still dance with the devil. But it's there in the Jasmine arc, too, where the overt comparison to organized religion asks the question with a slightly different twist: if dancing with the devil brings happiness, does it matter that it's the devil doing that quick step? And maybe it's there throughout the whole series - after all, Angel is the devil, and all these people come to work for him, and are corrupted to his world in their turn, becoming other than they were, for better and worse. Corruption is sometimes just change. And sometimes, it means having your whole body hollowed out and replaced with something terrible, as seemed to be the case with the women of *Angel*, over and over again.

The question is deathly important in this culture that says: you're worthless if you don't make money, but making the kind of money that makes you not-worthless usually means doing some pretty dire things for faceless entities out of the dark, hungry systems with a million mouths, petty awful hells that would like to believe themselves the whole earth. In high school, it's easy to say: that one is a demon and demons will never, ever be any good. That one is a vampire who only wants me for my body. But in the working world, everything is harder to see. That one will use me for the blood and sweat I can offer, but will give measure in return. This one is soulless and cruel and will destroy me, but I was assigned to his project by HR, so what the hell am I supposed to do about it? The office is hell - but it's the hell you know, a hell that feeds and clothes you, a hell that becomes day by day indistinguishable from a pleasant middle class living. And for awhile, before it got cancelled, *Angel* was about how to navigate that and still be a righteous man. And yes - I say man, because to be a woman on *Angel* was a wholly different narrative ribbon, from the first episode when a blonde damsel had to be saved to erase the taste of *Buffy* from our mouths. Women were lost, like Fred, or Girl Fridays, like Cordy, fairy tale girls, twisted and set on their ears, yes, but still damsels in whatever dress. However snarky Cordelia was or smart Fred might be, they all needed to be saved, and they all ended up as vessels for higher and genderless powers - in part because the virtues and problems in traditional masculinity and/or its deconstruction shows up most clearly when placed beside archetypal female behavior. Strong, yes. Also dead. And their paladins forever mourning them. *Buffy* and *Angel* were always mirrors this way, the one concerned with a feminine universe constantly besieged with sexually coded, penetrative or patriarchal (vampire or Watcher) threats, the other concerned with a masculine universe menaced with the loss of physical and spiritual integrity - to be invaded by the spirit of another, to lose the cohesion of the body or the mind.

And of course, in that binaried world of traditional gender roles, the Office is the purview of the Most Male, the jungle where he competes (no accident, I think, that Spike appeared at the same time, to be the younger, ambitious *All About Eve* sort of riposte to Angel's old man's *richesse*) for dominance and mates, where he does or does not become alpha. And that is hell, too. To become king of it, or to escape, or to never have played the game - *Angel* puts up answers to all of these: Angel, the collaborator; Spike, the iconoclast; Wesley, the lover and intellectual; and Lorne, who just chose to play his own field.

But back in the real world, there are office girls, too, trying to figure out what it means to be locked into a palace of glass and metal every day, what that means for them, trying to sort out their own story in all those narratives meant for men. And I was like that, trying to decide whether to be an artist or to be safe, if I could be safe and still be whole, be myself. *Angel* became wholly its own show as *Buffy* waned, and for viewers of my age, high school slipped further and further away, becoming like a fairy tale, a collection of stories that everyone more or less shares, but no longer as vital and present as the decisions you make in your twenties that affect everything else you will become. As I have done all my life, I looked at male archetypes and saw myself, needing the lessons that in previous generations only men were allowed to learn.

And what was *Angel's* answer to all this? I'm not sure it ever got to give one, given its cancellation. You could call it nihilistic and not go wrong: yes, you'll lose your soul and destroy what you love, but you can go down swinging. Sometimes the networks will swing their own axe, and all you can do is stand tall and beautiful as they cut you down. But I prefer to see it as a message of integration: Illyria could merge with Fred enough to love and grieve, Spike and Angel could redeem their pathological champion complex with regards to Buffy, chasing her blonde ponytail through a dark club and never catching her - as if they could ever catch her. Wesley could be loved by the ghost of Fred in just as strange and controlling a way as he loved her. Everyone gets what they want. Everyone dies. Everyone is lost, everyone is found. Yes, the world is always bigger than you, hell is always stronger. HR will assign you demons and your 401k is run by vampires. All these things are as true just as it is true that high school is hell. But you still have to live in that world, every day. You never graduate. The big snake and the prom were the easy parts. You must try to be a champion, though you'll never really manage it - that terrible, overused word - and never take the easy ways out constantly presented in the forms of Jasmine, Lilah and Lindsay, Darla, the ever-present Shanshu prophecy, promising a kind of reason and folkloric logic that the real world just never plays out: be good enough and you get your reward. In the end, *Angel* said gently: *kids, it just ain't so.*

14

And me? Well, *Angel* ended, *Firefly* got cancelled, the war started just about the time when Buffy was telling us we were all Slayers, and I dropped out of grad school. I couldn't find a job even in hell. But *Doctor Who* came back from the dead, and I moved to Japan, where I got lost for a few years, just like a certain waifish physicist I used to know. And just like her, I was saved by monsters - I started writing fairy tales and dark things on the walls of a cave, and eventually found the light again. But the funny thing is, there's never a point where I don't have to navigate the waters *Angel* was trying to chart - do I sell out when someone is buying, do you give up my soul and my voice for the chance at comfort, do I believe cynical old men when they tell me that this is the way the world is, and if I want to change it, I have to become part of the system first?

Or do I pick up a sword and head out to a dark alley where a hopeless battle awaits - hopeless, but forever worth fighting?

Stranger in a Strange Land

Every once in awhile, I end up reading a bunch of "literary fiction" books in a row, whether to see what's going on outside of genre or by some fluke of omnivorous shelf-grazing. Almost always, it causes a rash of contemplation about literary fiction as a genre - because boy howdy, is it a genre. And this time is no different. Due to what was staring me in the face in a certain guest room, what was on offer in the Frankfurt airport bookstore, and what I happened to pick up when I got home, I read, in quick succession: *A Brief History of the Dead*, *The Lovely Bones*, *Kafka on the Shore*, and *A Trip to the Stars*. Add to that the not-really literary fiction but certainly mainstream YA *Feed* by M.T. Anderson, and out of my own perversity a re-read of *The Secret History*, and it's a feast of angst and high sales and quotes from *The Los Angeles Times*.

To be fair, I didn't even finish *Kafka on the Shore*. I love Murakami, but this was so boring and uninteresting and meandering that I just had to give up, less than a hundred pages from the end, which I never do, because the tedium of it made me want to die. I seriously cannot believe this won the World Fantasy Award. Also, authors should deeply reconsider whether annoying 15 year olds (who talk like 30 year olds) and their bizarre sexual habits are fascinating enough on their face to justify hundreds of pages of examination. It sounds trite to say nothing happened in this whole book, but it's a buddy flick where the buddies don't meet and their endgame is some murky WWII event (it is Murakami, after all) of which only one (who is mentally disabled) is aware and then all of the sudden there are crystals and bizarrely helpful truck drivers and some kid is having sex with his mother and thinks it's awesome. But it's all so banal and flatly written that I don't even care - even less than I care about some of these other books, and that's saying a lot, so let's just leave it with a "not living up to his potential" comment on Murakami's report card. Guh.

Feed, on the other hand, was really and truly decent - though it thrives on the reader being young and thus never having read *Stand on Zanzibar* or any of the other SF novels that feature a constant stream of advertisement as a literary technique. Again, though, I have a problem with the bored, passive protagonist and his sexual fantasies being more or less all I'm given to hang on to as a persona. And the dying wrong side of the tracks girlfriend having actual serious thoughts about anything while the privileged boy goes on to... not have any. It's just kind of a tired trope. And the lesions were never explained, no matter how awesome the truffle line is. In general, I think that *The Great Gatsby* is great despite its execrable protagonists, not because of them, and I don't actually want to spend any time with mini-Nick or mini-Daisy, even on the moon. But back to this one in a second. Those would be the outliers, the best and worst of the lot.

I found none of the others to be bad books *per se*. Obviously, they're bestsellers of varying degrees and somebody loves them, they speak to someone. But I feel like, with every one, they were doing it wrong. Clearly doing it right for someone, but doing it wrong for me, personally, as a reader. And with every one I felt like I got a clearer idea of the actual difference between "literary fiction" and "genre."

The difference, I think, is rules.

I've commented before on litfic's obsession with suburbia, which Alice Sebold hilariously claims in the interview in the back pages of *The Lovely Bones* is somehow a neglected corner of Americana where all the real stories are and she had to learn as a writer to recognize it as a legitimate source of stories. To which, with all the class I can muster, I wave my brandy snifter and say: LOLWHUT. Look, I get that urban stories are legion - as long as that "urban" means "New York" and the protagonists are privileged white people, but suburbia is *where it's at* for literary fiction. The story of the repressed housewife being dissatisfied while her husband works miserably and her kids act out is getting to be nigh-on universal, no matter whether it's the 50s or the 00s. Hell, it's the plot of *Mad Men, Desperate Housewives, Little Children, American Beauty...* I could go on, but it's pointless. The siren call of the easy symbolism of an outwardly perfect row of houses and inwardly borked lives is resisted by precisely no one. *The Lovely Bones* is merely another entry in that restrictive genre of storytelling, and other than its otherworldly protagonist, it alters the traditional narrative not even a little. But besides having to sit through yet-another reel of how much being a wealthy white family in the suburbs sucks, what I really notices was a total lack of worldbuilding or rules of the game. And more, a total lack of interest in the same.

To be honest, Sebold seems to have no real interest in the afterlife she sets up at all. It's just a vantage point for the family drama, and half-baked serial killer thing (worst serial killer ever, by the way - there is no *way* this guy doesn't get caught in five seconds in the real world). And yet, what few rules she sets up (the dead can't affect anything, mainly), she breaks without any stated reason or justification. Those of you who have read the book will probably know the big Rule Breaking Moment I mean, when not only does our little Susie body-swap for no reason, without intent to do so or any possible sense of why she could, but she takes her last living moment not to talk to her tortured family about who killed her, but to bang a dude she liked in middle school, despite her only other sexual experience being brutal rape. Yay! Love is awesome!

But I just kept saying: why? Why can this happen? And what happened to the other girl's soul?

But Sebold isn't after that fish. She cares about a) the broken suburban family story and b) writing a scene she wanted to write without caring whether it fits with the universe of the book. Because she's not a genre writer, despite the genre window dressing, she doesn't recognize that the book has a universe, or care about rules, or worldbuilding - because it's ostensibly our world and doesn't have to be built. But for me as a reader this is just insane, because it's ghost time in the house, and the book just throws up its hands and says: *weird things happen! We don't have to DWELL ON IT! Let's get back to a suburban dad smashing things.*

Two final and beside the point points: one, the death of the serial killer was bullshit and I call shenanigans. There is an implication that Susie made it happen but it's fairly clear she didn't, at least to me, since it's all from her POV and she doesn't say she did it. But the refusal to decide whether the dead can or cannot affect things reaches its most ridiculous toward the end. This is not satisfying, for crying out loud. And by the way, a heaven where no matter what happens you cannot grow or heal or change, where you cannot grow up, ever, where you can meet other people but cannot be an adult, or sexual, or progress beyond the age and mentality of your death is not heaven. That's hell.

Ahem.

Same thing with *A Brief History of the Dead*. I got the gist of everything in literally the first 30 pages, which are easily the most interesting. I walked out and asked the owner of the guest room I lounged in: "Is anything going to happen in this book besides everyone else figuring out that someone has to remember you on earth for you to live in the purgatory city and that one chick is the last one on earth so everyone she doesn't remember is gone? Because I got that, and there's a lot of book left."

And he wouldn't meet my eye.

What I wanted, with these afterlife porn books - the genre element of choice in American fiction - was some exploration of the world put forward, of what it means to be dead, of why people keep their general economic status, still working in restaurants, etc. Why do dead people need to eat? Does anyone, ever, do anything but stare into the distance and act depressed? But the authors didn't want to write those books. They wanted to write about Antarctica or the standard "the connections that bind us all" or, you know, "emotions."

As a genre writer, it's funny how I put emotions in quotes. We don't like emotions or characters, right? It's all about the world. And the worst genre fiction does get mired in that, the fetishizing of rules and worldbuilding. But, you know, some attention to the fact that you've invented this fascinating premise and are going literally nowhere with it and exploring nothing in it would be nice. And I use quotes because the emotional arcs presented by these books are just not intense or interesting enough to justify flying in the face of logic so often. I can't listen to parents mourning their kid because she hasn't died yet because they're *eating* in a *diner* and people are *working shifts* there and they're all dead and *why*? But it's the emotional content of the scene the author cares about, not making it work in an invented world. (Don't even get me started about the fuzzy fade to white handwaving ending of that book, either.) Really? Parents miss their kids? Stop the presses. We have got to get someone on this.

A Trip to the Stars was probably the best written of any of them, but the best example of why genre fiction can't have nice things. Every five pages, the author picks up a genre trope, shakes it in confusion, and then throws it away. There's vampires, but they're gone within a few pages and no one cares. The whole thing is an embarrassing Mary Sue (Gary Stu, really) adopted kid's fantasy about how the protag's *real* family is *rich* and *awesome* and will take him away to a palace in the desert where he'll get a perfect education from genius tutors and speak Greek and Latin and be awesome at drawing and get all the toys he wants and *also* be awesome at sports and anyone who doesn't like him is inherently evil and despite all this he has tons of free time to wander in the desert where a spider will give him superpowers (that won't matter and will be forgotten) and his tutor will give him a *bably wolf* and also they're all *true descendants of Atlantis WTF*. (Actually, the Atlantis thing is especially awesome, because supposedly it's their sooper special "double O positive" blood type that makes them Atlanteans. I thought that sounded weird, so I looked it up. Turns out that "double O" just means O, as it's a recessive gene. That means, far from being the "rarest blood type on earth," it is in fact the single most common blood type on earth and it just so happens to be mine. So now, when my husband asks me to do things I yell: *No, for I am a true descendant of Atlantis and I do not do dishes!*)

The point is that Nicholas Christopher doesn't give a shit about making all this magical stuff jive with the plot, nor, clearly, does he even recognize the painful Gary Stuness of his story. He cares about the relationship between his two main characters (sort of) and the rest exists so that the back cover copy girl can list a bunch of cool things separated by commas that make the book sound epic. Don't you want to read about vampires in the Old West, alien spiders, Captain Cook, Basque separatists, astronauts, Atlantis, and *baby wolves*? I know I do! But none of those things matter to the book at all, and the minute one starts to matter, the author crushes them brutally and glares around daring you to remember that there were real fucking vampires like five pages ago and everything that's happening are coincidences that beggar the end of *Jane Eyre*. It's the real world, right? Shit just happens, and you don't have to explain it.

The Secret History is really a bit of a cheat on this list, because the *doin it rong* is completely different - though related. Once again, I question why I want to hang out with the cast that got rejected from *The Great Gatsby* for being too assholish. These guys, all of them, are literally the worst people ever. And there's no reason that the worst one, Bunny, who gets killed on the first page, should have been let into the sooper special circle of classics students that the protagonist has to shit angel feathers to get into, where you have to be charming and smart and attractive and be approved by the perfect amazing teacher, given that Bunny is a colossal shit. Who can't do Latin or Greek. What the hell.

But my main issue is that only one thing of any interest occurs in this entire book. It happens to be the only genre element - the kids do a ritual to summon Dionysus and homes *shows up*. That is awesome, my friends. It's tossed off in three pages of dialogue. I suspect if you asked Tartt, she'd say it's a nod to Greek plays where all the action happens off screen and is reported by a messenger. Yeah, whatever. It's the only interesting part of the book and it's what the book should have been about. We should have seen all those aborted attempts, and the group growing close and then fracturing over failures, not just be told about it by a bored 21 year old who talks like he's 90. Good grief.

But then, that would have been a genre book, right? If you center stage the weird shit, rather than using it as a fetching window treatment, then it's not Serious Literature. But what we're left with is a bunch of Literature that makes no sense because the authors are essentially operating a forklift they're not rated to handle. It's awesome! It goes up and down! It crushes things! Wheee! But if you don't read the manual, you end up with a messy factory, and everything is out of order and nothing makes sense. A novel should have its own internal system, its own logic that coheres, that connects with itself. It should not be full of random incidents of magic that connect with nothing just because watching people grieve for 300 pages is much harder to make interesting without ghosts or vampires. It feels lazy to me, intellectually lazy, to throw out scenes and leave them hanging, breaking all the rules of the world, with no explanation. And yet I see it again and again in these books.

I'm reminded of a speech from *Six Feet Under*, a show that for awhile managed to pull all off this afterlife/family drama stuff pretty well: *It may seem weird to you, but there is a reason behind everything that we do here...*

Choose Life

It is entirely possible that no other subject has been the beneficiary of as much spilled blog-ink as our genre's collective Rodney Dangerfield impersonation: we can't get no respect. Our authors only win Pulitzers when they ditch the kingmaking cycles and pen tomes of urban angst, professors stare down their noses at us, and yet by some arcane calculus, some writers of speculative fiction are allowed to rest tidily in the Literature section, judged by publicist-Goldilocks as not *too* magical.

I've been thinking about this for awhile, being a fantasy writer myself, and thus subject to Dangerfield Syndrome. However, I am also an academic, and I can't quite accept that what I write is just silly while the literature of miscarriages and adultery is, as the Internet says, serious business. I think there's a reason that SFF is not respected by the philosophical powers that be, and to fight their battles, you have to use their language, so hold on to your hats.

It all goes back to Homer. See, in the *Odyssey*, Odysseus hooks up with this nymph Calypso, and after nine years of snuggling, she offers to make him immortal and ever-young, a god in his own right - and Odysseus refuses. It's a key moment in Western literature, and one that sets up an essential choice that informs almost every human decision (yes, even what books to read). Odysseus praises the real world, the small beauties of his wife (which didn't keep him from a decade of adultery, naturally), the honor and pride of working the land of Ithaca, the joy of his son. He chooses life over apotheosis. For him, godhood is a kind of death, the death of his reputation as a warrior among men, the death of his marriage, the death of his personal excellence, and perhaps most importantly to him, the death of time and the ability to perform heroic deeds. When a god commits a wonderful act, it isn't heroism, it's a hurricane, a drought, a mysterious birth. Without the threat of death, nothing can be heroic - and Odysseus is a hero precisely because he chooses this world. That choice reinforces the reader's own reality, tells him comfortingly that this is certainly the best of all possible worlds, and that even divinity cannot outshine it. It's a powerful, even intoxicating message. The life you, humble reader, live is greater than that of an immortal and all-powerful god.

And so goeth Western protagonists, all of whom long to go home, escape the strange realms in which they find themselves, be they Dante or Dorothy. Their longing for home is a chief virtue, their rejection of the fantastic in favor of Kansas or Italy a valiant stance in the face of the forces of the Other, the false world, the shadows in the Platonic cave. Mimesis, or mimicry, representations of the real which are not themselves real, are demons in the divine machine. To reject them and all their works in order to embrace wife, home, land, children

- this is an essential human act that we must all perform in order to go on living in this, the real world. *You must choose this world.* Those who do not are beyond redemption.

But it is more than that. In some sense, to read and write fantasy literature is to commit suicide. The Freudian life-instinct can be summed up by the choice of Odysseus (or Ewan McGregor, if you prefer), while the death-instinct is to choose the unreal, the magical, the Othered, the shadows and the mimics. To turn one's back on the world is to leave it, and that is a manifestation of the death-instinct. How many of us were accused of escapism as children, buried in our favorite unreal worlds? How many literally turn their backs on the world in favor of their internal lives via the Internet, parents' basements, shut-ins, and antisocial anxieties? The choice plays out in every corner of our lives, and it is not at all surprising that it is very much alive in the literary world, whether or not any critic calls it by its name.

The cult of realism thrives on this deep-rooted division of the world - and if you don't think the world is divided thus, turn on your television and listen to a certain young woman slice up the country into real and unreal segments. This goes much farther than books - those who do not choose the dominant culture, sexuality, family structure, political mode, they are just as unredeemable, and their fiction is more often than not the fiction of the fantastic, where it is safe to show themselves. No matter how sad or ugly or dim or boring the day after day of a family on Maple Street might be, it is *morally* superior to a family of fey (of either definition) struggling to survive on Avalon. The former will be lauded as unflinching and astonishingly honest, where the latter may hope to be described as charming, vivid, and touching. It *flinches*, see? It chooses the Other. It chooses the death of the real, and according to the dominant paradigm of the West, that can never be more affecting than a pleasant dream. You cannot choose the other world - that's not how it works in Puritan land. You can't just kill yourself to get to Heaven faster - you have to suffer here to earn it. Fantastic fiction allows us to escape this world, and that is a mortal sin.

Which brings us to the great hierarchy, which isn't all that hard to parse once you know the Platonic-Freudian code - primary world fiction comes in first, because it ignores that there is any choice at all between the world of the self and the world of the imagination, between inner and outer realities. Next comes primary world fantasy (I'm including science fiction in the term fantasy), which includes magical realism. It, at least, is still rooted in the real, the honest, the true, and uses the shadows of magic to highlight the virtues of the real. In third place comes allegory - fiction which takes place in the scary territory of alternate reality, but is plainly meant to address issues at play in the real world. Secondary world fantasy comes in dead last, since it also ignores the idea of a choice between inner and outer reality, but in favor of the inner, and thus commits moral suicide by abandonment.

I don't think this is likely to change. It's a pretty deep-down instinct. And that's why I don't stress the Dangerfield effect too much. The fact is, I'm no Odysseus. I'd take a chair on Olympus and a chariot driven by mechanical bronze horses over scrabbling in the rocks in Ithaca every day of the week. I choose the interior world. I choose a quest. I choose magic. I choose invented histories. I choose epic battles between armies of wolves and spriggans. I choose witchcraft, ray guns, AI, and dark gods. I choose swashbuckling, cruel queens, and talking beasts. I choose cross-dressing orphan heroines. I choose unreliable narrators. I choose my friends. I choose endless space and alien worlds. I choose complex cultures in a range of species. I choose archaic skillsets and arcane religions. I choose sitting on that couch reading fabulously jeweled books and shoving possibilities into my head. I choose another future. I choose, if pressed, death - but hey, black looks good on *everyone*.

The Ending

There is this Ending. It is a Twist Ending. I feel safe in saying it is The Twist Ending. If you have seen advertising for a movie or heard word of mouth that informs you *OMG your mind will be blown*, there is a very high probability that This Ending is what lies in wait for you, crouching in a dark theater, hoping you'll come within its grasp.

I don't want to spoil any movies - or indeed, any books or television shows, so I'm not going to name names or point fingers. All of you have seen shows and movies and read books wherein The Ending has appeared, corpulent and tired, its baseball cap turned to the side, sticking both fingers up its nose and hollering *I R ART* at the top of its prodigious lungs.

You know The Ending. Say it with me.

He/She/It/They were dead all along/in hell/heaven/purgatory all along/were manifestations of multiple personalities all along/were crazy all along/were in a computer simulation all along.

ART.

All of these variations on The Ending are really the same ending: they weren't real.

Now, I know all you postmodern kidz can go with me when I say "real" and mean "real within the confines of a narrative that is obviously fictional and there for unreal in itself, however, there are shades of real, yo," so let's not argue about who killed who, okay? The point is, you may recognize The Ending. You probably knew it when it was a kid, eating paste and pencils in the back of the class, desperate for teacher's love, wasting everyone else's time with constant grabs for attention. Back in those days The Ending went by the name of And Then I Woke Up. In a twist The Ending itself might appreciate, *they're the same dude.*

Now, it's gotten to the point where if I even catch a whiff of The Ending, I run the other way. It is one of the most common endings in Hollywood these days. I'd go as far as to say writers and producers are obsessed with it. And they all trot it out like it makes them new and edgy and *OMG wasn't your mind blown?*
No.

Here's the thing about The Ending. It's a fucking cheat. It's like Lucy yanking that stupid football away over and over again and laughing demoniacally every single time. The Ending breaks compact with the audience. It says: everything you just watched and cared about and experienced vicariously didn't matter. You sat here for two hours and watched something whose sole purpose was to yank the football out at the end. None of the actions of the characters matter, or the characters themselves. Everything onscreen was irrelevant and unimportant, because even in the context of the film, it was not real, and no one could react to it sufficiently to solve their problems because they had no problems because they weren't real. There was no story, and most especially no threat, because this did not occur on the plane of the actual, and therefore was never subject to the rules of cause and effect. You just thought they were. You were given the tools only to *have your mind blown*, a joke shared by the producer, you, and the football.

Now, The Ending can work, I'm not saying *The Sixth Sense* and *Fight Club* didn't pull it off - but they pulled it off because something onscreen was real. The relationship between Bruce Willis and the kid, wherein the living child played psychopomp to the dead man - that was the story, not just that none of it was real ever. If it never worked, we wouldn't have to see every B-List screenwriter try it. Like any literary tool, in good hands it can be beautiful, and if it falls into the wrong hands? Doom.

And I think there has to be something going on culturally for The Ending to show up so often these days. Why do we keep wanting to play this out? Why do we keep wanting the world around us to *be made unreal*? I mean, in a meta-sense, The Ending is universal - at the end of every film, show, book, artistic experience, we wake up from the fictional world, shake our heads, and return to our real lives, which are often somewhat-to-extremely less awesome than the constructed world we briefly experienced. But I don't think that's it.

I do think there's a desire to suddenly depart from the everyday humdrum world, to suddenly have the curtain pulled back and find oneself in Oz, in a different story, where the rules are not the same, and all the threats and conflicts that consumed you vaporize immediately, become more than irrelevant. I think that's the whole instinct behind the current brand of Christian eschatology in this country. Wouldn't it be nice if your unemployment and unfulfilling marriage and angry children were all unreal, and you were just vaulted into a world where none of it mattered, but you, your essential person, still did? It's a kind of solipsism - the protagonist is always ultimately real, experiencing the unreal world. The protagonist goes on to the next reality, and all the bit players in his life are left behind. It's a wish fulfillment, though I'm not sure the wish is even on the level of consciousness - it's the most seductive part of that Freudian death-instinct. *The world is not real, but I am. The rules of life which I hate apply to others but not to me because I am the protagonist and they are not real. Everything I see and feel and experience exists purely to facilitate my personal enlightenment and development. I am the project. They are tools.*

That's a somewhat terrifying and sociopathic thought-line, but I think we can all look around us and see that a rather large number of people conduct their lives as though this were the truth and not just a disturbing ending to a film. I think The Ending plays into that fantasy, and when coupled with quality writing, that's why it can be incredibly satisfying to a mainstream audience. *Mind. Blown.*

Of course, the flip side of that coin is that most often, the protagonist is ripped from an interesting and exciting world, full of action and high drama, and forced to accept that they are stuck in the every day humdrum world after all, in an asylum or dead or in Kansas or whatever. If there is ever a question within the film as to whether a series of fantastical events is or is not real, the answer is it wasn't real, or at least not fantastical, Guillermo del Toro I'm looking at you. Which goes back to the old Odyssean choice - you must choose this world, every time, without fail. It's what society has to say to people who behave as though protagonism justifies anything they do and are. It's the Judgment. And seeing others get their deserts is also deeply satisfying to most people.

But it's not satisfying to me. It's And Then I Woke Up. It's a navel-gazing, narratively unfair playground cheat, and most often it's done stupidly and clumsily, with a logic that crumbles when the nearest breeze passes by. And worst, it's easy. It's not daring or edgy, it's just easy, flaccid storytelling, and I'm deeply tired of it. I would boycott The Ending, but by nature, it's a stealthy bastard, and we all have to keep up our defenses just to hold on to our damn football.

A Wrinkle in the Heart

I read *A Wrinkle in Time* for the first time the other night because it was so hot I couldn't sleep. As often happens when I read a book that I mostly found good but had some big issues with, I want to talk to someone about it. But this is not just a classic, it is a Beloved Classic, and while we can give Narnia and the Problem of Susan the stinkeye and admit that *LotR* is kind of hinky on the all kinds of scores, some books seem to be Beyond Criticism. You don't go taking your red pen to *The Phantom Tollbooth*. You just don't. It's not *nice*. And everyone loved this book as a child. The shock that went up on my Twitter feed when I said it was my first read was intense. My friends get this soft, dreamy look on their faces when I mention Charles Wallace.

And yet, why didn't I read it? I obviously own it. (The whole series, though I've only read the first one so far.) I've obviously heard of it and been vouched for its quality. Though when I think about it I seem to remember other people saying: *yeah, I loved it, but you should not read it. You wouldn't like it. You would have Issues.* And so I didn't. But now I have. And I want to talk about it! But you can't talk about the stuff we loved as a kid in a critical way. (Not that everyone hasn't gotten Cool Points from shitting all over *LotR*, my beloved adolescent books, in the last several years.) And I didn't *not* like it. Some of it just bothered me, as an adult reader in the 2010s, rather than a child in the sixties or seventies, for whom I suspect this was as revelatory as a book could get. So, I am going to talk about *A Wrinkle in Time*, and I beg you not to get too angry or comment with the popular refrain: *yeah that's true but I loved it anyway.* I know you did. Everyone did. You should keep loving it, for it is lovable. And we all want an Aunt Beast. (And a mother like Mrs. Murry.)

It really is highly readable - I peeled through in one night - and full of endearing characters. I can see why this book matters to people so much - firstly, best family ever. I mean, it's like the opposite of Harry Potter (or I suppose it's really the Weasleys, down to the red hair) and other orphan narratives where the protagonist clearly Does Not Belong. Meg is so utterly a product of her family, she belongs there, and is loved for who she is. Bookishness and geekiness are good and encouraged Murry traits. Mom is an awesome scientist, and so is Dad. Sporty brothers are viewed with slight suspicion. It's the family we all want to be in, and few of us are.

But... despite Mom being a scientist, she stays home and takes care of the kids while Dad has adventures. She is perfect and beautiful (uncomfortably, Calvin's mother is explicitly not beautiful, and this is kind of a shorthand for her not being as Good as a Murry - though good heavens, a woman who has had seven children and lost all her teeth might have reason to be cranky), but domestic, cooking beneficently for her family while doing her experiments. She is not employed by the government; she is not even allowed to be involved in the rescue of her husband for no defined reason. (I mean, really, she knows him better than any of her kids, all of whom were tiny when he disappeared. Why can't she go? Dad can be a Player.) I know in 1962 this must have been super-advanced, female-role wise, but now it feels discomfiting. I recognize that I react incredibly poorly to the "woman who stays at home being awesome and carrying on while her husband is away" trope for obvious personal reasons (I basically won't even read *The Time Traveler's Wife* - this is a thing which triggers me, and I don't use that word lightly). It's especially squirmy when considered alongside the issue of Meg.

I suspect everyone loves Meg. Identifies with her, because she is an outcast in school, and even in her own family feels different, all the while she is assured she isn't. (She is though, as we'll see. She's the only one, essentially, without superpowers.) We love that type - especially when they only think they are not smart, while actually being pretty great. (I can't recite the periodic table, yo.) But here's the thing: everyone in this book is special *but* Meg. Even Calvin, who really is just some rando Charles Wallace ran into, even Calvin has a special gift and is destined to be wonderful, destined to be part of the family and obviously Meg's future husband. Calvin's gift is communication with the alien, Charles Wallace is clearly Jesus or something (having looked up the wiki, it would seem we never actually find out why Charles is special, nor what happens to him, which is *maddening*), so incredibly marvelous and perfect that he must be protected at all costs. Meg's gift is... being difficult and kind of pissy. And loving her (male) brother. All the men are endowed and stalwart and gifted with particular talents. Meg's talent is an especially female one - loving her male relatives and... well, I got very tired of how many times she "wailed" "cried" or "stamped her foot." This is very infantilizing language, removing her feeling from anger or passion into the realm of tantrum. Charles Wallace is always described in adult terms, though he is five. Meg in childish terms though she is at least 14 (in high school).

Again, I'm sure back in the day having a girl as the lead at all was amazing - but Meg is not the hero of her own story. She is a Girl Having Adventures, yes, but those adventures are all about other people, she is never the point or the mover, and everyone around her is a Male of Import. More import than Meg, always, more power, more agency, more options. It was painful to me to see her so infantilized and sidelined, down to essentially fainting for a whole chapter because she's not as good at traveling as the men - even Calvin! Who has no reason to be naturally awesome at anything the Murrys are! Calvin bothered me, as you can see. He gets very little development for how central he is to the plot, and is introduced so suddenly and is so great at being a Murry he makes Strider look like a subtle debut.

In structural terms, the book felt very rushed at the end, and I found myself gaping at (spoilers) IT's revelation as a giant brain. Really? That's IT? It's become so cliche now to have a giant floating brain that I can't see it as scary or even interesting - plus the word IT makes me think of King's novel, and amps my expectations. I felt a whiff of anti-communist preaching in Camazotz, and wanted, really, a whole lot more to happen in those sequences. We get pages of Charles falling under the influence, but very little else. I loved Aunt Beast of course, and wanted more there too. Every single piece of the book was so interesting, but I never got enough of any of it, or enough specificity. Maybe that's elsewhere in the series, explaining what is going on with everything.

And the God stuff... eek. Narnia was subtle, comparatively. Angels and Jesus and God, God, God.

But for all that it is incredibly compelling - like *Babylon 5*, it seems to be more than the sum of its parts. The gender stuff is as ever hard for me to let go of (even the Mrs. W's are genderless in their true forms, not really women), even if they and the structural irritations are perhaps products of their time. It was lovely to see a portal science fiction tale, the tropes of portal fantasies transferred over to science fiction. Some of the passages, most particularly Aunt Beast and the Mrs W bits, were just charming. And I am still quite seriously considering naming my incoming boy-kitty (at some point soonish from darling Betsy) Charles Wallace. (Arrrg, how could MLE leave us not knowing what and where he is? I swear here and now never to do that ever.)

And yet. And yet.

Some childhood novels one can read as an adult and find wonder there. And some are hard to read as one might have when one could just black out the bits that bothered. I feel like I have missed a beautiful and moon-colored train where all the other children can shriek in delight and trade tales of tessering, leaving me to stand on the platform mumbling "But..."

Say Yes

The biggest idea in *The Girl Who Circumnavigated Fairyland,* the one that sits at the center of the book like a seed, is saying yes.

I've talked a lot about how this book came to be written - what was once a book-within-a-book in *Palimpsest* became a crowdfunded online serial novel became an Andre Norton Award winner became a bestselling print series. It's a great story, but it's a story *about* the book, not the story *of* the book.

The literary purpose of including that little fragment of Fairyland in *Palimpsest,* of dredging up the protagonist's favorite childhood novel and creating a new one rather than just making her an *Alice in Wonderland* fan or a *Wrinkle in Time* enthusiast, was to talk about saying yes. It's what November took from that book as a child, to always say yes to adventure and magic and things that seem strange or outlandish. And in our culture, we simply don't have too many narratives hauling that line.

After all, saying yes is dangerous. It is frightening and unsafe. You never know what might happen. Saying no means nothing has to change, and the outside world can be kept outside.

A portal fantasy goes: a child (or adult, *Farscape* is also a portal fantasy, though still one about coming of age) discovers or stumbles into a magical world. He or she, while frantic to get home, ends up coming to love the magical world and saving it, often from its own worst impulses or native tyrants.

And the thing is, if at any point in my life, including this one, I found my way into another world, my first impulse would not be to reject it and seek a way home. It would not be, like *Buffy,* to elevate " a normal life" beyond all other sources of power and awe. I just don't know how to tell that story. It doesn't interest me. As a child, I wanted magic, desperately. I would have given anything for a door to open in a wood and let me out of my life. I never understood the need to end the dream and get home - perhaps because I never understood "home" as a metaphor for "safe." Not all homes are safe. Not all places of safety are home-like. But I would have run wild through a magical kingdom and never looked back. Talking animals? Yes. Witches and monsters? Yes. Dark queens? Absolutely. Give it right here. I would have said yes to all of it.

There are exceptions, of course. Portal fantasy is enormously popular. The film version of *The Wizard of Oz,* for example, is an exemplar of this mode, but the later books are altogether stranger and more interesting. But the film is what seizes our culture's mind - because in it Dorothy would always choose our life over the Technicolor alternative. It butters us up, tells us that our lives are the better lives. Our world and the minutiae of it better than the most beautiful dream. It teaches us to say: *no, thank you.* Part of the reason fantasy is so reviled,

I think, is because it gives us this idea that the world is more than what we're given, that it can be anything, that the rough material of work and hard going is not the whole substance of this universe. Dreamers don't make good workers. So you teach them that no matter how miserable, what they've got is the best, and the Other is terror and lies.

Well, to be bold, fuck that.

If I was going to write a portal fantasy, if I was going to get my Joe Campbell on and ship a kid to Awesomeland to do deeds of derring, I wasn't going to roll like that. Especially since I was going to be sending a girl. Too often in books like this, (especially in the classics of the genre) girls are acted upon, rather than actors, their choices are few, reflecting the real world, where a girl's power is often located purely in her ability to say no: to suitors, to her social inferiors, even to herself. I wanted my girl to choose, to find power in saying yes, to make her own story - and of course her own ship.

Yet September, the heroine of Fairyland, is not particularly "badass." She's a kid who doesn't know who she is yet, as most of us don't at 12 years old. But she knows what she wants, which is everything wild and magic. In many ways, what *Fairyland* and *Palimpsest* are both about is want and the satisfaction of it. *Palimpsest* is the very adult version. *Fairyland* is a more universal story, younger, more playful and innocent, but no less canny and feral. September is strong and loyal, and embraces everything she finds, even when it hurts her to do it. Her story is not even particularly about saving Fairyland. If the Marquess's scheming managed its goal, Fairyland itself would go on. Without spoiling the end, what September saves is the *possibility* of saying yes, for herself and everyone else.

I wrote a book about a girl who never said no. When she first enters Fairyland, it isn't because she falls through a hole in the earth or wanders through a closet or chases a rabbit. It's a choice, and however dark her journey becomes, she never wishes to take it back. The Green Wind shows up at her door riding a flying leopard and asks if she wants to *go*. If she wants more than she's been given. If she wants to leave this world and grasp for another, a mad and gorgeous place, sight unseen, results uncertain.

And she says yes.

Our Jane

There are books it is difficult to talk about. They are so near to the bone of the reader that to discuss them is to discuss the inner workings of one's ventricles or pancreas - certainly these are topics permitted in polite society, but it makes one squirm in one's seat.

For me, *Jane Eyre* is one of those books. It seems to me to exist within its own Red Room: a terrible, beautiful liminal space of particularly feminine power, of particularly powerful femininity, where ghosts and nightmares and impossible hopes flit about the curtains - enough to make a young girl faint. It is a book that, for a certain kind of woman, slowly stitches itself into her heart as the pages are turned, and when it is finished, she cannot imagine a world in which she did not know the contours of Jane's face. I am surely not the only reader to imagine so - how then to introduce a book so well known and well loved, which certainly needs no help from a digital-age cherub like me?

As best one can, I suppose.

There is a slow, peculiar canonization which occurs in literature, that Vatican-of-the-mind. The pun is sly and appropriate: it is both the process by which books ascend from the shelf into the Canon, and by which they become the vast, sprawling secular scripture of humanity. Canon tunnels through pages like an earthworm, turning a bawdy play concerning twins and mistaken identity into liturgy, a pardoner's wicked lies into hagiography, a Gothic romance novel into a holy book. It is elusive and capricious, and often blind, as is the nature of worms. It is the alchemy through which characters who never lived become ours, become as real as neighbors, become the small gods of this world. Hamlet, our patron saint of melancholia and indecision, Mrs. Dalloway, intercessor for socialites and suicides, and Jane, our Jane, Lady of Lowood, Thornfield, and Ferndean, Our Lady of the Plain-Faced, of Equal Spirits, of Remarkable Coincidence.

Harold Bloom, that famously compulsive list-maker, allows but four women into the pantheon of his Canon: Jane Austen, Virginia Woolf, Emily Dickinson, and Charlotte Bronte. Bloom's Canon is hardly canonical in itself, but it does seem to represent the collective view of (white, male) Criticism as to what is and is not eternal, what has and has not been visited by the Worm. Surely ladies need no more than four - what do they have to talk about, besides babies and embroidery? Why, four is a surfeit of riches! The list would not have been much argued, save for temporal issues, in the time of "Currer Bell." Four, like evangelists, rampant in the margins of male experience - and of these I humbly submit that Bronte is our winged lioness, forging her strange and circuitous path through the critical desert so that we may follow, bright as the sun.

Jane Eyre is subtitled "An Autobiography" and so it surely is. A story of the self, and like any good saint's life, it teaches us how to live, promises the possibility of enlightenment at the end of all things, and transcends the single soul at its center to become a story of the Self: the human anima, its metamorphosis, its progressions through archetype towards cohesion.

In short, our Jane is a Campbellian hero. Jane Eyre is referred to as a romance only because it contains a marriage and a central heterosexual relationship - but this conventional structure conceals Eyre's bones: the great mythic cycle underlying male initiations and heroism from time immemorial. Women's myths are often called romances.

Eyre is, no less than Luke Skywalker or Frodo Baggins, a disconsolate and orphaned youth living out her early life in obscurity, unaware of any extraordinary feature in her person. Jane takes her ordinariness one step further, and proclaims her plainness throughout the novel, to an almost fetishistic, emblematic extent. She is The Fool, Key 0, innocent and victimized by her aunt and cousins to a degree which would impress even Cinderella. And though, as heroes will, she is forcibly removed from her home and set on a path to strange and otherworldly experiences, I would argue that her "call to adventure" comes before the perforation of Jane's adolescence into the Reed Household and Lowood, in the terrifying Red Room.

Here, Jane is locked away into an entirely othered space within her familiar house. It is sensual, scarlet, even uteral in its lushness. It is hard not to code such coloration as indicative of menstruation, of the coming of age that all heroes must vividly endure. Yet it is also a place of death, where the former Master of the house perished, and Jane is overcome by loneliness and ghostly visitations. She is confined within a powerful and perverse symbol of femininity, confronted with death and sensuality in one awful moment - she crosses the first threshold of adulthood, of the mythic hero/ine, swallowed into the abyss. Yet Jane is a young woman, not a young man, and she is not, in her case, confronted with femininity as a stand-in for the ultimately unknowable, dark, and threatening cosmos. Femininity is not other for Jane, of course. It cannot truly threaten her, though the onslaught of incipient womanhood holds enough terrors for any soul. Instead, she crosses into her own knowable self, descends into her own darkness and fear, and emerges again, full of the strength with which she defies her dubious benefactress and enters the new world. She will repeat this act, of descending into the dark and erupting again into the world at large, three times, like any hero worth her pages.

Lowood, the dreadful, bitter school into which the reborn Jane is delivered begins the "road of trials," and slowly accumulates her hero's tasks. She is starved, falsely accused, surrounded by wasting disease. Yet she also draws to herself a hero's companions: Helen Burns and Miss Temple stand beside her, nearly angelic examples of the kind of submissive, quiet, undemanding woman Jane will never be, both elevated by their suffering. They are not heroes, they cannot understand why Jane will not submit to the punishments and cruel pronouncements of Mr. Brocklehurst, who is her first brush with the strict, brutal god-figure that will come to its full flowering in Rochester. Campbell notes often the importance of the hero's encounters with the "Goddess" in whatever form, his merging with or consumption of her, his cleaving to the other in order to produce the final result of the quest-cycle: a single cohesive soul. It is only appropriate in Jane's case that her encounters be with a God as dark and compelling, as frightening and seductive, as sadistic and beckoning as any Vivien or Eve.

And one by one, Jane's fellows are taken from her, Helen by death and Miss Temple by marriage. Having survived the literal underworld of Lowood, itself a twisted, cold mirror of the Reed household, Jane, of her own volition, ventures once more into the wild. She trades the drafty halls of Lowood for the drafty halls of Thornfield, and takes a young girl not entirely unlike herself under her care, becoming a governess, that archetypal position in Victorian literature.

Thus, Jane comes to meet the dark God of her tale in earnest - and like every hero who has stumbled upon his damsel in distress, here is Jane, stumbling upon her demon in distress, as Rochester falls from his horse at her very feet. Rochester is almost a parody of masculinity - more what is indicated by the word "Byronic" than Byron himself. He is capricious, mercurial, cruel, and manipulative, his features dark, his desires inscrutable but surely base, his moods unpredictable, given to lies and tricks. He is demonic, no less than Morgause or Lilith or Circe, and a reader may question, in our own half-enlightened age, why a woman of Jane's spirit, who would not countenance Brocklehurst's abuse, accepts and is deeply attracted to the imp of Thornfield. Yet there is something perverse in the hero's soul which seeks out the dark deity of their own shadow, to fuse together with it. The Self seeks the Shadow - there is no more central mythic conceit. If the Shadow did not tempt, it would be nothing.

Jane is again given a glimpse of the strange and otherworldly when she hears the unearthly cries of Thornfield's other tenant emanating from the attic - but she is not yet ready to witness the extent of the Shadow's perversity, to examine it or integrate it into her soul. She has yet another hero's task before her, one which has its genders reversed once more, for this is, irrevocably, a story of women.

The Campbellian model makes much of father figures and the necessity of the hero reaching atonement with his father, making peace with a wrathful parental figure and thereby freeing the last of his soul to enter adulthood and the final stage of his adventures. So too must Jane find peace with Mrs. Reed, hardly less a monster than any fairy tale stepmother, and the narrative at

Thornfield is interrupted to give her this chance at reconciliation. Jane behaves in a manner of which Helen Burns might have been proud, forgiving her warped mother-figure even the offense of pretending to kinder relatives that Jane was dead. Mrs. Reed does not reply in kind, recalcitrant to the end, but Jane has risen above the mire of her abuser, and leaves unburdened to plunge again into the adventure of Thornfield.

But the Shadow is a Shadow, and cannot help but betray the Self. Rochester has betrayed every woman he has touched, from the pitiful Bertha in her lonely attic to poor Adele's much-maligned mother. He is prepared to do the same to Jane, even to damn her eternal soul, for any marriage with the bigamist Rochester would by Christian tenets be adultery on Jane's part, but she is delivered by the truth of the previous wife, the previous Self betrayed, and once more rises from what has become a dark and dreadful place to enter the wilds again, her third and final flight.

Jane takes her "magical flight" through the moors and sleeps beneath the stars, the hero in the wilderness, starving, alone, awaiting vision and deliverance. It is here that the narrative takes a turn for the nearly-unbelievable coincidence - unless one understands Jane's true nature as a hero. She must find her family in the wild, she must be granted what Campbell calls "the ultimate boon" of her inheritance, very much the equivalent of a magical sword or cap of darkness, and more she must refuse it, sharing her new wealth equally, as befits a pure and unadulterated heroic soul.

At this point Jane enters the downhill slope of the final stage of the hero's journey - The Return. She is practically in lockstep with Campbell here: "the refusal of the return" and "rescue from without." She is nearly ready to marry the quotidian and uninspired St. John, stubbornly refusing to return to Thornfield, when she hears Rochester's ghostly voice cry out to her in extremis and flees back to him. It is her other self which cries out, the incomplete hero who must rescue the maiden to be whole, who is incapable of refusing that thin, ghastly cry. She "crosses the return threshold" to find that nothing is as it was, Thornfield, like the Shire, a hulking, broken ruin, burned and hollow. She discovers the story of the failed hero - Bertha - who could not integrate herself with the Shadow, who could not tame it, who let it cage and destroy her.

But Jane will win out, and is not, in the end, destroyed by the demonic Rochester. She discovers him maimed, blind in both eyes and missing one hand. He is crushed, humbled, brought low, a penitent Shadow, nearly, but not entirely, shattered by the last woman he brought on the journey of integration.

Harold Bloom is deeply disturbed, as were many of Bronte's contemporary critics, by Rochester's final state. He is the outward world, the patriarchal, the world of male power, and he is brought to heel, broken down and blinded. It is this treatment of the Byronic Rochester, whom Bloom and other critics stubbornly identify as the hero of a book named for Jane.

Of course he is not intact. He could never be. Jane has internalized him, and rightly so. She is the hero, and the hero must contain the Shadow. She has become The World, complete in herself and all things, content. In Jane's world of inequality between men and women, between classes, Rochester could not begin to be enfolded into Jane, could not begin to enter her and produce the heroic, cohesive soul, were he not brought low. In his intact state, he was a demon who devoured women and eradicated them - he ends the book a tamed imp, his horrific revels finally done. Jane herself is the "mistress of two worlds," in Campbellian terminology, having done what any hero does at the conclusion of their astonishing and harrowing quest: taken a spouse as a reward, and taken a child from the spouse. It is a long and honored tradition of princesses and maidens and redeemed women that Rochester joins, and he is in august company. It is only the reversal of genders that causes such paroxysms of critical anxiety. Jane rests her sword at Ferndean Manor, her demon conquered, her line assured, beatific and smiling, mistress of a land of plenty. No king in his hall has ended better.

One might ask what a book written in 1847 can possibly have to say to the savvy reader of 2007, for whom the idea of class as a bar to marriage is at best quaint, for whom "governess" is hardly a viable lifestyle choice, to whom the fact that a woman should speak plainly to a man is no surprise at all? Why should a woman of the twenty-first century love Jane, who, at least in the West, can choose her husband freely or not at all, own her own Thornfield, change her plain face with little effort, and is rarely compelled to avert her gaze from anyone?

Because we are all Jane. She is family. She is ours. She is the small child in us who must suffer through nightmarish schools and the loss of childhood, through parents who ought to care for us but do not, through unsatisfying jobs, unhappy love affairs and demonic lovers, through cold, wet nights on the open moor, through grace unlooked for, through happiness undreamed of, through integration, through darkness and into light. Like a hero, she blazes a path. Like family, she shows us the way.

And to read and discuss *Jane Eyre* is an act of spiritual instruction, like counting the beads on a secular rosary. And I say to you that when you are lost, when terrible places to shame Lowood tower high above you, when mothers turn against you and lovers betray you, when the moon on the moors is freezing and you are starving for bread and revelation, when you are in need of Remarkable Coincidence, call out to Jane - for her, three miracles are less than the work of one afternoon's reading.

My Commitment to Sparklemotion

The newest trend among vampires seems to be removing any downside at all from actually being a vampire. Gone are the days of Nosferatu or even Dracula - apparently vampires can walk around in the daylight now, whether they sparkle or not (*Being Human, The Vampire Diaries, Twilight*), are universally hot (everything ever), functionally cannot be killed and honestly no one even tries anymore, can see themselves in mirrors most of the time, and can even touch crosses without going up like a roman candle (*True Blood*). There is literally no bad in being a vampire except for the blood drinking thing, and being a vegetarian who only drinks cow blood or whatever is pretty much *de rigeur* for your modern vampire.

So... essentially you just live forever, right? That's it. You live forever, are super strong, and smoking hot.

And yet these vampires mope around like this is the greatest burden ever borne by preternaturally attractive man. The moping was because of the downsides, kids. Never seeing the sun. Being unable to have sex or connect with humans. Being hideous. The whole moral compass of vampire literature is that yeah, you live forever, but it sucks. And beneath that is the Christian assumption that you stole eternal life from its proper channels (Jesus) and took it for yourself through the devil. So it's a black reflection of life in the paradaisical hereafter. (Also no hereafter for the vampire if you get staked.)

There is no reason to get upset because you get to live forever while not being hunted to death by righteous men, having to avoid delicious garlic, while also having every girl or boy in a mile radius fall madly in love with you. That is not the curse of the ages. That is awesome.

So seeing vampires behaving as though their life is any kind of monstrous travesty (I won't make her a monster ZOMG!) is really pretty boring. Most humans don't think twice about using others for their own ends and they aren't vampires at all. Having to live on blood, which is basically all that's left of the mythos, is not an angstfest. Some Scottish people are eating black pudding *right now* without being even a little bit horde of the damned.

I just wish there were any other plot. One vampire wants to be nice and only eat cows and every other vampire is harshing their squee. They want to be as much like a human as possible. Except vampires *are* humans now, except hot and immortal. Literally no other difference. But they're acting out the same old plots like they're Bela Lugosi. It's way postmodern, if anyone noticed onscreen, which they don't. Like 19 year olds acting out stories about their grandparents' radical activities in the 60s, when they in fact live in a world where all those issues are passe.

I have the same contempt for this plot that I do for the portal fantasy wherein the stupid kid just wants to go home. It's exactly the same story. Once turned into a vampire, with the whole world opened up and turned upside down, become something new and endless and fascinating, the stupid vampire just whines about wanting to be human again. *Shut up.*

Being human? Not that awesome. In fact, we pretty much suck, and we don't even sparkle a little. We're violent and amoral and devious and angsty. Just like a vampire. Only we die, and we still have to eat meat to live until that happens. And yet any character who up and says: "You know what? Being a vampire rules" is immediately a villain and treated with contempt by her maker. (*True Blood, Angel, Being Human, Interview with the Vampire,* and *all of everything ever.* Don't even get me started on how vampires are apparently 99% male now, and yet the character who enjoys being a vampire is usually female. Or Ian Somerhalder.)

Given this new breed of vampires, there should be, you know, *a new breed of vampires.* For example. Watching *The Vampire Diaries,* which is terrible, there's a scene where the receding hairline vampire high school guy mumbles and looks at his feet and then tells the boring high school girl that he's "not very good at small talk."

Well, you fucking well should be, shouldn't you? You're four hundred years old! You should be *awesome* at small talk! You should be like a social Olympic athlete! You should be all: *sometimes I small talk a tree, just for fun!* You should be able to walk into a room and own it like fucking David Bowie, my friend. What have you been doing all this time? *Mumbling?* That doesn't even work for mortal boys! *I am done with you, vampire failure.*

Vampires should be pretty much like mean girls, all the time, only amazing at it. Flawless. They've had time. Like when you put a penny in a bank account and a thousand years later you're rich. Social capital, it is the same. Those high school kids should never know what hit them because they are *amateurs.* Vampires should not be at the approximate social stage of a particularly awkward 14 year old with anxiety issues. They should be devils in blue dresses. This is the metaphor: the cool kids are all vampires, and they fuck with you because it's fun. Because they're demons and they like it. They keep going to high school over and over not to pick up some awkward 16 year old virgin, but because they can get away with shit in the maelstrom of high school that adults would never put up with. They are Chuck Bass. All of them. All the time.

But no, we get the same old mopey crap. Vampire Dorothy wants to go back to boring human-Kansas. And the werewolves turn into gross CGI monsters instead of actual wolves and are never, ever as cool as vampires even though I literally do not know a high school girl who would turn down a guy who was an awesome wolf sometimes. The only thing better would be a were-pony. I'm sick of that trope, too. If we've decided as a culture that where there is a vampire, there is a werewolf, then werewolves need to up their game a little, instead of being the also-ran in the monster rally. I mean, the material is all there - vampires are sex and death, werewolves are life and sex, they really do go together - but no one ever does anything with it but yell: *Look! A werewolf! Now back to the vampire moping on the double!*

I demand better.

And this has been my complaining about the state of vampires in our fallen world. We now return you to your regular sparkly programming.

Why Not Moose?

I preface this by saying that on my better days I *am* a pagan (I like to think of myself as a non-practicing agnostic) and I have nothing but affection for other pagans. Do not be offended if your name is, in fact, Raven Silverwolf or Silver Ravenwolf or Sparkle Glitter Starlight Wolfpuppy. All that I am about to say is filled with love and concern for you.

It's easy to mock pagans. We stick out. We're kind of dippy and strange, we wear funny clothes (at least a few times a year), we insist on lecturing you about how St. Patrick actually murdered Druids and the whole "snake" thing is a smokescreen while you're trying to chug your third mug of green beer in peace. A good portion of us have read too much Tolkien for our own good, and our version of church seems to involve buying a lot of weird stuff at stinky shops. We're easy targets. But it doesn't help when a vocal portion of the "community" (a word I use loosely, as there is a great deal of variety in pagan beliefs and groups, and I certainly haven't noticed a "community" pitching in when I'm out of incense over here) insists on naming themselves ridiculous things like Raven Summerhaven and Wolfheart. And forcing their Kinko's co-workers to call them by that name in public. (Sometimes they spell it "Ravyne," which makes my brain bleed. But then I don't spell it "majick" either, so I'm out of the club, anyway.) Now, there is nothing wrong with new names, and the Native American tradition of animal names is a long and noble one. But in addition to making the rest of us look like a pack of rabid D&D players who got their hands on a copy of *Let's Go to the Zoo!* somewhere along the line, these names show a stunning lack of creativity, or even an understanding of the traditions of which they claim to be a part. Mostly, it's about looking cool.

There would appear to be only five to ten animals deemed attractive and noble enough to name oneself after, if one is to be a proper little pagan. Ravens and wolves top out the list, followed by lions, hawks, bears, owls, the occasional deer or crow. A handful of others pepper the landscape - I am not even going to address the bile-summoning trend of naming oneself after dragons, griffins, or any other mythical animal which can be found in a fantasy paperback featuring bikini-clad chicks with swords. Some pagans also choose flowers or trees, or gods and goddesses, but at the moment, I want to address the much more common HELLO- My Name Is (fill in animal here) phenomenon.

I would venture to say that very few of those named thusly actually feel a deep spiritual affinity with ravens or wolves. Liking Poe is not a deep spiritual affinity. (And I am far from convinced that the raven predilection doesn't come from reading *The Mists of Avalon* one too many times. Yeah, I liked that book, too, guys. Fiction is fun.) But we, as part of the western tradition, invest certain animals with qualities of nobility and courage, regardless of their actual nature. For instance: the wolf was reviled in Europe for centuries - hence the typical "lone wolf" image, though wolves are pack animals. (Know what you call a lone wolf? Fucked. It's cold in the tundra without your mates.) Those who choose a wolf name rather more often simply feel cast out by society, and latch onto the idea of a shunned but *essentially honorable and powerful* creature.

And there's the problem. Wolves are no more noble than scorpions. They'll happily rip your face off between munching on fluffy rabbits and sweet little mice. But wolves are furry and gorgeous and they look off into the distance as though they contain some unspoken wisdom. Bitch, please. They were thinking about how nice some *noble* caribou would taste right about now. But this seems to be the prerequisite for liking an animal enough to name yourself after it - that the animal is adorable or fiercely beautiful, which reflects well on the *namee*. No one ever names themselves Salamander Mangymoose, or Swift Ostrich, or Starmanatee. Yet these are perfectly lovely animals - they just don't make you look dark and cool, do they? Yeah. I'm onto you.

Even more strangely is the phenomenon of the "fluffy pagan." The main tenet of pagan belief, I think it's safe to say, no matter what cultural spin one puts on it, is a reverence for nature as the literal expression of divinity. Fluffy pagans believe that nature is a happy, bouncy place where little bunnies cuddle up with the fuzzy tigers and no one ever gets turned into a goon or, well, eaten. The vast majority of members in the Ministry of Silly Names are more or less fluffy. Yet they continually choose *predatory* animals for their namesakes! Or even better, carrion birds like ravens. Nobody wants to be a prey animal, no matter how genteel they think the law of the jungle is. Birds of prey are not whistling Mary Poppins birds. *A spoonful of sugar makes the hamster I ripped to pieces and chewed up last night go down...* These "totems" are being chosen for their coolness factor, not their nature - which is *not* inherently naughty just because they enjoy a nice titmouse or fawn for dinner. These are human judgements and human moral compasses - it's called projection, look it up. No one ever thinks: *I am a loner, and sexy in my aloneness. Therefore, my animal name is... Orangutan!* Yet the orangutan is a creature who lives alone, seeking out others only to mate - but their fur is an unattractive shade of orange, and they shit at unfortunate times when you visit them at the zoo. So *ixnay on the rangutanay.*

Another excellent example is the hyena.

Hyena are wonderful symbols for the average pagan. They are matriarchal, fiercely pack-loyal, and skilled hunters. They scavenge when they must, but prefer to hunt. Yet they are scruffy and ugly and make irritating laughter-type noises, and so there are a dearth of pagans called Hyena Hoarfrost. But lions? Oh, *everybody* wants to be a lion, they're so pretty and strong and *noble*. And bullies who scare off other animals from their kills more often than hunt down their own. But why actually read a book about nature when you can read a Dragonlance novel? It's more important to have a name that makes you look cool.

Only, sweetums, it doesn't make you look cool. It makes you look just like everyone else. It makes you look like you aren't serious about your faith. It makes you look like a Hot Topic shopper. I speak most of all to the Ravenwolves. Please stop before you put your eye out. No one thinks it sounds mysterious and sexy, no one thinks you actually embody the traits of these animals. If you do, I have a nice rotted sparrow carcass for you to snack on. At least *try* to be creative. Come out of the RPG. Put the Marion Zimmer Bradley down. And understand that it is just possible that a mystical name is a private and powerful thing - and thus should *stay private*. You are not Neo. You do not get points for forcing everyone to call you by your handle.

Or come to me. I'll give you a name *no one* else has. You'll be the snazziest kid at the Sabbat. Otherwise, Bob, Sally, and Jenny - let's lay off the sparkles and velvet portion of the freedom of religious expression, shall we?

The Lost World

All right, *Lost*. We need to talk.

I'm going to try to get through this without any spoilers, just talking about the show in general terms. I do not consider it a spoiler to say that there are genre elements in *Lost*. But if you haven't watched anything and have somehow managed to avoid any information about the show at all and want to keep it that way, this essay is not for you.

Without further ado.

Lost, fuck you.

I'm not going to complain that you've been making shit up all along - I know you have and I expect that for long-term storytelling. It's fine. I'm not going to be like *OMG we don't get answers it's just like Twin Peaks*, because it's obvious we aren't getting answers and I don't need an Exposition Episode and *Twin Peaks* had kind of a badass ending that you just know *Lost* would never have the balls to try. But I do know what's wrong with *Lost*, particularly what's wrong with *Lost* Season Six, and I'm about to throw some truth down here.

Lost is a science fiction show.

Now, they haven't wanted that label from the beginning. First, they assured us that everything had a real-world explanation and it was not science fiction or fantasy at all. This is obviously crap at this point, but they continue to insist in multiple interviews that *Lost* is a character-driven drama and not a genre show at all.

Oh, I get why you don't want the badge, kids. It may get you the geek love, but no one will call your show art and the big meanie procedurals and high-budget crime dramas will kick sand in your show's face and laugh at you. There is a genre bias ~~enforced by this kind of bad storytelling and mealy-mouthed interview sidestepping crap~~. But *Lost* is science fiction, or at least it fucking *was* until this season, when we suddenly landed in magical fantasy land and got a Dark Lord and a freaking *glowcase* and vague mystical nonsense and this is my angry face. I don't normally come down on the side of "get this fantasy shit off my screen" but damn, yo. You cannot resolve a science fiction plot with glow-elves and a Dark Master. Most of the problems with *Lost* have in fact been because its creators are, frankly, genre snobs, and refuse to believe that anyone is interested in the mysteries of the show but are instead merely invested in their "characters." I put that in sarcasto-quotes because these characters are terrible, boring, flat, and idiotic. And the only ones anyone was attached to are dead or sidelined. Thanks for killing off all the non-whites and non-males except Kate, too._ They do not get that the only people still watching are people who are interested in the island mysteries because they are genre fans. Everyone else peaced out a long time ago.

Incidentally, it's not like *Lost* is alone in this. Every time some producer claims a show isn't science fiction while standing in front of a huge spaceship set, baby robot Jesus cries. Yes, *Battlestar Galactica, I'm talking to you.*

But here's the thing, guys. If you don't want to get tarred with the SF brush, you don't get to play with our toys, either. That means you do not get any of the following exciting action figures: monsters, immortal beings, time travel, alternate universes, glowcaves, Egyptian mythology, electromagnetic magic, insta-healing, psychic powers, Dark Lords, Lords of Light, magical touched by an angel fatecakes, teleportation, mystical islands, or bodily possession.__ Get your sticky hands off them - you'll only break them. Make a sitcom and shut up, if you want to howl about not being SF. Make a gritty procedural. Make *Thirtysomething*, I don't know. But don't make an SF show and then prance around telling everyone it's *super realistic* while trying to conceal your painful giant quantum rabbit erection. You can't trot out all those shiny SF baubles and then refuse to develop them or treat them seriously. I've said it before: the difference between realism and non-realism is that realism has no interest in consistent worldbuilding or rules, or even making anything have narrative logic, because those artists think their work takes place in the real world and therefore requires none of these things. The real world is already built, yo. It doesn't need explanations.

That's why nothing in *Lost* makes sense. Because to make it make sense, you have to admit it's a science fiction show and explain why things happen. You have to treat your own story with respect, and not just wave your hands in the air and blabber about your characters which you never bothered to make engaging in the first place *because you were writing a science fiction show and the mythology made up for the lack of awesome characters.* Jesus, it's like Golden Age SF Excuse 101.

But the thing is, in their bitter, black hearts they know that the SF toys are *completely awesome.* There is literally not a single realist show that could not be made more awesome by adding robots, monsters, time travel, or magic. You can try to come up with one, but you will fail. Why do you think Buffy and her unfortunately stepchildren *The Vampire Diaries, True Blood,* etc are so loved? Because they are *90210* with vampires, and that is better than just regular *90210.* Likewise, *Lost* is *Survivor* with SF, and that's what made it great. The tropes are interesting and fascinating and they get the geeks in front of the television - and geeks will love you forever, even if you make bad art. Geeks forgive. Geeks endure. This is also why most long-running realist shows throw in a genre episode - under the guise of a dream sequence or a crazycapade or whatever - somewhere in there. These things make an audience hold their breath.

But in an attempt to avoid being genre-shamed, *Lost* has been trampled into the ground and made truly terrible (I'm sorry, this season is just unforgiveable on the heels of the amazing Season Five) by what is, in essence, a bunch of loud kids running into the SF playroom and busting up all the toys because they don't know how to use them. I'm afraid the lesson of *Lost* will be the same as *Twin Peaks* and *The X-Files*: never make a mythology-based arc show, because it will only end up disappointing the audience. No answers can ever satisfy.

Only if you suck at writing things, people.

The lesson should be: if you use SF tropes, you have to treat them as seriously as you treat realist tropes. As you do character motivation and miscarriages and adultery. You wouldn't *never* reveal who someone had an affair with - that would be stupid storytelling. Or much less reveal their face but never give them a name. That makes the audience disengage. Causation exists. Treat the SF in your show as a character. If the SF travels in time, then you have to close all the time loops and make a stab at having it be important to the overall narrative. If the SF makes people immortal, you have to give us the how and why and more importantly how it affects them. Just like if a person in your story got pregnant, she would eventually have to have the baby or people would be upset and confused. Do the characters get closure? Then the SF gets closure. You don't just get to drop things like they're hot because *they're the SF parts so you think they don't matter.*

Damn. I don't want *Lost* to kill arc-y shows and make people be all smug about that shit so all we have left on TV is episodic procedurals where everything is the same every week in case someone tunes in to something they've never seen before and *jumps out a window in panic and terror.* But it will. It and *BSG*, with that unforgivable ending.

Just know, from here on in, when someone says their show isn't science fiction when it obviously is, what they mean is their show isn't *good.*

Lies do not become us, gentlemen.

Blowing Off Steam

There comes a time in the life of every young novelist when she starts to think zeppelins are *really* cool, and corsets and goggles and vague gear-based science seem to lurk around every corner, opening their jackets to her nubile gaze and revealing a lining sewn with all the books she might write involving Victoriana and steam-powered rockets.

Parents, talk to your children about steampunk.

It's everywhere these days, isn't it? Anime, *Doctor Who*, novel after novel involving clockwork and airships. Young women going about in *bustles*, for heaven's sake! But it's just as easy for the kids these days to get impure steampunk, cut with lesser punk materials.

Let me say it now and for all time, for the protection of your little ones: you can't have steampunk without steam.

Most of the product on the street these days would more adequately be termed clockpunk or gearpunk - though the golden age of clocks was about a century too early to bear the ubiquitous Victorian sticker with which we plaster everything from the Enlightenment era to Belle Epoque. If there's a corset and a repressed manservant, by god, it's Victorian. Steam power itself seems rather inconvenient, bludgeoned out of the way by corpulent balloons and quasi-Dickensian dialogue.

It is my understanding, poor, un-hip child that I am, that steampunk correlates precisely with cyberpunk, substance of choice of the last generation: literature which addresses and delineates anxiety (hence the *punk*, also ubiquitous, also nearly meaningless now) concerning new technology, computers in the first case, steam power in the second. Yet in almost everything I've ever seen called steampunk (besides the powerfully adequate *Steamboy* film), that eternal gateway drug, there is no actual steam power to speak of, and precious little anxiety. Because we, in our current, painfully neo-Victorian culture, think all that old-fashioned stuff is *so damn cool*, well, the actual Victorians must have loved it, too, right?

Dare to tell your wee wastrels that it's not all quaint manners and cufflinks - steam technology caused horrific scalding and often death, thrilling explosions and the utter terror and unfathomable joy - and which one often depended entirely on whether you owned the factory or worked in it - of a world which was changing so very fast, devouring itself in an attempt to lay just one more mile of railroad track. Again, I return to *seriousness* as a necessary addition to fantasy: if you want Victoria in your coat pocket, if you want the world that comes with her, all that possibility, all that terrible, arrogant, gorgeous technology, *take it all*, make it true, be honest and ruthless with it, or you're just gluing gears to your fingers and running around telling everyone you're a choo-choo train. Get punk or go home - and think, for just a precious second, about what punk means, the rage and iconoclasm and desperation, the nihilism and unsentimental ecstasy of punk rock. I've heard the punk suffix mocked soundly by everyone I know - *but we should be so lucky as to live up to it.*

If you're going to go prowling for tophatted villains at night, seek out the pure stuff, the real, filthy, ugly, euphoric sludge at the bottom of a spoon, because that's the Victorian era, that's steam power, that's a world shredding itself to death on the spindle of industry, hoping to wake up to a prince in a hundred years. No one wants to get screwed with a bag full of Drano and flaccid research.

But gears are so *pretty*. So *easy*. Why, you hardly need to know any science at all! Just stick a gear on it and it's golden! Come on, Mom, just one clockwork automaton, please? Don't be such a hardass.

And you can have them. They can talk like C3PO and everyone can eat gearcakes with brass icing for tea, and it can be a beautiful thing, but you mustn't call it steampunk.

#shitsiskosays

Today I'm going to Think Real Hard about *Star Trek*, that old SF past-time. It's like playing on your childhood swingset. It's a little small for you now, but it still makes you smile.

I've been slowly rewatching *Deep Space Nine*. It's been fascinating. On the one hand: Oh 90s! *You were the best!* With your adorable *we are so dark* plots that seem like Strawberry Shortcake Goes to Space by today's standards. On the other, in many ways 2012 has already overtaken *DS9* as The Future goes, barring, of course, space travel and replicators. Culturally, though, we've zoomed right past the twenty-fourth century by the second decade of the twenty first.

I've been struck particularly by two things missing from the DS9 universe - one unpredictable in the 1993-99 span of the series, and one predictable but unattractive from the creators' standpoint.

Nobody uses social media, and nobody wastes time.

As I watch everyone interact on the station, the lack of social media sticks out hugely to me simply because it is how so many of us interact with each other now - and especially over long distances. There is no hashtag for DS9 workers to tweet LOLSisko macros or talk to families back home. Everyone uses voice/video communication rather than text despite the security issues this obviously poses (and of course a social network of any kind poses security problems in and of itself, but provides rich narrative opportunities in that arena which I've yet to see explored much) and the fact that we are seeing even now many people shy away even from the telephone when given an alternative. We have the videophones of science fiction past - and no one much cares. We use it sometimes, but it's far more of a pain to make yourself presentable onscreen, get the kids and dogs to leave you alone for long enough to Skype, and carry on an etiquette minefield of a conversation when a quick text or email will do for most business.

This doesn't begin to cover the constant "come here and see this" requests, where said person will not be able to come there and see that due to falling plot. We live in a world already where no one need come and see anything, a quick picture upload obviates the need for O'Brien to come squint at your shit in person. Part of the reason, I think, that *Minority Report* continues to be a watchword for interface technology is that it showed a new(ish) way for people to interact with technology. In *DS9*, instantaneous information tech is available and evenly distributed, but the writers do not live in a world, yet, where anyone has begun to figure out what to do with it. So walkie talkies are still, in 1999, the model for communication. *DS9* cares about physical presence in a way we are already beginning to leave behind.

All of the episodes involving Jake's incipient writer-hood (besides being pretty weaksauce in general) make much more sense if one imagines him as a blogger rather than an intrepid boy reporter for... a newspaper? Magazine? I find it sort of touching that the kind of 30s reporter that Jake seems to aspire to be is still considered worthy and important - he wants to write our brand of McCarthy/Hemingway realist fiction (when we hear his plots, they do not involve spaceships or aliens even though those would be realism for him) and even more amusingly, he's terribly famous in the future he glimpses on account of having published a single short story collection. In fact, the war correspondence he so longs to write - and he believes he is the only one who can write it - would be one of many, many voices escaping from occupied DS9 in the post Arab Spring networked news hivemind.

I do think the presence of a TrekTwitter would be deeply erosive to the power structure on DS9, though I'm not wholly sure that's a bad thing. Everyone in power is good and believes themselves a hero - even when they are deceitful and manipulative, it is always in service of the greater good, where the greater good is defined as the survival of the Federation. Can you imagine the subreddit for the station? How many atheists would tear down Sisko the messiah, how every decision would be questioned, mocked, dissected where the actors and the acted upon could see it? Every show of this type has a "view from below" episode at some point - but part of the point of the barrage of opinions and information we now sort through every day is that the view from below is as available as the A narrative, at all times.

But it's not there. At one point someone asks for a high-speed data connection and this is treated as a pretty serious request. But all I could think is: for *what*?

This absolutely feeds into my second point, which I think is far more endemic to SF in general than simply the lack of anyone predicting Facebook in 1993.

We do see hobbies on the station: O'Brien and Bashir, who are basically married by Season Two, like to re-enact famous battles in the holosuite. Sisko likes to re-enact baseball games. People gamble, they play sports, they play instruments, they buy prostitutes both virtual and real. But the hobby we see most often is reading books (followed by cooking food, which is interesting and I think a right call in a world of replicators - real, cooked food suddenly has a tremendous value and becomes a status-flag) and we never see anyone just wasting time.

Battle re-enactments are eminently useful for military officers; likewise strategic sports and even Picard's mystery-solving programs and the crew's bafflingly low-tech poker games, though that's getting further afield than I'd like. Gambling is almost always shown as a social activity (as opposed to online poker) in which many other kinds of important information can be had. Reading books is mentally stimulating and often the books themselves are classics even by our own standards, such as Shakespeare. (Most people, no matter what their profiles say, do not read Shakespeare to unwind. Apparently all Starfleet captains do, however. As a totally irrelevant aside, this jives a bit with my experience with Naval captains, who often know a good deal of Victorian poetry and classical prose, but they learned it in college and despite being able to recite Coleridge as a party trick, I never knew any during my more intimate years with the US Navy that cracked open *The Rime* for a good time.) In fact, the pastimes we see are very Victorian in nature. They are parlor pastimes: reading, talking, playing live instruments (something we already see drastically less of than even a few decades ago, especially as compared to how many people can play Rock Band vs can play a guitar). It's all over Aubrey and Maturin up in there.

Nobody sits around and plays *Farmville*. Nobody gets embroiled in a flame war concerning the portrayal of Klingons in human vids or just sits and watches vids with their feet up. Nope. The brave men and women of the future read (super old) books, talk to each other face to face, and even in their VR fantasies practice for things they will have to do in real life or, admittedly quite realistically, have space holosex. There is no *WoW*. There are no video games at all unless they are evil ones from Risa that will suck out your brains.

Because of this, and because of the lack of a social network, it is possible to be alone in the *Star Trek* world in a way which I would have to deliberately take action to achieve in my world. Even when we are alone, most of us check a number of communication vectors and leave them live - Twitter, email, text messages, Facebook, our blogs, Reddit, news feeds. We are a baby hivemind spinning our training wheels. To be alone as profoundly (to me) as Sisko, Kira, and the rest often are, I would have to make a decision to shut down all of those streams. (And I do that sometimes. But it's a choice. The Internet is always on. Actually, in my house we have nineteenth-century nights where all the power and screens are shut off and only pre-electricity activities are on the table. You know, reading books, playing live instruments, talking, cooking, playing cards. It's a bit hilarious that those nights are the closest thing I can get to living on DS9.)

Sidebar: Interestingly, the whole notion of the Great Link seems to present a very high-level version of that interconnected, networked state, much like Asimov's Galaxia. This is a concept that used to horrify me, being a good 14 year old "rugged" "individualist" American. But now I live in the baby-version of that world, where I can plug into the world's thoughts at will. It's addictive; very hard to unplug once you're there. And the Great Link is a wholly, constantly networked culture - even their bodies are open source. They do not need to eat or work or sleep or have sex or die. When they're not getting up in the Alpha Quadrant's grill, they simply are.

And in terms of *DS9*'s universe, the Great Link is at best squicky and at worst an abomination. That connectivity, that lack of need, is presented as a big part of their Otherness, the reason that not only are they bad because they engineer species and want to fight the Federation, but that their being is essentially suspect. Not like our upstanding heroes, who never waste a moment, never let a consideration of others get too much in the way of Doing the Right Thing.

Anyway. I know wasting time is not necessarily narratively interesting, (though it can be - how one wastes time says a lot about a person), but *Star Trek* is at least in lip-service a post-scarcity world, and the Federation is not at war until Season Six. Wasting time and/or fucking around would be a lot of what people did with their lives. It's a lot of what we do now, and we're not even close to post-much at all. No one is frivolous in the future. No one exhibits poor or even mediocre time management. All are paladins of self-organization.

Wasting time has a unique pleasure (some call it slack) that we as humans are kind of addicted to. We're starting to do it collectively on our social networks now, to waste time in a connected way. The universe of *DS9* is culturally incredibly old-fashioned - all the aspects of life that were important to a nineteenth-century officer can be found in spades, both in-show and in a meta-sense. In a world with faith in its higher-ups, as *Star Trek* purported to be, it is terrifying to see the paladins playing *WoW*. They should be defending justice even in their sleep - and this too is a very old idea.

Much continues to be made of the fact that we now have *Star Trek* pads, ubiquitous, available, and to be honest, better than those on the show, which showed piles of them required to convey basic ship business. But more than the pads, in 15 years or so, we've leapfrogged the social norms of *Star Trek* on the back of the Internet. It's amazing to me just how quick the transition was - of course we're still in it - and that more recent *Star Trek*s have not and probably will not engage with this new reality either. *Star Trek* is a butterfly in a glass. It is no longer meant to predict or exhibit the future, but to quietly stand for the world of the past, as much as the Shire ever was. It's not exactly revolutionary to say that about *Star Trek*, but *DS9* still gets props for its realistic portrayal of war (I actually think the war bits are sort of trite and easy - the Dominion is never for a moment meant to be seen as having a point or being in the right) and grittiness, since of course grittiness = quality in terms of much contemporary media.

But it strikes me that, though she wears a pretty technodress, underneath *DS9* is Grandma telling us kids how it was in her day, and that no matter how many fancy doodads we get, her day will go on forever.

The Silent F

Once upon a time, there was a kerfuffle about whether Science Fiction Poetry Association is, or ought to be, inclusive of fantasy poetry. Mainly because, in response to a review of *Star*Line*, someone suggested that, respectfully, *science fiction rules, fantasy drools*, which brought up memories of the suggested name change years ago to the Speculative Poetry Association or the Science Fiction and Fantasy Association, and to which the collective response was: LOLZNO.

I'm not here to write a thoughtful essay explaining why a little fucking respect for other sub-genres might behoove all of us within the non-realist community, or that the Rhyslings have been dominated by fantasy poetry for years, or even that maybe, just maybe, everyone should focus on writing poetry that doesn't embarrass itself and stop arguing about terminology. Though I usually refrain from even discussing things that are already drama storms, I'm rolling up my sleeves - I aim to make trouble on the Internet.

Because you know what? I'm fucking sick of it.

I'm sick of being looked down on by science fiction authors for one damn reason or another, the endless accusations from the SF camp that fantasy isn't as rigorous, or Important to the Intellectual Development of the Species, or h4rd-c0r3, or whatever it is they hate about fantasy this week. Once, at a convention, another author turned to me on a panel and told me that my entire genre was just "kowtowing to Daddy Tolkien." The rest of the panel laughed and nodded agreement. After making some generally rude remarks about Daddy Heinlein and Daddy Asimov, I actually went to check the convention booklet to make sure it was a Science Fiction and Fantasy convention, because I had never felt so unwelcome as a fantasy author.

Because the simple fact is? *I cannot think of a single instance where fantasy authors en masse have risen up and demanded that the "S" be removed from SFWA or SFPA or any other organization claiming to represent all of us.*

And yet every so often, someone has to barge in and tell all of us fantasy writers to GTFO, so they can have their rocket club without us.

Good grief, *why*? Who cares? Is SF such a delicate flower that it will bear no other genres before it? Where is the threat here? Why must an entire group of writers be expelled in order to keep an *acronym* sacred?

I'm sick to death of being the silent F in SF, of being told that what I do is somehow on the face of it less rigorous and deserving of serious thought (the academic attention debate, where we gird our loins to prove ourselves worthy of deconstruction, always seems to come back to worrying about respect for science fiction, since, you know, Tolkien is the whole of fantasy and he gets plenty of academic love) than slimy alien fic. At this point, the point of *yet another dude* telling the fantasy writers in his midst to leave, I can't even dignify it with another analytical argument. It's clubhouse behavior, that's all. It has nothing to do with keeping the SFPA pure and free of icky, girly fantasy.

This doesn't even get into the insidious and intellectually dishonest implications in the old saws about how SF is about *the future* and fantasy is about *the past*, or the terminology we use - hard and soft - to describe each... or, even, how gendered this *whole discussion* is, with men trumpeting a rocket-shaped horn and laughing behind their hands at us girls and our silly fairy tales. Nevermind that both genders write both genres, somehow these conversations always seem to fall uncomfortably into a formula of a male SF author rudely calling out fantasy authors, and female fantasy authors trying to respond calmly and logically, explaining the virtues of accepting them into the club they had foolishly thought welcomed them, while not being listened to in the least, and receiving rudeness their male brethren simply do not in return for their peacemaking efforts.

Well, you know what? I am many things, but a gentle peacemaker I am not. At times like this, I'm pretty sure the F in SF stands for "fuck you."

Fantasy is an amazing genre. It contains some of the greatest literature written in the history of the world. It embraces possibility and strangeness and passion and magic - and sometimes there's even *science* in there. Rigorous science, even. It's as hard as you want it to be. I am a fantasy writer and a fantasy poet and I will *go to the mat* for my genre.

It's not even controversial to point out that fantasy as a genre right now is dynamic, growing, innovative, and bustling. Current SF? A bit anemic, a bit derivative, with a few stellar books here and there. So much so that all Neal Stephenson has to do is cough and he is assured of a place on the Hugo ballot. (Shit, I feel bad just *typing* that. I don't want SF to be a dwindling genre with a dwindling and increasingly curmudgeonly audience. I love SF. But of course in screeds against fantasy, no one feels the need to say they love fantasy, no, really, some of their best friends are fantasists. So why do I feel guilty pointing out that this is not exactly the Golden Age?)

But it's all about labels, right? SF Clubhouse. Fantasists Keep Out.

The fact is, fantasy is *by far* the more inclusive term. It could easily be argued that science fiction is an exclusionary term while fantasy is inclusive. All science fiction is fantasy, not all fantasy is science fiction. And yet we never go around screaming that SF authors should go soak it, mainly because that is *dick* behavior, and doesn't do anybody any good.

I mean, it sounds ridiculous to even say it, right? **I hereby move that the SFWA and SFPA be changed to the FWA and FPA in order to welcome *all* non-realist writers under their umbrellas.**

Why, it's like calling it herstory instead of history, or something!

And yet, that makes a hell of a lot more sense than kicking out anyone who doesn't have enough ray guns or alien cats in their work. But it doesn't even get brought up at meetings, because the SF guys would have a collective coronary. But we fantasy writers, we just take it and take it and don't even ask for that silent F to be pronounced. Nobody is afraid of pissing off the fantasy contingent.

Well, I'm pissed off. I'm, dare I say, mad as hell, and not taking it anymore. Fantasy is here to stay. It's only the oldest kind of literature for fuck's sake. So pull up your big boy pants, learn to play nice with others, and in the words of the post that started all of this, *get over it*.

Who Watches the Historians?

The London Blitz and the evacuation of children from that city has served as a jumping off point for 70 years of British fantasy. The tales of children fleeing the bombing into the countryside are innumerable, as though that diaspora was itself a journey into Fairyland.

I find this fascinating. My favorite permutation is definitely *The Thing in the Forest* by A.S. Byatt, but it's a pretty common theme in fantasy literature, especially British fantasy literature. But what's even more common - and I've wanted to write about this since seeing the otherwise excerable *Hellboy* - is how many works of science fiction or fantasy begin with WWII and the Nazis, find their source and legitimacy there, root themselves in that history as firmly as they can, wrap themselves up in the warm narrative arms of that war. From *Hellboy* and *Indiana Jones* to the *Justice League, X-Men,* and even *Sandman,* many comics and pulp-style media, (hell, *Doctor Who* does it too), if they do not literally begin in WWII, they seem to be driven back to that wellspring.

Now, I'm no comics expert, so I'm just ruminating here, on what I've noticed watching and reading and ingesting culture. But man, does it seem to be consistent. It's where we seem to find legitimacy, in a medium which is often not considered legitimate. It's the equivalent of the medieval attachment to the classical era - if you were writing legitimate literature in Chaucer's era, you damn well set it in Athens or Italy, and you damn well referenced the classical fathers.

I think there are a couple of things going on here. First and simplest, in the Land of Literature, the most Serious and Worthy of subjects, is War. War, as they say, is Srs Bzns. And comics are not. So if one anchors a comic in that most Serious and Worthy of all Wars, one automatically ups the SB quotient by at least a couple of Real Writer Points™. Superheroes, after all, are always running about fighting Evil during times of peace, and that's a little decadent, isn't it? I think our culture has been terrified of being decadent in the eyes of the Greatest Generation (which, gag me, I hate that phrase with a passion) since about September 1945. Real men fight wars, they aren't gothy loners with parental issues. The masculinity issues of many comic book writers past an present notwithstanding, fighting for a country is always more noble than fighting for your own fucked up reasons. It has to be, in mainstream culture, or no handsome young boys would sign up to die in the desert.

But more than that, WWII has somehow replaced every other war in the history of the world as *The War.* In America, anyway. And this one's easy, you don't have to sprain a brain stem to figure that it was a delightfully clear-cut conflict from the point of view of our current gerontocracy, and the enemy was nice enough to outfit themselves in Evil Theme, just like a comic book villain. Black and red and silver skulls, lightning bolts on their lapels and a whacked out obsession with the occult. I mean, really, is there a comic book villain that isn't either Hitler or Mengele in modern drag? I mean, it's so *easy*. It's so archetypal. Three generations of cinema and novels have kept WWII at the center of the American consciousness, as *Call of Duty* and its slavering ilk will attest. It's practically the only example of clean-cut, no ambiguity, cartoonish evil available. And America sidled in, brawny and square-jawed, and saved the day. This isn't complicated or original as far a analysis goes. Our inability to even recall WWI in the face of such a juicy war, a war where no one questioned us, where they begged us for help, shot up the Batsignal for years, a war so awesome that it took 60 years for people to start scratching their heads as to why we, allegedly not an empire, have 135 military bases on every continent in the world. It's breathtaking, the simplicity. It's why we love it, even though it was a horrific war that when you get right down to it was about as awful and bloody and ambiguous as every other war ever. But on this side of the Atlantic, it's all America vs. the Nazis, and Stalin doesn't figure, nor Japan, really, unless we need a giant monster created by radiation. The whole story is reduced so that it can be used as a bedrock, as fertilizer, as justification, and as a wet dream for hawkish policy-makers.

And comic books, of course, had their boom during and after that war. They began there, it is their mother's teat. But I find it interesting and disturbing that these specific stories reach back to it like a scrawny effete kid pawing his burly daddy for affection. Why pulp-inspired spec-fic? Why comics? What do they specifically glean from that era, what is specially theirs? I'm not sure I know, beyond what I've enumerated here. I think it's a little ugly and very predictable, no longer at all rich or interesting. But it's there and I doubt it's leaving any time soon. Nothing else satisfies like the Nazis when you want the kind of war that'll let you sleep easy at night. It's as though the world began in 1939, and nothing before then was real, real enough to create all the things a comic book hero needs: secret weapons, deranged scientists, radiation monsters, occult artifacts, dark geniuses. And that's why fleeing the Blitz is Fairyland - WWII is the eternal Real World in this subtle genre, and to leave it is to enter the frightening unknown.

But the unknown is always more interesting.

I find myself thinking a lot about this as I'm planning a new series of novels set in the early Stalinist era. Because, you see, when dealing with Russia, that is the easy period. It's archetypal, it's a somewhat obvious choice. But man, it's hard to choose other than totalitarianism when it comes to magical realism. The two want to go together, like, well, comics and WWII. My own personal obsession with Russian history is the era of Tsar Nicholas, just before the revolution, the Russo-Japanese war, the 1905 Duma, which, if you avoid Anastasia and Rasputin, is a largely open field. But I have a hard time rewinding the book 40 years. Can you have magical realism in an era most people view as magical to begin with? Was WWII the birth of the non-magical world?

I don't know. Easy choices are easy for a reason.

Regeneration X

The funny thing about real life is how much it's like a television show. If you look, you can find every one of us in that strange, hyper-colored world. Reflected, distorted, blown up, writ large, but we are all there. We cannot help but find ourselves there - and not just find but *seek*. We live a dozen lives a day that are not our own, through books and movies and television, and we need so desperately to believe that it is not wasted time, that it means something more than the deepening of the couch cushions. We want to believe that life can be as circular, as karmic, as rich and deep as art. That in life, too, themes repeat poetically, and sorrow ends. That is, in the end, what fan activity is: seeking ourselves, seeking meaning in stories. We choose our idols our of dozens, hundreds, and clothe ourselves in the appropriate vestments and icons. We buy, say, an absurdly long scarf, or Converse shoes, to identify ourselves as this acolytes. In a very real way, television is the new mythos. It defines the world, reinterprets it. The seasons do not change because Persephone goes underground. They change because new episodes air, because sweeps week demands conflagrations and ritual deaths. The television series rises slowly, arcs, descends into hiatus, and rises again with the bright, burning autumn.

To some this might seem horrific, the destruction of serious thought. I don't think so - and I am a classicist by training. Persephone is my co-pilot. But part of what classicists do is to see how old stories take on new shapes, how they remain the same despite the constant warping influence of technology. Television has become something new, has grown up and grown more serious, shrinking to a standard of 13 (talismanic 13!) episodes rather than a rambling 22, 24, 39. It breaks myth into bites small enough to chew. It has become the best way to tell a long story onscreen.

And *Doctor Who* is a very long story.

I'm a New *Who* girl. I never watched the old show - having been born in 1979, I just missed it on multiple levels. I was only peripherally aware of *Doctor Who* at all, despite moving in science fiction circles for most of my adult life. But I lived in southern Virginia for awhile, and there just isn't much to do down there. I saw a little blue box at the video store and decided to take it home and see what the fuss was all about. And it seized my heart like few other shows. I don't think *DW* has ever touched the heights of the ninth Doctor arc again, but it was enough to grab me like a hook to the heart, and keep me going through less ambitious cycles. There is an ache to the first season, an urgency and a mythic spread most shows don't even try for. And then there was the little detail that, at least in that first season, we were all allowed to have stories: women and queer and polyamorous and every sort of freak. We were right there, on the screen of the world, next to the straight white heroes, and we weren't less than they.

I bought a scarf. I bought a brown coat, and it wasn't because of *Firefly*.

Yet it's always been hard for me to express what I see in *Doctor Who*. After all, even in its new incarnation, it is often silly, nonsensical, and emotionally stunted. The writing is uneven, the plots preposterous, the aliens range from sublime to infantile. A love of *Buffy* or *Farscape* is comparatively easier to defend. The *Doctor Who* fan must forgive so much. And yet, what is there, behind it all, is so primal that all the wobbling styrofoam costumes in the world cannot hide it. Because that delicate viewer-identification dance that moves back and forth through all television shows is peculiarly expressed in *Doctor Who* - perhaps even perfectly so. Because if this Doctor or that companion is not a mirror held up to your soul, well, wait a few seasons. Everything changes.

Though I understand that the regeneration theme began as a necessity of casting, the grace of it is occasionally breathtaking. We say: *my Doctor. Your Doctor.* Because among the 11 of them, one is always us. Nine is mine - his sadness, his weird intensity, his guilt, his desperation for connection. Maybe Ten is yours - his nerdy ebullience, his enthusiasm, his endless apologizing, his acceptance of fate. The Doctor is all of us, he lives and dies as all of us, and we need him to - because, no matter the anvil-imagery of the Doctor as Christ, this is actually a far older, and far simpler, story than that. Everything changes.

We all regenerate. I am not the same woman who first saw Rose ascend. Years go by and I become someone new, with the same memories, but a new face, a new self. When I first watched the Doctor dance, I was a Navy wife, unhappy and stuck and reaching for something, anything, that connected me to the world. Now I am on the verge of marrying again, living on an island in the sea, writing books and adventuring in an unobtrusive little box. I am bigger on the inside than I am on the outside. Who knows who I will be with the twelfth Doctor rolls around? The Doctor and I change together, evolve, learn, grow. Sometimes our lovers, our friends, our enemies, our companions will stay with us for awhile. Sometimes they will come and go so fast, with such flashes of light and love that you flounder in their wake. You can set your internal clock by the cycles of the Doctor. Because it wouldn't be mythology if it weren't played out in large and small in every sphere of our lives, in ugly military divorces and post-collegiate ennui and lost jobs and pirated BBC shows - and thus in the stories we tell. We are born, we fight our battles, we make terrible mistakes, we lose our companions, we die in vain and otherwise, and are reborn to do it all over again. It's the old sacrificial king rag, in which Christ is just a first-chair flutist - but oh, how sweet it plays on the Gallifreyan pipes.

And then there's the companion, whose face changes, too. The new incarnation of the Doctor insists on playing out a male Doctor/female companion dyad

(Jack was always his own man, just stopping by for an arc or two, and that is sad, because no woman is given the same autonomy when faced with the Doctor). This is deceptive - it makes it look like the story of the Doctor and the companion is always one of a tempting trickster, a Hades, beckoning Persephone down into the dark, infinite otherworld of the TARDIS. The amoral alien ever in control, offering riches and adventure and awful beauty to an innocent young girl. And on that level, it works for a subset of viewers, who are either innocent and young and want to be tempted, or older know-it-alls who want to dazzle a nubile maid. And if we watch that story, we can change with her, from a shop girl to a doctor to a lost soul to a Doctor again. The companions are always ascending, always, moving upward, around on their own wheels. But there is another story going on underneath it. The companion is not innocent, she is not agog. She pulls the Doctor out of grief and into another cycle of living, she is, ineffably, the life force, pushing him through the hero's cycle again and again. Even though he wants to rest. Even though the moment he sees her he knows he will die in her arms, if not this specific girl, one like her, when she has changed her face the way he changes his. She is Hades, literally, his death come to take him on one - or two, or three - final rides before it's down into the dark again, and the painful rising towards light. His wheel turns down as hers turns up, looking into the vortex of time and becoming the light of the world, the goddess of terrible, awful light - and when their wheels touch (and they always touch, once a season, ever so briefly: cheeks pressed to the same wall, caressing the same watch, sharing the same mind) and she passes it to him, it drags him back into shadow, into change, into the momentary oblivion of death. In some sense, perhaps, the seasons only exist to move these two icons, the Queen of Life and the King of Death, or the Lord of Light and the Queen of Air and Darkness, towards each other, to merge for just a moment, and inevitably part - which is the core of every tale ever told. There is no he or she in that. There is only a binary system, seeking itself, repulsing, destroying, creating, and seeking again. I look, have always looked, at the Doctor and seen, not fathers, husbands, brothers, men moving and shaking, but myself, the brainy post-traumatic girl moving so bright and fast through the lives of others, appearing and disappearing like magic as I moved through three countries and five states in the space of a few years, writing and re-writing stories until they came out right, offering to take people with me, over and over, until someone said yes, talking constantly so that no one knew how afraid I could be, how lonely I was. Apologizing, always apologizing. I always looked at him and saw me, looked at the companions and saw my mates in life.

And yet I can't help but remember an old girlfriend, miserable, eyes streaked with tears, insisting: *All I ever wanted was to be someone's companion. I'm not like you. I'm not a Doctor.* And being horrified, because her wheel was spinning nowhere near mine, and I didn't want a girl to stay in the TARDIS and make cookies, and I couldn't see how the wheel that started with a lost shop girl could ever end with golden light spilling grace out into every cell. Letting her go because I couldn't love her in anything like a normal way. Because if this stuff wasn't universal, there'd be no sense in writing silly space stories where it happens over and over. Everything repeats. Everything changes. It all depends on which wheel you're on. Sometimes you're on your way up, into the heavens all full of angry robots you can turn to stardust with a wave of your hand. Sometimes you're on your way down into hell, with demons turning and turning in the dark, just waiting for you to come within reach. Life consists mainly of jumping from one wheel to the other. The Doctor does it, roughly every 13 episodes. And so do we. Life moves like that, in patterns, in shapes familiar and strange, and at no point does the curtain close and the screen fade to black while lurid nebulae keep on bleeding into the black. Sometimes ratings are low and viewers miss the old flash and crackle. Sometimes our demons are ridiculous and ugly, sometimes they are boring and keep showing up no matter how far beyond them we think we have grown. Sometimes the jokes fall flat and a plotline that should have been profound runs smack into a wall of tragedy and failure and mindwiping because Life and Death cannot live in the same body but *ye gods* how we wish they could. More than we wish for there to be a perfect world where we can have our impossible lover, we wish for this world to be one where we can be both human and divine, Light and Dark, Donna and the Doctor, both wheels spinning together. Sometimes everything seems stupid and tawdry. Sometimes the sonic screwdriver is a beeping piece of light-up plastic. Sometimes it can do anything. Everything changes.

The Doctors and the companions are push-pins on a map. They regenerate constantly, every year, winter into spring. Our reactions to them, our identification with or repulsion by them, our need for them, our rejections of them tell us how far we have come, how far we have to go. They are silly, and unsightly, and self-indulgent, sublime, and glorious, and utterly necessary for the sacred acts of self-mythology.

And they tell us that there is always next season, when ratings will be up, and the smiles will return, and everyone will be reunited. We'll ride a blue box into the sunset, the tale finally illuminated by two wheels, one falling down into the past, one rising upward, eternally, into the future.

The Dark Side of the Moon

Writing and Publishing

The Breaking of the Vessels

I was listening to an author give a TEDtalk about writing the other day. About demystifying writing, to be specific. It was great - right up until she ran full-speed into the wall of the most mystifying of writerly myths, one that sends me up the wall and around the block, only to come back and shred my copy of *The Republic*. (I keep copies around for cathartic shredding. You'd be surprised how many obnoxious ideas got their start in that book.) Because this is not only a horribly pernicious idea about writers, it's also one of the oldest - Socrates got in on this idea way back in the goat-shearing, oil-smearing day.

Allow me to paraphrase.

Writers are vessels. They simply open up and let the muse flooooow through them, the divine spirit of Art reaches down and works the writer like a puppet, making words out of nothing, shimmering gossamer out of rough mortal matter. The job of the writer herself is mainly to be an empty conduit, ready to be filled like a fire-hose at any time with white-hot, spurting fonts of Literature.

Sounds like a pretty sweet gig.

I mean, seriously, how much more work could I get done if all I had to do was ~~lie back and think of Athens~~ basically just hold still while a cherubic demi-god sticks her hand down my throat and works me like Kermit? That would be so awesome! Why go to college or hell, even learn to read? No need, my good sir! Just point me to the nearest type-a-writer!

But it doesn't work like that. It really, really doesn't. Oh, sometimes it *feels* like it does. When things are really going and the connection between your brain and your fingers is on fire and everything is just flowing and the world in your head is just opening up on the page so perfectly... but the point is it only *feels* that way. And usually, you have to throw out half the stuff that felt amazing while you were writing it. It's a metaphor - any action performed well can touch that zen of perfect union between mind and body and work and the present moment. But no one talks about how accountants are vessels for the true, con-centrated spirit of math. (The other side of that is, of course, that it often feels as though you have no control over it, that it can come and go as it pleases. That's still just your brain, kids. Some days it works, some days it doesn't.)

The fact is, writing is a lot of hard work. Even "automatic writing" (another phrase I hate) is work. Whether the muse shows up or not, you have to sit at that computer. And it doesn't always, or even often, feel like pure zen creamy goodness. Before you even get to that computer, you have to think long and hard about what book you're writing, follow plotlines in your head, create characters, design plots, research endlessly. And before that, it helps to get an education in something interesting so you can write about something other than writing.

But despite its absurdity, this is a myth about writers that persists, over thousands of years. That metaphor for what it feels like when the writing is going well has been turned into what a lot of people - including, apparently, writers, who ought to know what a metaphor is - think about the writing process. (Incidentally, Plato was a failed playwright, and I have to think there is some bitterness that comes out in his treatment of poets as empty-headed baubles for gods to play with. Would that he had had a successful play!)

The most pernicious thing about this myth is it implies the author does not own what he or she creates. The muse did it. The author just took dictation. Authorial intent is all but dead in critical circles anyway. This effacing of the authorial self is bizarre and laughable on its face - of course the author did it. They planned it all out. Miss *Eat, Pray, Love* planned it all out, however she wants to talk about her vessel-ness. An author is not empty, they are not driven by embodied characters to write things they would not otherwise write. These are *metaphors for brain processes* - but talking about them as literal realities makes us all look a little flighty and a little crazy. And indirectly leads to the awesome I'm-an-artist-and-I-can-drink-all-day-and-fuck-whoever-I-like-because-I'm-an-artist-and-I-need-to-court-my-muse. Vomit.

Maybe I'm extra-sensitive because women have been viewed and treated as empty vessels by various folk for just about all of ever. Maybe I just hate Plato and hearing his twaddle spouted by people who have *a vested interest in mystifying writing* so that they can sit on high on the lecture circuit and talk about higher powers. Because the other subtle implication of the vessel argument is an awful Calvinist creeping notion. Only some of us are chosen by muses and demigods and Literature. *The rest of you can work as hard as you like, but all your work is nothing next to a Truly Chosen Artist who has been Touched by the Divine.* It's classist and upsetting and it's what underlies this whole stupid line of thought. Some of us are chosen. Some of us are not. Aristocrats don't work, but are rarified spirits. Plebes work themselves to death and yet can never be so wonderful as a prince on his throne.

Well, no. Sorry. Keep selling your Platonist screed. I'm not buying. I've never bought it, even when people called *The Labyrinth* automatic writing and insisted that I must not have thought about it at all since I wrote it so fast. No. It was hard fucking work and I nearly collapsed from it. It is possible to work hard very very fast. It doesn't mean that I had a secret hook-in to the red-light district of the collective unconscious. It doesn't mean anyone does. We all just write what we know how to write and hope it means something to someone else. No one has a magic writing wand. No one has an underpaid, statuesque muse without a union to do the work for them. (Ever notice how muses are always female? Inspiring is women's work.)

I also think there is a certain amount of distancing that some authors want.

The author of *Eat, Pray, Love* can dismiss her success as the work of a vessel under the weight of a higher power and it means she doesn't have to listen to criticism, or take responsibility for the unrealistic economic model for good living she set up, or do anything but be a special snowflake that was chosen by a glittery, kindly, oddly enough very economically savvy goddessy thing. It's so much easier to do publicity that way, you know? So much easier to write the next book if you just believe the work is already done for you.

And that's the thing. It isn't easy. It shouldn't be. It's scary and hard and it takes forever. Own that, for fuck's sake. flex your bicep and say: *hell yes, I wrote that book. Not my characters. Not my muse. Me. Every verb, every article. I've got the carpal tunnel to prove it.*

Writers aren't fragile Mina Harkers, occasionally filled up with Dracula's literary fluids. We're Rosie the Riveters. We *always* have to roll up our sleeves and do the damn work.

Now, if I could be a vessel for the glimmering, diaphanous spirit of True Copyediting, *that* would be awesome.

32 Statements About Writing

1. Writing is fun. Like learning a dead language, it is a far too time consuming, exhausting, difficult, and humiliating thing with which to occupy yourself if you're not having fun. People who tell you it's not fun are, to be frank, joyless husks of once-living flesh, and should be given no more attention than your average lurching zombie.

2. *Not* every writer is an experimentalist. Some writers wallow in tradition like a bikini-clad stripper in a mud-wrestling ring. There's no shame in that. There's a lot of pressure to "break new ground." Don't worry about that. Write what you are driven to write, and if it turns out to be a troublemaker who'll never, ever be any good, prone to tearing things up and chewing through the canon like a meth-addled alligator, that's what it'll be. But if it wants to sit in the corner in bifocals and pet its Shakespeare, that's ok, too. The literary world doesn't like its subjects to experiment *too* much. You may find yourself rewarded for bifocals. Don't be afraid to be a duck of a different color, but some ducks are just mallards - and have you ever seen the green on the head of a mallard? That's beauty.

3. Learning to write is easy. Alphabet + vocabulary + syntax. People write every day: checks, notes, memos, grocery lists. That's why everyone thinks they can write a book. By the time they're 20, the average person has written well over the requisite 70,000 words. Learning to *author* is hard. Learning to create a book out of nothing is hard. It's something to proud of if you can manage it, but if you can't, that's ok, too.

4. Read more than you write. But writing isn't math - you don't have to show your work.

5. When you stop taking pleasure from literature as anything but a lesson-plan, it's time to quit. Take up painting instead. Or accounting.

6. Every story has already been told. But you haven't told every story. Originality does not lie in plot, it lies in voice, and yours is the only one of its kind.

7. All writing is confessional.

8. Genre is irrelevant. Write. Let others sort out what section of the bookstore you belong in.

9. Don't be afraid of the "I" in poetry or prose. The "I" is magical. It allows the reader to experience the work as though she wrote it, as though she lived it. All art begins in the primordial "I." Don't turn your back on that wellspring.

10. It's ok to be lazy. Procrastinate. All things in their time - if the work is alive in you, it'll demand your attention. Don't force a birth at five months.

11. On the other hand, write something every day, even if it's a grocery list.

Groceries can be poetry if you allow it. Carrots and ice, lemons and salt.

12. If you don't write every day, that's ok, too. Cultivate zen when it comes to output anxiety.

13. Don't talk too much about writing, or write too much about craft. It'll keep you from your real work and make you neurotic.

14. Language is more important than you think. It is not a tool, it is, in the end, the sum of literature. Language has a taste, a texture, a smell. If a painter used only beige, white, and grey, the viewer's eye would slide off the canvas and start examining the wall. Strive for eggplant, oxblood, and burnt sienna.

15. Poetry and fiction are not opposites. They're more like fraternal twins who have it out on daytime talk shows every other week. And Poetry's a hair-puller. Don't feel you can only spend Christmas with one or the other - gas up the Chevelle and eat tofurkey at Poetry's house and a big greasy side of ham at Fiction's pad. You'll start to notice that they have the same nose, the same strut, the same taste in ceramic figurines...

16. The company of other writers is a tricky thing. It always starts out with Chinese firecrackers and leviathans in a local cafe, and before you know it you're an Iowa Writers' Conference, and half your members are brawling in a Des Moines alley over book deals and who slept with who.

17. Publication is not the point.

18. Don't rely too much on revision. There is value in the first flush. The cult of revision has many members. They won't miss you.

19. Listening to what works for other people only gets you so far. At some point, you will be struck dumb by good advice.

20. Do not listen to people who habitually use words like "my process" and "the craft."

21. Good writing is not always economical. Sometimes good writing blows all its cash on video slots and all-night steak buffets, and shows up at its best friend's house at 3 am with two black eyes, asking for beer money.

22. Workshops can be circle jerks. Or a circle of jerks. Find one that is neither.

23. Art is a way of life. It is also a career, an obsession, a trade, a magic act, a lie, a simulacrum, a habit, a ritual, and a virtue. Don't let other writers define your terms for you.

24. Experiment like it doesn't matter. It doesn't. You live at a unique time in the history of the written word - everything is permissible. But don't be surprised when you discover that the world of publishing is essentially conservative, and is made uncomfortable by anything truly radical. Have a Plan B, like automotive repair or appliance sales. A real writer can find poetry in a muffler or a washer-dryer combo, too.

25. You are not entitled to a book deal. Maybe it'll happen for you, maybe it won't, but one universal truth is this: no one likes an asshole who thinks he's

owed something.

26. Cultivate perspective. There is only one extant copy of *Sir Gawain and the Green Knight* - that's how close it came to being snuffed out forever. Most manuscripts, no matter how brilliant, are destroyed by the vagaries of time and weather. Paper rot cares nothing for beauty. Write, get it into the world however you can, even in the tiniest press. Then hope rain, mudslides, and drunken librarians pass you by. That's the best you can do.

27. Don't write to an audience. The audience isn't the one you have to answer to, in the end. Let that shit go and write what thrills you.

28. Own your work. No matter how it looks now, remember that when you wrote it, it lit up the page and melted the pen. Self-hate is a waste of time.

29. It's ok to suffer for your art, but don't make a fetish of it.

30. You know how to write. Don't let washed-up hippies mystify it with half-assed quasi-koans or barricade it behind a wall of awards, endowments, and prizes for which you have neither slept with the judge nor studied under the fashionable poets.

31. Shut up and write.

32. Lists are useless. Your mileage may vary.

Touch the Puppets

This is a phrase I used during a recent writers' workshop; I want to pass the savings on to you.

I first heard it while indulging in my favorite activity: writing while listening to director's commentary. Oh, it is wonderful! What's the point of a DVD without commentary? Due to years alone when I lived in Japan, I am somewhat phobic about silence and empty houses, and a commentary makes me feel like someone is there, talking about really smart things, and yet, it doesn't distract me from work. Occasionally, when, say, Guillermo del Toro or Baz Luhrmann is talking, I get great ideas about use of color and theme, about combining the surreal with the real. It's really the best of all worlds as far as whilst-working entertainment.

So, awhile back, possibly even in Japan, I was listening to an episode of *Farscape*, and the actors' commentary. Ben Browder was laughing about the Rygel puppet and exclaiming: "Oh man, they were always nagging at us to touch the puppets. It made the puppets seem real, and us seem more sympathetic." And at the time, I thought - heh. Neat. It is *totally awesome how real all the puppets seem in the Farscape world.*

And during in workshop, it popped right back into my head, in a somewhat oblique, metaphorical way, and it's now one of those phrases that I think about when shaping a story or a novel.

See, I'm a fantasist. Which means there are strange things afoot at the Circle K in my books pretty much all the time. My work is full of things that would take some pretty sweet puppetry to realize in any kind of corporeal way. So is yours, if you write SFF or horror. And no matter what else you're doing in a novel, no matter how many plates are spinning and motifs are on fire on your little pulpy stage, you gotta touch the puppets.

It makes me grind my teeth when the fantastic element just sits around wheezing its animatronic pistons and looking weird and little more. It's so easy to let it happen - to let folkloric beasties be mere walk-ons, running by the camera at top speed as if to say: "Hi! I'm a dream-eating tapir, colloquially known as a Baku! Aren't I cool and weird?! Those wacky Japanese! Bye!"

Sometimes it takes me awhile to realize what's bothering me: that nothing fantastic *matters*, just by dint of being fantastic. It's not real, not subject to the same examination as the human/mundane/reader insertion character.

If you're going to bother to write non-realist work at all, you have to sit down and figure out why you're doing it. It sure ain't for the money, so there must be a reason you need to have tapirs. If the only answer is: *because it's cool?* You're in trouble, and you had better find a way to make readers think it matters, or we're likely to wander off. The best SFF connects because it combines crazy stuff with genuine emotional content - and the very best wrangles the whole thing so that you couldn't have gotten tot he emotional climax without the erstwhile help of a Baku.

How do you do that? You touch the puppets.

The beasties, fairies, ghosts, aliens, AI, whatever - the protagonist must interact with them. She must be moved by them, to disgust or revelation. She must talk to them, touch them, eat with them, be threatened by them. They must become her friends, her enemies, her lovers. It must *matter* that they are there. They specifically, not interchangeable pointy-ears. This might seem like a basic rule, but often, as I have read a great number of books for review over the last half-year, I've gotten the feeling that the author is really turned on by something in the book - but it sure isn't the fantastic element. It's the high concept or the literary allusions or the very human desire to blow shit up. The rest of all that fantasy crap is just set dressing. Paper dragons, cardboard gods, tissue-paper ghosts. Matte paintings for the characters to walk off into. Non-Playable-Characters mechanically pointing the way to the end of the chapter.

When confronted with the tapir walking around in circles announcing "Our village is in peril! Our village is in peril!" the hero can walk right by on his way to the battle and the author can write off "awesome tapirs" on his or her book checklist. Or the knight can stop and grip the thing by the shoulders. *Why are you like that? What happened to you? Why do you eat dreams? Do they taste good? Do they give you indigestion? Did you ever want to be a mechanic instead?*

To me, one of these options is compelling, and one is boring.

Of course, the key to that is a really good answer from the tapir. It's hard to substitute any phrase or advice for "make it good." But touching the puppets can be surprisingly simple - a line or a paragraph, simple brush-strokes that imply the world. It's not just the hero that has to touch them, it's the author. Take a breath and look around, ask questions, let those creatures/magics/world/ships be fully in the story, rather than marginalia.

Or start writing realism.

Puppets are particularly a problem in the "Josephine Normal stumbles upon Magical Kingdom Type #441™ and stares goggle-eyed at the array of suitably wondrous creatures around her" sub-genre. Which is a totally legitimate and time-tested plot frame. We all love our Alices. But it often feels like the hero is standing still while a filmstrip of *mysteries from afar* flicker by. But all it takes is reaching out a human hand to touch the inhuman skin, and, as if by magic, the mysteries grow eyestalks and a sad, down-turned mouth, possess private tragedies and public humiliations, long histories and phobias and desires of their own. And the hero seems invested in the world, in discovering it, in fighting it, rather than simply paying the minimum of attention in history class. WALL*E worked because we believed in the private life of a robot, and believed, not coincidentally, in his overwhelming desire for touch. *The Sixth Sense* worked because we were so deep in the psyche of the fantastical element that we literally forgot how to see with normal eyes.

Advocate for puppet rights. NPCs need love, too. They are ends in themselves, not means to an end. *Or at least you have to pretend they are to lift a book beyond the tired and mundane.*

Touch the puppets. Make them real. Otherwise you're just playing with dolls.

The Devil and Ms. V

I firmly believe that one of the circles of hell consists of a single endless undergraduate poetry workshop. They are harrowing by intent and design, so it should be unsurprising that your humble narrator was scarred by one or two in her time, and in times of extremis, draws out the lessons of those humiliating jungle-years with which to instruct and terrify. This is one of those times. Hearken, children! For what I have to say will chill your heart.

The devil of my early writing was man I shall henceforward refer to as Dr. S.

Dr. S was obsessed with the idea of Cliché. I capitalize it because he did - you could hear it in his speech, the awe and fear with which he regarded it. It was a word that came to haunt me, a floating neon noun ready to pounce on my carefully-typed pages and scald them with accusations. It was his main criticism of anything he did not like, lines, images, subjects. He was as vigilant against it as a savvy hunter against hidden panthers - Cliché may leap upon you at a moment's notice, burrowing into your verse without pity or hesitation, and if you are not so well-read that you say your night-prayers not to God but Ginsberg, you will never even know it is there. Dr. S outlawed an entire index of words from our available poetic vocabulary at the beginning of the semester. I will not reproduce it in full, but among them were: "ocean," "tears," "love," "gossamer," and "blood." These are necessary tumors to remove from the under-graduate body, of course.

In later years, it seemed odd to me that a man so feared of cliché in poetry could embrace it so in his person. For Dr. S was particularly fond of the follow-ing activities: elbow-patches on corduroy jackets, writing poetry about his fatherless childhood in the Midwest, running the campus literary magazine like his personal Chilean junta, and sleeping with his students. It is entirely possible that there is a factory somewhere deep in the wilds of Iowa where such men are stamped out by the dozens and neatly shipped to educational institutions across the world.

Needless to say, Dr. S hated my work. Poetry should be about parental issues, edgy sex, and the Midwest, not magic or myth, after all. Eventually he threw up his hands and declared that if I wasn't going to change for him, I wasn't going to change for anyone, and I might as well just do what I do and languish in the purgatory of the unpublished. My response was, I believe, unprintable in such an august venue as the one in which these words abide.

However, despite my personal differences with the dastardly Dr. S, his phobia of Cliché was communicable, and I inherited it full-force.

It is a valuable phobia to have. In poetry, you cannot hide. Your words are naked and unprotected: if you dare to say a woman's skin was white as snow, you will be caught out and arrested, and no judge in the world will remain steadfast at your side. It's no more than you deserved, really. And because poetry is so vulnerable, so unguarded, most poets of any quality have figured out how to avoid it, or at least to slow down when they see a critical patrol car in the distance.

But in fiction, you can hide.

A novel consists of so many words that you can get away with murder, so to speak. And if you did not bend under the whip of Dr. S, if you did not discover along the way a phobia, nay, an allergy to Cliché, you may toss about as much snow-white skin as you please, and be forgiven for it. And as I have begun to review books as well as write them, I have come to believe that Dr. S did not make a small hell of enough young writers' lives.

What is a Cliché, you might ask, so that I may identify it in the wild? A Cliché is something repeated so many times in so many pieces of media that it has lost all ability to move or impact the audience, and is therefore utterly useless to the writer. "Get away with murder," for example. No one who reads such a sentence is really struck dumb with the raw unfairness of such a thing, the injustice, the violence condoned, the amoral, godless universe implied by such a phrase. Nor is it funny. Yet it is used and re-used as though it carried some kind of mantric power. This is silly, slovenly writing, and I shuddered to type it. Nevertheless, especially in genre literature, such proliferate like foul mushrooms. Not because the writers who use them are bad, or lazy, or anything of the sort. They simply are not poets, and have never been strip-searched for unoriginal phrasing. After all, in a work of a hundred thousand words, what does it matter if a thousand or so have been chewed to death by three millennia of decomposing authors?

It mattered to Dr. S. And it matters to me. The world could do with a little phobia, and if novels could be as naked an accountable as poems, we would all have to endure far less rubbish.

As a start, allow me to fire the following items from the English Author's lexicon: "vise-like grip." "His/her blood ran cold." The word "eldritch," applied to anything, unless you are Terry Pratchett and therefore making a joke, or H.P. Lovecraft, and therefore dead.

Skin may be any color, however, it may not be compared to: snow, milk/cream/any dairy product, ebony, porcelain, chocolate, coffee/café au lait/any caffeinated beverage.

Eyes, especially if they are green, may not "flash."

A heroine may have red hair. If you pay a tax, it may even be "flowing red hair." However, if she does, she may not be "fiery" a "spitfire" or any other combustible substance. She may not be spunky, sassy, or in any other way defined solely by her hair color. If she has flowing red hair and a fiery personality, under no circumstances may she be named Molly. Or Kate. Or Annie, for god's sake.

A sword may be many things. It may slice, dice, and julienne. It may cut tin cans and tomatoes with equal ease. Try hard to resist giving it a lineage, or allowing it to be of dwarven/elvish/eldritch make. Or glow. In fact, try writing a fantasy novel without using the word "sword." It'll be good for you.

If a hero is spunky or sassy, like his redheaded friend Molly, if he is a scrappy, clever, tricky type, he may be named anything but Jack. If he is an orphan, Oliver is right out.

This one may seem too easy, but like smoking certain vegetable substances, we rarely narc on each other, even though we know it is illegal: if a certain young man is destined for great acts of heroism, he may be raised anywhere but a farm.

The phrase "genre hack" was created for addicts of this sort of thing. This is only a beginning. Search inside yourself - you know others lurk there, panther-like, ready to pounce. They lurk in me, too. Our vigilance must be tireless. It is not that any of the above are bad in and of themselves. But they have been done so many times before - why would you spend precious time that will be counted against you at the hour of your death creating more of it? Life, and the warranty on your wrists, is too short for unoriginality.

If this sort of thing continues much longer, I shall have to institute a Neighborhood Watch. And you know, Dr. S just doesn't have the vacation time.

Voodoo Economics: How to Find Serenity in an Industry that Does Not Want You

In the antiseptic, sour-smelling halls of psychology, there is an entire wing devoted to Anxiety. Within that wing is a dingy corner containing a dry mop and a broken drinking fountain bearing a sign that reads "Please Love Me." This section is wholly devoted to Writer's Anxiety.

There is a hierarchy of Writer's Anxiety, and since this is a magazine which splits its favors more or less equally among the tiers, it is this hierarchy which concerns me as I sit down, fresh from my latest rejection, to tell you all how I keep the temptation to rip up paperback copies of *The Sword of Shannara* and choke myself to death on their pulpy remains at bay.

The first tier of Writer Anxiety can aptly be described as "Oh, God, Let Me Get Published." This pupal stage in the development of the author is fraught with misery and self-doubt, characterized by a willingness to do any number of unsavory things for the chance at a stapled, mimeographed contributor's copy and a steadfast conviction that publication vindicates all.

The second tier falls under the fluttering banner of "Oh, God, Let Me Keep Publishing." This intermediary stage is full of dread and attempts to scry the market using arcane methods of haruspicy and blog-reading in order to keep oneself relevant and employed. These tiers often snipe at one another in a morbid kind of Misery Olympics - is it more wretched to have no credits to your name and a burning, thwarted desire for them or to have to deal every day with a hostile market that could dump you onto the landfill at any arbitrary moment? Meet me at the con. We'll compare ulcers.

It was not so long ago - about four years - that I was squarely in that first tier, just hoping against hope someone would see in my work what I saw, that someone would reach down from the gold-paneled heavens of New York City and say: *yes, you are what we want.* That didn't happen.

How can I say that, when I, in fact, did get a two-book deal with Bantam Spectra, followed by a third, when I've gone from total unknown to multi-award-winning author on the cover of *Locus* in less than four years?

Because the industry doesn't want me. And they don't want you, either. The word industry is applicable here only with squinted eyes and foil-wrapped antennae affixed firmly to the skull. Imagine, if you will, that instead of the effete, latte-sipping literati we surely are, that we all work together in a steel mill in, let's say Ohio, oh, round about now.

The glory age of our employers is long past. Most of the field has either gone out of business or merged or found other, cheaper workers who will not insist on decent pay and benefits. The world is actively, eagerly looking for some way to completely replace what we make with something more energy-efficient, modern, and interesting. Every once in awhile our employers land a big contract, and that keeps the rest of us afloat for awhile, but it's been on the downhill for a long time. Take a look at some of the steel towns in Ohio. It's a metaphor, but it's also a mirror. The difference is, if steel production ground to a halt today, it would be a problem.

There are more writers today, producing more text, than ever before in the history of the world. It can't have escaped notice that this entire article is pregnant with the assumption that its audience is primarily other writers and aspiring writers. More books, more blogs, more everything. If everyone with literary aspirations were to, at this very instant, wake up, laugh, and get a banking job, the publishing industry could go for decades, even a century, on just those who are working now, reprints, and endless new editions of the ten most popular books of all time. No one would even notice.

We're selling steel to the steel barons, kids.

So when I say it didn't happen, what I mean is that the barons will never look down at me and say: *yes, you are what we want.* Let's be honest, I don't even sell machine-grade steel. I sell Damascus steel, folded and intricate, dug up from the earth, practically useless, desirable only to lovers of the arcane, the beautiful, the old. No one slammed a fist down onto their desk and shouted: *what we need here is a woman writer with too much education to natter incomprehensibly about fairy tales!* It doesn't work like that. It's a ghastly game, trying to predict how an author will perform, betting on her like a horse. And how she runs! As long as she can, she runs. But usually, it's not that long.

I've been questioning myself a lot lately. Questioning my steel, if you will. I choose to write the aggressively strange, almost virulently outside the mainstream. Does this hurt me? Does it, slowly, kill me? I can't tell. I just can't. I try to recall Ted Chiang's words as I was working on this article: "I once heard that, on average, published novelists earn only slightly more than migrant laborers. With prospects like that, why not just write what you want?"

It doesn't always get me to sleep at night.

I contracted to write this article at the beginning of the summer, when I felt like I had something to share about finding serenity, finding the zen of choosing yourself over your industry, of pursuing your strange, unseemly niche until it carries you where you ought to go.

But a funny thing happened. I got rejected. A lot. A couple of projects I believed in made the rounds and went precisely nowhere. Now, I know we're not supposed to talk about our failures - we manufacture a propaganda of success that promotes a narrative where every worthwhile book gets published, but Virginia, it just ain't so. But it's a funny thing to stare at the title to this article for a couple of hours when all your awards and buzz add up to the same rejection letters you got when you were waltzing with the mop in the Anxiety Museum. Kind of like the universe smirking in your direction. *How does that serenity taste now, kid?*

And it's taken me a couple of days, it really has. But I'm here to tell you: it tastes fine.

When you work in a steel town, you either cling to the mill and drink for all you're worth or you embrace the new world: new technologies, new economies, niche markets and products no one has thought to want before. The only other option is death. And proximity to death brings clarity: they don't want me. They don't want you. There are no job openings and there are lay-offs by the thousand, every day, that you never hear about and no pundit weeps over. We are the ones full of want, full of desire. We transmit our want to them like to fickle gods and like gods they accept us or turn away for reasons we cannot scry.

I would like the equation to be simple. Want made manifest in glorious books = success. Straight-to-RPG Tolkien knock offs = failure. But we all know otherwise. There is no equation, unless it's spin around three times, sacrifice a chicken, shut your eyes real tight, throw your book into the air and hope it was the right chicken. In the face of that kind of chance, that kind of future, where every book is an act of voodoo and faith with no hope but a fool's hope?

You spin around three times. You sacrifice a chicken. You close your eyes and write your book. There's nothing else. Nothing else possible. And there is a zen to be found in embracing that, even if what you were put on this earth to write isn't a bestseller that engulfs you in praise every day. Life is a lot like a publishing contract: a thing full of promise, a cauldron into which we throw all our best ideas and acts, and out of which comes utterly unpredictable results. Children with eight arms, Chinese gymnastic teams, even recursive books about folklore and griffins. Yes, and bestsellers, too, but you can never be sure if it was the onion or the eye of newt that did the trick.

Every book *is* an act of voodoo, gorgeous voodoo, sympathetic magic, of stupid, blind faith. Our job is to maintain that faith just long enough to produce about a hundred thousand words. And that's as it should be. Faith is not always answered. That is also as it should be. We are wicked fairies, all of us. We must pay our tithes to hell, and some of those tithes come in the form of failed books, rejected manuscripts, bad reviews.

When I got my first acceptance - not a short story, not a poem, but a full-blown (and largely forgotten) novel called *The Labyrinth* back in 2004, I sat very delicately on my couch and closed my laptop. I realized something in that moment that I am trying very hard to remember right now, when I fear for my ability to keep working in the steel town I have chosen: *publication was never the point.* The point was the work, the book, the voodoo, the faith. The point was the sheer joy of creating something out of nothing, crystal out of gross matter.

They will never really want what I have to give. My job, insofar as I have one, is to make what I have to give glow so brightly that they cannot turn away from it.

And that's your job, too.

That's it, right there. That's the serenity that this life will offer, and not too much more. There is never a time when you are not scared for your next contract, never a time when you do not fear for your future, when you stop praying to the motley gods of union-workers and Ohio steel towns to let you keep working, please, just a few more years. Even J.K. Rowling, she of the blessings and grace you hope for, worries about what she'll do next. It's a serenity that is hard to hold on to, it requires steadfastness and a world-champion grip.

Fate, all three of them, are stone cold bitches. They laugh at awards and ash their cigarettes on them, they gobble up all your fervent hopes and ask for more, always more, without giving a damn thing back. It's their nature. And it is ours to be fodder for them. The only other option is death.

And you know what? Even if you don't feel it, even if you've had your baby chucked out of the big city this very week, especially if you have, *you say these things anyway*. When someone asks you silly questions for an online article. When your spouse is tired of your lack of income. At night, when you're sure you'll never sell another book. You say it anyway. Everything true bears reminding. It's a mantra, it is specifically designed to heal the broken soul. And it becomes true again in less time than you think.

How to Write a Novel in 30 Days

Here's the thing - I am a fast writer. I think this is a skill I developed in college, a combination of stress and a vital part of my personality: I am incredibly lazy.

Because I am incredibly lazy, it is very easy to convince me not to work, since I don't want to work anyway. Which led to an abnormal number of papers completed the night before they were due... and then the early morning hours before they were due, then the not so early morning hours[1]... And if *even once* I had failed to turn in a paper, failed to churn out 20 pages on gender anxiety in *Sir Gawain and the Green Knight*, if I had even once failed to get an A, I think I would have rethought my methods and come to some sort of conclusion about work ethics.

Didn't happen.

So what my brain learned was not what it should have learned, namely that this sort of thing is about as risky and dumb as huffing whipped cream canisters. My brain learned that there was no deadline it couldn't meet.

This is a dangerous thing for a brain to know, and I recommend failure to meet deadlines to everyone. Human behavior means doing something until it doesn't work. This sort of thing still works for me. I do not expect it to work forever, and frankly, it giveth and it taketh. You get the work done fast, but your body is shredded and you end up with the interpersonal grace of Gollum on a meth binge.

But you're not going to listen to these warnings.

The 30 days is an arbitrary number - it is kind of an absolute minimum for me[2]. I haven't pushed myself to see just how fast I can turn out a novel, but I don't trust myself with less than 30 days. I'm not *crazy*. Obviously, Nanowrimo influences that number (50k in a month, at something like 1400 words a day, is not actually very hard if you're a fast hand at the keyboard and don't have a day job) and now it can be told that I did Nanowrimo in 2002... sort of. See, those were heady days. I was 23. I was all balls-out and brazen and come-here-world-I'm-gonna-take-a-bite-out-of-you.

You know, totally different than now.

---

1 This is where being a classicist *really* pays off. Ain't no English class (see what I did there?) can lick you - you know most of it before you set foot in the room, and your base of knowledge is broad enough that you can sound damn smart in a number of varied fields. I in no way mean to imply that in graduate school I did the research and the composition the day the paper was due. That would be *crazy*.

2 I've done the 3 Day Novel competition - they expect you to produce something like 30k words, and that's a novella at best.

So I just did it on my own in early October and I clocked in at a lot less than 30 days. The result? The beginning of my career and a novel called *The Labyrinth*.

The key, really, is to never learn you can fail.

I really enjoy timed writing - with deadline from without (editor) or within (online project, personal goal, etc). I think it's because I enjoy obstructions. Things created within boundaries, where the boundaries become part of the object, creativity fueled by restriction. It lights me up inside - your mileage may, of course, vary. This is not how I write every novel - it took me six years to write *The Orphan's Tales*. As I said, I don't recommend this: first of all, no one will think you can have possibly produced anything good in that time, because time spent = quality, obviously, and no other factors come into play. Second of all, you absolutely have to play by this first rule. No exceptions, no hall passes.

Rule 1: Be a Genius

Guys, I cannot stress this enough. See Kerouac's *Belief and Technique for Modern Writing*. Rule #29? *You Are a Genius All the Time.* (Yes, I have that list nailed above my desk.)

I don't care what kind of writer you are. I don't care how many rejections you've had, I don't care how long you've been doing this. For 30 days, you are a genius. Everything that flows from your fingers is pure light. You do not have the luxury of not being a genius - not being a genius is laziness and sloth and you just can't tolerate that shit right now.

Writing this fast is an act of unadulterated, blind, idiot faith. Faith in yourself, in your voice, in your story, in your sheer ability. If your faith falters, you lose time. In my experience, if you're working on a 30 day cycle, you can afford to lose maybe three days (non-consecutive, if you lose three straight days you'll never recover) to self-doubt, internal criticism, and not being a genius. More than that and you're running up against words-per-minute, and when you get down to it, typing speed is actually a big factor. Us Millenials who grew up in chat rooms have generally fabulous-fleet skillz, but seriously, this is no time for long-hand.

2. Tell Everyone

Make sure everyone knows what you're doing. This will provide the heady ingredient of shame to the proceedings, and I find that shame is an enormous motivator. If you fail alone, in private, no one will ever know, and you can claim that writing a novel in 30 days is impossible, for hacks, etc, with impunity. If you post to your blog and tell all your friends, you have to admit to it if you fail. This is assuming you are not subject to the major reason for speedwriting: you have a deadline and you watched *Alias* reruns instead of working until the last possible second.

It's also important that your partner and social group knows not to expect you to be anything like human for the next month. Fortunately, you're a genius, and geniuses are never expected to conform to primate behavior standards[3]. Just, you know, apologize later. If you are very lucky, you might have a partner or friend who is willing to provide any combination of the following salves for your chafed genius muscles: food, quiet space/leaving you the hell alone, a clean house, inspirational backrubs, crazy-ass genius sex.

But probably not.

3. Be Crazy

Jeff Vandermeer said that one ought not to try for much more than a transparent style when writing at breakneck speed. I, rather predictably, disagree. If anything, I'd suspect this doesn't work so well for complex *plot* than complex language, but that's likely because I find language easier than plot. Pick what you're best at, and make that the focus of this marathon. I rather think that no technique is better suited to beatnik-pomo-style crazy writing than this - let go of your internal editor, of the ways writing is "supposed" to be (hint: it's not supposed to be done in 30 days), any ideas your English professors might have given you about literature, and just open your brain onto the computer. Direct flesh-to-motherboard communication. Remember, this is blind faith we're talking about. You are St. Teresa, and *you are here to be transfigured*. This is *radical, revolutionary trust* that what you are creating is worth the world.

You may not actually end up with a novel at the end of the month. But you'll have something. Kerouac said not to be afraid to be a crazy dumbsaint of the mind. Quite so.

4. Sacrifice Your Body

Come on, you weren't using it anyway.

The fact is, this sort of thing is a horrific strain on your human suit. You stay up late, you eat whatever is easy, you have to ice down your wrists at the end of the day. You burn your brain out, no joke. Make time for recovery afterward. Get out of the house occasionally, to Toby and my Starbucks, or the front lawn, or a laundromat. Look up at the sky. Accept the fact that you will fall down on your household chores - which is why this sort of thing is usually a childless writer's gig - and that several times, you will literally want to die rather than write another word. Keep going. Talk to marathon runners. Rejoice, and conquer. Die, if you have to. Then get up and get back to work.

---

3 *Do not drink alcohol.* You are not that kind of genius.

5. Don't Fail

You don't have time to fail. You don't have time for writer's block. You don't have time to wibble.

And if you don't fail this time, you'll never learn that you *can* fail, and every time you don't fail, your faith in your ability to not fail will grow until one day you'll wake up and you won't be a failure at all. It's kind of awesome, if you can manage it. But the key is not failing, and the key to not failing is stupid dumb-fuck faith that you *won't* fail. Life is circular like that.

The reason I don't credit Nanowrimo is not because I don't think quality can be produced in 30 days. That would be a silly opinion, considering. It's because *they* don't think quality can be produced in 30 days. Their whole site is about producing crap and having it be okay to produce crap. It is okay. But I don't have time to produce crap. Life is too short to produce crap. And the only way I know how to do this is to be absolutely convinced that what I'm writing is gobstoppingly amazing.

And I can only maintain that sort of conviction for short bursts.

Say, 30 days.

Ghostpigs

I took a job editing a magazine because I thought it would be interesting to work on the other side of the editor/author divide for awhile, to see first hand what the selection process is all about. I thought it would be educational - and it was. I'm not a mean person, I'm don't reject stories for fun. I want to find awesome stories because frankly, it sucks to read bad ones all day. Finding the readable jewel is always a rush. However harsh I may seem, I actually don't want to crush spirits under my pointy literary heel. That being said.

Holy shit guys, what the hell is going on with opening paragraphs?

I swear to god, in every workshop I've ever known, they've said: you have to make your opening paragraph awesome because editors will kick it if it doesn't grab them right away.

I know I have heard this. Like, a *lot*.

Yet 90% of the stories that have crossed my desk have first paragraphs that tell me nothing about the story, have no interesting language use, and little bearing on the rest of the story. It's no coincidence that the other 10% are the ones that were accepted, asked for rewrites, or in my I can't decide yet file.

Dudes, a short story is not that long. You do not have 50 pages to hook a reader (you don't, really, in a novel either, but that's another post), you cannot lazily dick around for a page and a half before being all *check it out ghostpigs*. Because no one ever made it to the *ghostpigs*, who were buried under: "Robert walked down the street. The sky was cloudy. All the houses were brown. He thought about work."

Oh my God.

Don't bury the lede. There is no reason not to open with: *Ghostpigs motherfuckers*. You know how Ezra Pound famously cut the first 200 lines of *The Wasteland* so that it began with *April is the cruelest month*, one of the most famous lines in poetry, which Eliot, not ever having met a ghostpig, stuffed under a pile of 200 other lines which were *not* the most famous lines in poetry? Yeah. Do that. For serious. Because I should never be scrolling up to see *how long is this story, really* after a single paragraph about Robert and the brown houses.

And why would you want to sideline the ghostpigs? (Incidentally, it's a little known fact that just because some venues accept horror stories doesn't mean they are ghost story only publications. *I know. It's fucking crazy.* But there are horror stories which are not ghost stories. Some aren't even slow meandering literary midwest/New York stories with a ghost thrown in at the end so that you can sell it to a genre magazine. *I cannot believe it either.*) Don't you want readers to be like *hold up I have to put everything else aside to read this now*? Don't you?

And if you want to hold back your awesome, then wouldn't it make more sense to start with something at least stylistically interesting, so that by the time the ghostpigs are shredding on diamond-crusted 12-necked bone-guitars, at least people are like: I trust something supersweet is on its way because this author can clearly write. I cannot begin to understand the logic that turns every story into the literary equivalent of a mullet: *boring stuff up front, awesome to the back.*

Honestly, this goes double for poetry, only where it says paragraph? Insert line. Your first line had better be amazing, and the second one, too, because that's about all you have before I start to not trust that you know where you're going. And if the first couple of lines rhyme, they had better be interesting and, um, fresh rhymes, because your standard a-b-a-b malarkey doesn't really cut it unless the content is stellar. You have even less time in a poem than in a short story to prove to a reader that this is worth their time. And in all stories, poems, books, you really do have to prove that this thing right here is worth the reader's time - that it will give them something more than the equivalent amount of time spent watching movies or speed-cycling or knitting or watching paint dry. And while I'll give a novel about 50-100 pages to prove that, I will give a short story one to two pages. And a short story that is in a mass of dozens I have to read in a few days less than that. It's not mean, it's not unfair, it's reality - if you can't write a good page, you probably can't write a good story, and after enough stories, it's pretty easy to tell the difference between a story where I can lop off the first two paragraphs and have something great, and a story *with no ghostpigs at all.* I am telling you this not to be a big bad mommy editor, but to make it easier for you to sell me a story.

Raise Your Gauntlet of Rock

It's funny how music terms get appropriated and become general terms - like punk, which accompanies any given noun to create a dizzying cabaret of sub-genres. Or like metal.

Most of my friends use this word about as often as they use the word awesome, which is to say *constantly* and with overweening enthusiasm. "That's pretty metal," Jack will say when he wins a game decisively. And he means it's good on the level of bone-crunching, passionate, bombastic, anger-filled music that might or might not be from the devil, that has shredding virtuoso guitars and thumping drums you can feel in your pancreas. I *dig* that as an adjective, especially since, like writing, playing metal is way harder than it seems, and writing fantasy is just as likely to be written off as not *real* music/literature.

I wonder about the motivations involved in the invocation of punk in our wide and diverse genre. I've been thinking about this since yesterday, more or less nonstop. It speaks to me of a deep longing for all that punk represents, and a deep anxiety that as a group, we ain't got it. Maybe we feel there is something inherently not-very-punk about sitting at a keyboard for 12 hours and writing about ray guns and fairy socio-political constructs. It doesn't look cool, like playing a guitar, there are no video games to simulate it, and despite the shine the *idea* of writing has, the reality is so boring that three generations of filmmakers have bent over backward trying to come up with a way to show it on screen that doesn't make the viewing public nose-dive into their popcorn and came up with, collectively, a fake nose and a montage. So we invoke people who are somehow ineffably cooler than us, hopeless dorks that most of us were and are. That's ok -music is usually trying to get itself taken seriously in a literary way, so it's fair game. But we must want it, god, we must want it so bad if we keep using the word like it's an amulet against the world. (Secretly, though? Writing *is* punk rock. It's hard fucking core and we are kung-fu lycanthropic nuns with mean hangovers. But don't tell anyone. There's only so much depilatory cream to go around.)

But we have to earn it if we're going to wear it, you know? No $200 ripped skirt with patches pre-sewn on. Even though it's a vague and subjective thing, what is punk, what is metal, what is not - well, what is not is usually pretty obvious, but what is is often less clear. Insert pornography test here. I'm not sure myself if I know what the hell I'm talking about - someone said to me yesterday that fantasy was by definition not metal, and ~~I killed him with my pen~~ sputtered indignantly for a long while, trying to explain the secret hardcore of fantasy. Though I think, given that musicians have been arguing their own terms since at least 1977, I can be forgiven for not having a Recipe for Metal.

But I have an idea of what the dish looks like when it's done. It's something bone-crunching, passionate, bombastic, something so honest it hurts, something hard, virtuoso, thumping, pounding. You feel it in your pancreas.

And somehow, it's the key to something. Like a pile of mashed potatoes. Something awesome and terrible, something fantasy can be. Something we can be. And my challenge to myself as I work on my sixth novel is, at the end of every chapter, to ask myself:

"Is this metal?"

And move forward only if the big, antisocial, spike-booted, string-shredding, pen-stabbing imp with a steel bar through her face who lives somewhere to the left of my spleen says: *Fuck yeah, it's metal!*

I challenge you to do the same.

And you don't stop.

Have I Ever Told You About My Love/Hate Relationship With Confessional Poetry?

The art
of confession's to focus attention on what's
confessed while leaving the secret
mutations untouched. I once put the hose
of a vacuum on my penis and turned it
on. Honesty makes me feel so clean.

—Bob Hicok

Some of you know I started out as a poet. Some of you might have surmised as much from reading my books, which generally treat plot as a back-door lover, to be treated with suspicion and kept in ecstatic servitude. There's training to be had in poetry just like there's training to be had in fiction, but the training in poetry tends to be more like acting class: find your deepest, most horrible, painful, darkest experience and drag it up for the joy of the crowd, who is really only there to see real, honest tears and breast-rending. Kind of like NASCAR fans.

It's like the Xtreme Sport version of Write What You Know.

In the days before I got the bright idea to start writing novels, I ran that particular obstacle course. I dutifully ate the scorpions and walked the highwire, dredging up my childhood abuse and past relationships and anything else that seemed suitably dire to please a professor. It really makes for an alarming personality type: someone who has lost all notion of appropriate social filters, and views their private pain as public discourse.

You know, a blogger.

The thing is, I never learned my lesson, even when I turned away from what I had always been taught was "real" Literature, the literature of displayed agony, and started writing about monsters and pirates. And honestly, I think it makes me a better writer. Most literary rules are better off bent, and combining the ritualistic self-flagellation of confessional poetry with genre tropes makes a much more delicious cocktail than either the bucket of emo-blood or elven mead alone.

Because you have to write what you know. And most of us know two things: what we've read and what we've done. What we've read is speculative science and folklore. What we've done is starve for love, bloody ourselves black for parental approval, take stupid risks for stupider reasons, get lost the dark of life and maybe, if we were lucky, found our way into the light again.

Cue the old "you got chocolate in my peanut butter" ditty.

A lot of contemporary fantasy fails to satisfy me because it does not have the creamy center of genuine emotional experience. Most contemporary realism fails to satisfy me because it lacks a crunchy exterior of awesome. It's not enough to create a magical world, you have to show me the hand of god in that world, and the author is god. If there is no emotional core, I don't care how many tribes of elves you've invented. The fact is, none of y'all know what it's like to be a young, blond farm boy dreaming up at the stars when a wizard shows up to dump the fate of the world on your shoulders and also hands you a crown and a girl. Life doesn't work like that. The best books serve two masters: they show us what life could be like if everything was different, and they make us recognize ourselves with a start. They make us say: *yes, that's what it's like.*

To strike that balance, you must be like unto a World of Warcraft heroine: wear sparkly, leathery, fantastical armor that nevertheless shows all your secret parts.

You may not know how it feels to cast magic missile, but you do know what it's like to irrevocably lose someone you love. To be abandoned. To be betrayed. To find joy and grace at the end of suffering. Those things are universal, and a legion of poetry professors exist to help you dredge up the details of those experiences. So use them, not the generalized Life Issues™, but the genuine and specific things that have happened to you - let it hang out, let your fetishes and your griefs and your hoary, bloody innards fall all over the page. The best writers can't fool anyone. We know what they want, what they've never had. No one ever thought Delany was a straight, monogamous guy. Stop caring who sees your private places - or care, and teach yourself to be an exhibitionist. Readers are sadists - they're there to see the wreck, and they want to see you cry.

You have to put your penis in the vacuum cleaner. Honesty will make you whole.

And *then* put in the dragons.

How to Sleep with a Writer

Carefully.

First of all, you must be prepared to see yourself dressed up in her clothes. In drag, in costume, in spangly eyeliner and a fedora hat. You have to steel yourself, and accept the following with equanimity:

She is going to write about you.

It takes a strong person to bear this: you'll see your private jokes, your secrets, your childhood, the angle of your penis, the heft of your breasts, your personal griefs, your complaints, your house and your profession ground up and mulched, composted and laid out bare, for *anyone* to see, in her books. Her books are naked, and she will make you match her. It will not be comfortable. She'll use everything you are - but she's fair, she uses everything she is, too.

Every time you touch her, she will store that touch away, to be accessed later, spooled out, smoothed over, given to characters she hasn't even thought of yet. Every time you fight, she will mentally catalogue your turns of phrase. If that seems inhuman, well, she can be like that. Computers are not so ruthless about retaining information.

Of course you will have to comfort her when she has gotten rejections, tell her she is brilliant at least 17 times before she believes it again, suffer sympathetic pregnancies every time she struggles to bring a book into the world. You will have to feed her when she forgets to do it herself, and bear up under infrequent money, critical disasters, and her quitting the whole business at least once a year. And naturally, if you fail to love her books, or pretend to like them for the sake of peace, she will never forgive you. Until the next book, which is so wonderful, not at all like that one you hated.

You didn't hate it. But she won't hear you.

If you leave her, cheat her, crush her, neglect her - she'll write about that, too. Even if you think didn't do any of those things. And even if no one else knows who she means when she uses that fateful pronoun, *you* will know.

If you stay with her, you will eventually see pieces of yourself, tiny slivers - the way you take your coffee, the way you talk to your mother, the way you rub your eyes when you're tired - exalted and debased, deified and debauched, in any number of stories, any number of heroes, any number of villains. You will hardly develop a new habit before she's written into her heroine.

If you stay with her, you can look back, in 30 years, 40, and see how well she will have preserved your lives together, how faithfully, how accurately, and with such variation. Butterflies under glass. In her very secret places - which are only pages, where she keeps all her most secret things so that she can show them to the world - she will have dressed you both up as everyone in the history of the world. You could never have lived such lives as she has written, full of griffins and monarchy and grief.

You cannot castigate her for any of this. She will just smile at you and say: "Why are you so angry? It's only a story."

And there is no arguing with that - it *is* only a story. But it's also you, your soul and your marrow and your life with her, and she knows it, but she won't let you spoil the tale. You made the choice when you slept with her the first time - you belong to her, and she will use you as she pleases.

My advice is not to do it. What sane person would sign up for that?

Anatomy of a Sex Scene

When I began writing my third major novel, *Palimpsest*, I found myself faced with a frightening task: I was going to have to write sex scenes.

But wait. That's not scary, right? I mean, everyone's doing it. No one would think any less of me. Come on, baby. Just one scene. Just one little description of your main characters rolling around a tawdry bed, or on the floor, even. If you fade to black, you don't really love your book.

But I'd never done it before. My previous novels had been fairy tales. Dark ones, violent ones, old school folklore with blood and witches and horrible things being done to very young children. The way fairy tales ought to be. But the thing is, writing fairy tales is an automatically respectable activity, like volunteering at a local animal shelter or recycling. You are Contributing to the Folkloric Tradition. Parents will bring their kids to your readings. The kids, bloodthirsty wee goblins that they are, aren't bothered by a little cannibalistic witchery. They were weaned on Hansel and Gretel. They'll dress up as your most bestial characters and pass out in an orgy of cocoa and graham crackers, snug in the knowledge that their mothers love them and would never leave them in a dark forest at night. It's good family fun. Fairy tales are all about sex but do not contain it - it's all in code, a dogwhistle for adults. Sex is subtext; the text is candy, or magic, or even marriage.

And because of that textual play, it's easy for an author to hide in fairy tales. I can write down my whole life and so long as I put a wicked queen and a magic mirror in, no one would ever guess that I'm being naked and intimate with them. The fourth wall is robust and muscular. But as I wrote *Palimpsest*, very conscious that I had made the choice to write a book about sex, I knew the jig was up. No more kids at readings, no more parents happy to entrust a sliver of their little ones' psychological development to my imagination. No more automatic respect as a Soldier of the Grand Tradition.

But that's not what scared me. The nakedness involved in writing sex scenes - the good ones, the ones that make you shiver - is just so overwhelming. And I don't mean describing body parts or caught breath or eruptions of various kinds. A writer can't help but bring her experience to bear on everything she writes, and writing about sex is like laying your entire sexual being out in front of a reader, all your kinks, all your nights, ugly and beautiful and awful and perfect. It's an unbearable bareness, and even if there's a wicked queen and a magic mirror, the minute the queen shrugs off her black gown and kisses her huntsman, there is no escaping the essential intimacy of what is about to happen: the author is whispering her deepest notions of sex and self and skin and suffering to the reader, and to me, that is hardly more intimate than sex itself.

It's leaning out of the page and saying: come into my world. This is what it looks like. This is what it feels like.

And that's a terrifying thing.

But it's the key to a good sex scene. A Venn diagram of raw, close-to-the-bone intimacy. Author-character-reader. The author brings their sexual experience to bear on the content of the scene (and the unspoken law of exchange is that the wider the author's experience, the richer the sex they write becomes - but that's an even more frightening thing to address in our conflicted culture, where writing erotica is more acceptable than reading it, and both are morally superior to watching it), the characters are stripped literally and metaphorically, shown at their most vulnerable, at their most naked and unguarded and helpless, and the reader is carried along through it, experiencing a single sex act through a multitude of lenses.

Hell, I've had lovers who haven't seen me as naked as my readers will when this book comes out.

For all the snickering and arguments about legitimate literature, I think writing about sex is an act of fundamental bravery. My readings will be more uncomfortable places next year, while I read these scenes out loud and listeners look at their shoes - because its hard to admit that it's not just words, it's not just a book, it's blood and bone and life and a mess of personal history, and that's why we look away, not because we don't want to see, but because we want to stare, and it's almost impossible to believe that's allowed. Writing about sex is an invitation to stare, and while it takes spine and spleen to take the invitation, to extend it has been one of the scariest and most exhilarating actions of my young life.

Step into my parlor. Everybody's doing it. No one will think any less of you.

The Future/I Mean/Wow

This is a difficult essay for me to write. I almost didn't. I almost kept quiet, suffering in silence, weeping in the small corners of my house and bearing within my solitary soul the knowledge of this horror, these crimes.

If I didn't have love in my heart, I would just look at the trainwrecks that come across my desk and cry lollerskates for honor and glory. But I do know love, humanity, and puppies and kittens and everything. And I can't stand by. This is a greater issue, one I've been quietly observing for years, in workshops, in anthologies. But now I'm an occasional editor, and it's my job to witness this thing.

And if it's my job to suffer for poetry, by *god*, y'all are going to suffer with me. So.

What the hell is wrong with science fiction poetry?

Now, I'm a card-carrying member of the Science Fiction Poetry Association (I actually don't think we have cards) and I've won a Rhysling Award. It's not like I'm not *invested* here. Everything I am about to say is because I want SF poetry to grow up and mature and be good, so good it breaks your heart. I want it to be awesome. But I went through my entire poetry slushpile last night, and it was 90% SF poetry, and 100% the same as all the SF poetry I've had to read in workshops and in anthologies for quite some time. It's that heartbreaking sameness that deeply creeps me out. It worries me, because I don't think anyone is conferring on the rules of SF poetry. And yet, the vast majority of the SF poetry I've seen seems to think that simply explaining an oft-used science fictional concept and putting those words in a column is sufficient to create poetry and access the great profit and literary respect available to science fiction poets everywhere. And since haiku is for some inexplicable reason *super popular* among the SF set, they're also often extremely short. And/or have puns. In fact, almost all the SF poetry I have ever read goes a lot like this:

STATEMENT OF SF CONCEPT.
PUN.
PEACE OUT.

That is not a poem. That is not even content. And I am not actually exaggerating. This is what I see, every day. Now, of course, there are some exceptions - it is unnecessary to howl a catalogue of all the amazing SF poetry I am ignorant of in my general direction. There are always exceptions. And obviously, *your* poetry is wonderful and delicate and perfect. It's those other guys, the vast majority of SF poetry that has burned my eyeballs, that I'm talking about. If I didn't see this 900 times more often than I didn't, I'd be having breakfast right now instead of writing this. I've had to come up with positive things to say about poems of this kind for years in workshops, and I can't take it anymore.

Time travel.
You know?
Yeah.

I know that a lot of people in the SFPA hate fantasy poetry and think fantasy poets like myself should not be allowed in the clubhouse. But I find that at least when I'm presented with a fantasy poem, there is more effort involved than just using a big Science!Word and taking a Lovitz-style bow. They're trying to say something about the fantasy concept, or how fantasy and real life come together, or something, anything, beyond: *elves man. WTF?* And I look at an SF poem and think: this is your cry to heaven, your expression of your deepest self, what you are desperate and aching to say, what you *must* say, because it burns you not to, and you could not find it expressed anywhere else the way it sparks and flames in your soul?

Wouldn't it be awesome
if the world ended?
I'm so there.
KURTZWEIL, YO.

I feel like this has something to do with the whole "SF stories are *idea stories* and shouldn't have, like *characters* or *feelings* because those are *gay* and also for *girls.*" Because poetry, despite having been written by straight white dudes for many eons without any problem, falls into the category of things that are gay and for girls, at least in the minds of people who make statements of that kind on forums and private email lists and such. So maybe there's a defensiveness about the very act of writing an SF poem - poems almost always deal in emotion and rich images, it's kind of poetry's thing. So obviously, the way to make these poems Proper SF is to strip away any feeling, or adjectives, or speakers which might be characters, and to put in a pun because Douglas Adams made that ok, and poems have to have wordplay, right? (Puns are arguably never funny. But puns in SF poetry are definitely never funny.)

Space elevator, man.
So weird
right?

I mean, there's a reason that fantasy poetry has dominated the Rhysling Awards for the last several years. No one wants to be the one to say this, but when you put contemporary fantasy poetry next to contemporary SF poetry, there's just no comparison at all. And perhaps it's possible that there's a reason we don't get to play with the big poetry kids. And I'm not saying fantasy rules, SF drools. SF can be awesome. I've been an SF reader my whole life. But somehow, the idea has gotten into a whole lot of people's head that the *idea* of SF is enough. You don't need sophisticated language or passion or a connection to human experience. Just say the idea, then go on break.

Humanity is a virus.
I am so deep.

I mean, maybe this is it. This is the ultimate SF. All idea, nothing else. Pure. Unvarnished. Unadulterated. The ultimate proof of that horrible meme that says that SF is better than all the rules of literature.

You know, this one time when I was in college, I had this idea that meaning in literature was like, the man getting me down or something. (Don't even smirk like that.) I had a reasoning at the time, that language could be beautiful on its own and perfect logic from one image to another wasn't strictly the most important thing ever, and emotional meaning could arise from non-meaning. Dude, whatever, I was in college, and it's not that dumb. But then my professor told me about the language poets, and how they had this idea before me (*shocking*) and he gave me some of their work to read and it was all green/czechoslovakia/cumulus and it was terrible. And I thought: oh, it *sucks*. That's the part I wasn't understanding. Surrealism is fine but we need *some* meaning. And I went on to be a mildly famous genre writer who posts stuff on the Internet.

I wish that lesson on all of us. If you take away everything but the *OMG idea* of SF, it sucks. You need something else, some meaning, some feeling, some voice, some beauty, some ugliness, some violence, some pain, some apotheosis, some damnation, some glory, some putrescence, some desire, some need, some disappointment, some loss, some girls, some gays, some love, some sacrifice, some ambition - *some point*.

Singularity, dude.
Like, whoa.
Like, Turing, and stuff.
Can I be on BoingBoing now?

It's the End of the World as We Know It

As Amazon has progressed by leaps and bounds, some more ethical than others, to take over a goodly portion of the literary market share - I keep hearing the same thing pop up in discussions of ebooks and Amazon and the iPad and the like.

Hooray! Traditional publishing is dead! (which old witch, the wicked witch...)
To which I say: what?

To be sure, technology is changing. To be sure, the world will be different in five years than it is now. But I do not understand the joy with which a sizable portion of the Internet is heralding the "death" of the industry that employs most of the writers they know and love, and a whole lot of other people besides. I do not understand how people can be waiting with bated breath for publishing to die, unless they genuinely hate books, storytelling, and quality, and just really love reading the slush pile.

The general meme seems to be this: with the advent of ebooks, which are definitely going to be the dominant form of book publishing forever and ever, there will no longer be any need for traditional publishers. Each writer will become something of an autonomous press, self-publishing through Amazon and Apple, who are totally awesome indie champions of the little guy, unlike those horrible corporate presses, hiring their own editors, copyeditors, typesetters, marketers, and artists, and putting up their work directly for sale online. Then: profit!

I find this to be a horrifying dystopian future, and I'll tell you why.

Now, I'm not actually trying to be a shill for The Man, here. But I am living, breathing proof that those evil NYC presses will buy weird, not terribly commercial work, and will keep buying it. I also have a vested interest in online publishing, as I've had a lot of success with it. So listen to me now and believe me later: you do not want this to happen, either.

As has been pointed out many times by people better with numbers than I am, the costs of publishing an ebook are not zero. That is, if you have any interest at all in a quality product. No one goes around suggesting that everyone should become their own autonomous cheesemakers and cheering the death of the cheese industry. Why? *Because that would result in a lot of shitty cheese.* The idea that we should all be hiring our own massive staff of personnel instead of letting the publishers do it is bizarre on the face of it.

First of all, it's financially ridonkulous. Professional editors of the level I work with now make money. Grown-up money that I cannot pay them, because I am not a rich person and never will be. Let alone copyediting, typesetting, and cover art (which is vastly important, don't be fooled). I have zero interest in paying out

$7000 to $15000 before the book gets published, and almost certainly seeing minimal profit (especially since that 70% Amazon deal everyone's so sweet on has a whole lot of strings attached). I like it when someone else does that. Publishers are risk-assesors, and they assume the risk, which is not insignificant, while I create the book. The "hire your own editor" handwaving strikes me as the strangest of this whole memescape. Really? Hire my own? With what money, without an advance? I suspect there is a pernicious undercurrent here that editors and copyeditors and artists and typesetters might not really need to be paid either. We're all in it for the love, after all, and most people aren't clear on what those behind the sceners do, anyway.

Not to mention, a beginning writer on their own has no idea who the best heads in the business are, who to hire even if they had the money, to make their book better. What is far more likely is that they'll get taken in by the many scams out there, spend the money anyway, and still have a terrible book. It takes experience and time to know who to work with - and experience and time are exactly what people seem to want to cut out of the process.

Publishers also, very importantly, pay me an advance. This is how I live and eat. I like advances. I don't get big ones, but I still get them, and that's damn important. I do not like paying the equivalent of an advance to others in order to publish my book. Because then I wouldn't have any money with which to live while I write the book, see? Banks do not write checks to under-30 chicks who want to write about fairy tales. The idea that writers are going to make more money by getting Amazon's royalty rate, when most ebooks a) sell a tiny fraction of what print books sell, and b) sell fewer than a hundred copies, when not backed by a publisher, is sort of hilarious. We are not even there technologically yet. Most people can't afford a $300 machine on which to read books. And we'll probably never be there culturally, where reading is held at such a premium that there's millions to be made for everyone.

Also, most writers, in this wonderful future, won't bother with that staff of experts. They're the ones who say that $7000 number is ridiculous. Why? Because they don't think editorial matters. It's extremely expensive and most people don't really think they need editing anyway. To the author him or herself, their own work *shines*. Every syllable. But what happens when a writer refuses editing? I think we've all seen it, with Anne Rice and others that have claimed this right: too popular to edit. The books are crap. Editing is a good thing, a highly necessary process, and perhaps if we discussed our editors in public more, they wouldn't be seen as so expendable - and by the way, an editor does not merely suggest setting this Hamlet thing in Denmark instead of Spain and correct your spelling. They advocate for your book, and have their hands in every decision down to the type of paper used to print it. Did you like those Kaluta illustrations in *The Orphan's Tales*? Well, my editor conceived the idea, got the artist, and got him paid. I could never afford Kaluta on my own. If I hear one more person toss off editors like their completely irrelevant to the process, I'm going to have to smack an Internet. This is not an auteur kind of gig. It is a team effort, and that is a *good* thing. What happens when one person has all the power to make artistic decisions without input from anyone else? *The Phantom Menace*, that's what happens.

The author is generally the worst person to edit or copyedit their own work, and almost certainly the worst person to package it. I have seen self-published covers, my friends, and they would wake the dead. Bad photoshop, bad colors, stolen art... it's bad, kids. Bad. But all we authors see is our baby - because we haven't gone to school for graphic design or marketing. I heard a writer quote his own Kindle book as having cost him $70 to create. Well, that means it's raw off his hard drive, and that scares me.

I've read the slush pile. And in this Orwellian post-publishing dystopia, you will be, too. The mass of ebooks will be unedited, badly written, and horribly presented. And while this is an unpopular thing to say, that's pretty much the state of self-publishing now. There are a few great self-published projects, and they are buried in an Everest of trash. Essentially, a reader acts as an acquiring editor, sifting through the mediocre, offensive, awful, and laughable for one good book. And readers will usually give up after a few burns. If you think this isn't so, ask yourself: why isn't publishing already dead, when ebooks have been available and viable for more than a decade, when POD has been thriving and Amazon has been encouraging people to self-publish through them for some time? Because there's more to writing a book than typing.

Quality alone does not penetrate the signal to noise ratio. And what will happen is not some anarcho-syndicalist commune of happy writers doing all their own work. Scams to prey on the dreams of what seems to be just about everyone to be published will drastically increase, and many writers who can make a small living today will have to quit or become hobbyists with drastically reduced output, because they will not be able to afford marketing and editorial for their books out of their own pocket. This seems obvious, but I guess it's not. Remember how money flows toward the writer? I do not want to live in a world where instead of being paid to write, I pay to write.

Now, what about *The Girl Who Circumnavigated Fairyland* you say? Wasn't that a huge success for me? Didn't I make that work, donation model, online publishing and all?

Yes, I did, though you'll notice not through Amazon. Why people think that one giant corporation is better than another is beyond me. But here's the thing about Fairyland that I don't think is widely grokked: I don't think even *I* could repeat it.

Fairyland was what the kids like to call a perfect storm: financial crisis, quality product, an already established name that is associated with quality fiction, and an Internet wildfire that spread the word like crazy. If any one of those things fell out, it would not have succeeded the way and to the extent it did. There are a whole lot of crowdfunded project out there that didn't get that kind of publicity, or picked up by - wonder of wonders - a Macmillan imprint. You know, that company that's "afraid of ebooks" and "terrified of the future."

And people still sent me my spelling mistakes every week. Because I am a crappy copyeditor.

I have another completed YA novel cooling its heels on my hard drive. I couldn't sell it. I could put it up online or I could wait and try again with a rewrite down the road. And maybe if I put it up it would be a success and maybe it wouldn't - though almost certainly not a success on the level of *Fairyland* - maybe I could even get my own editor. One that would do it for the love, you know? And maybe I will, at some point. It's a choice I have, in this industry - the choice is mine, not Amazon's, not Apple's, not geek culture at large already deciding that there's only one choice. But it's still a better move to wait, because *many more people* read print books than online books right now. We in Geekville often forget that our gadgets are not universal. And especially more kids read from the library and from paper books. Publishers will get you into bookstores, and that's still important. They will get you read. And they will pay you to keep writing. And they will pay editors and everyone else, and so many people will eat.

Where I stand right now is a pretty good spot - I take the hybrid approach, using both traditional and non-traditional models. But that would be impossible if I had not already established my name through paper publishing. Or as near to impossible as makes lightning and lotteries. So while I've been told many times in the past week that I should chuck all those mad, bad, and dangerous to know publishers and go it alone, it's really not in my interest to do so, since I still live advance to advance. *And it's not a viable option for most writers just starting out out there.* I'm not just thinking about me, here.

Now, look. Publishers have a lot of problems and they need to improve. The status quo has a lot of crap in it. Where I think change could best happen right now is on the contract level. If, for example, e-rights became a subsidiary right I could administer separately, like audio rights, then you'd see a revolution in ebooks as we all experiment. Right now, however, you more or less cannot sell a book to a major publisher without giving them e-rights, and that sucks. But babies and bathwater, you know? Publishing has brought you literally every book you've ever loved, and the party on their grave is not only pre-mature, but in pretty bad taste.

So why leap over all the fascinating intervening steps and crow that publishing is dead? Frankly, it feels ghoulish and threatening. It feels like a lot of weirdly sour grapes. It's definitely ignorant of just about everything involved in producing a book. But hey! If not for those damn publishers, everyone would have a book out and be super successful and keep all the money for themselves, mwa ha ha! There's a lot of kind of nasty subtext out there to the tune of: if the publishing industry doesn't work for *me*, it doesn't work at all.

But the world isn't built that way. There's no conspiracy to keep good authors down. Amazon and Apple are not your Robin Hood. They don't care about you or your art. They want to make money, and so do publishers, and so do I. I think some of this comes from the idea that it's distasteful to make money off of art. That idea is offensive to me. I can't make art without food and a roof. Turning up one's nose and declaring that an ebook should be free or minimal cost because well, one doesn't *like* paying for mere *data*, that sounds like enemy action to me. People pay for programs from Microsoft and Apple and independent developers. That is also mere data. It's all mere data, in the end.

So my stomach's been in knots for a week, not because my sales are in danger, because they aren't, but because reading the comments on blogs, on Amazon, I keep seeing people taking delight and joy in their own fantasies of how my livelihood is going to die in a fire.

Funny thing is, if this future came to pass and the market were nothing but self-published autonomous authors either writing without editorial or paying out of pocket for it, if we were flooded with good product mixed with bad like gold in a stream, it would be about five seconds before someone came along and said: *hey, what if I started a company where we took on all the risk, hired an editorial staff and a marketing staff to make the product better and get it noticed, and paid the author some money up front and a percentage of the profits in exchange for taking on the risk and the initial cost? So writers could, you know, just* write?

And writers would line up at their door.

I Am a Fantasy Writer

When I wrote my first novel, *The Labyrinth*, it honestly never occurred to me that I wasn't a realist, a mainstream, salt-of-the-earth, if slightly cracked earth, writer.

If you've read *The Labyrinth*, you might find this slightly difficult to believe. It involves talking animals, doors that eat people, a sentient maze, and queer angels. But for someone like me, steeped in classics to the point of leaking golden apples and bull-sex machines out of my very pores, all of this seems quite normal to me, the stuff of Literature. Of course, contemporary ideas tend more towards the Theban (the urban angst of sleeping with *just* the wrong person) as opposed to the Olympian (the celestial angst of having slept with just the right person in the form of a cow or a shower of gold coins, and then she gave birth to a Minotaur and/or a banker and you know, both are very inconvenient houseguests.)

But what did I care for Thebes, when there were nymphs and satyrs in that nice wood over yonder?

And then a publisher picked it up. And my editor started saying things like "dark fantasy." This turned my head completely around. Sure, I was a little surreal, funky, even, but I felt "fantasy" was taking it a bit too far. My ex-husband very gently poured me a cup of tea, sat me down and told me that, strictly speaking, animals don't talk, mazes are cute little things made out of cardboard they put up for Halloween carnivals, and angels are supposed to be androgynous and sexless, so they can't really be queer. Oh, and there's no such thing as angels, anyway.

You are not a realist, he said. Realism doesn't have alligators preaching the gospel.

Then realism is stupid, I said, and it was a crocodile.

Nevertheless, I was uncomfortable with the idea of myself as a fantasy writer. I had a whole host of ways of getting around calling myself one:

"I'm interested in things that transcend genre, no matter what that genre is."

"I just work here. I write the books, and other people tell me what genre they are."

"I'm an interstitial writer."

See, because even though I am a reader of fantasy and science fiction, I had been so indoctrinated into the literary/academic system which says all fantasy has embarrassing cover art and involves elfsex, and can never be as good as the most unassuming realist novel involving *real* things that *real* people do (despite their being *fake* people doing *fake* things and no more real than Frodo himself) that even while writing, as I currently am, a novel which features rather heavily a Japanese dragon, I couldn't bear to have that label applied to my complex, atavistic, folklore-based snake-beast. Fantasy, after all, is for people who couldn't get over reading Tolkien in eighth grade. Let a professor tell you often enough that you'd better start writing about your childhood trauma and quit this fairy tale bullshit and eventually, you'll do it, and you'll believe that you're doing the right thing, the adult thing. The label has been so derided, even by people safely under its umbrella, that young authors like me already know not to touch it with a ten-foot dragonlance before we're even out of the gate.

Under the genre tent, new circuses go up every day, new ways for us not to call ourselves the F word, even allowing SF as a term to engulf us completely for a variety of strange reasons having to so with "hard" techno-lit being somehow more legitimate than "soft" magic-lit. The invisible Other F is a marginalized one. We embrace all these new words in order to avoid the big one - slipstream, interstitial, mundane SF, infernokrusher, magic realism. Of these the most offensive by far is magic realism. If it has magic, baby doll, it ain't realism. But in the gentrification of books, the realists can take the most visible sign of fantasy and call it their own, and more call it "edgy" and "fresh" when it is theirs, and "cliché" when it is ours. I know few writers who are not to some extent guilty of this three-coconut game of genre identification, and I certainly do not exclude myself.

But I was at the World Fantasy Convention last weekend. It's awfully hard to avoid the label in a place like that. And at the awards banquet, these amazing people whose books I have always loved got up and talked about what it was to create these things out of whole cloth, to walk in dreams all your life, and bring them out of yourself so that others could share them. They talked about this community of dreamers, who dream for everyone who doesn't quite know how. And I could not think of a more honorable profession, a more beautiful and sacred avocation than dreaming for the world, than being the source of new folklore, of new myth, and the continuation of all the old myths, and all their showers of gold. I was, for the moment, moved and proud beyond words.

And I realized that truly and honestly, even as a humble reader I will always find a story about a pirate-woman who is half precious metal (*Lighthousekeeping*) more interesting than one about gay cowboys and their bouncing baby angst (*Brokeback Mountain*). To me, that is as obvious as pairing bacon with eggs. So I'm going to quit calling my eggs matzo balls, because those just don't go with bacon, children.

The fact is, I am a fantasy writer. I make up stories about witches and monsters and yes, preaching crocodiles and queer angels. Are they better than "pulp" fantasy? I like to think so. But if you think realism doesn't have a pulp segment, you haven't seen a Nicholas Sparks movie recently. I hope, for your sake and that of your family, that you haven't read the books they're based on. Realism is a restrictive genre with strict rules and conventions - it's *fantasy* that's free. Nowhere else is the entire history of the world - bull-fuckers, bankers, minotaurs and all - at my fingertips. Realism says I cannot have a dragon if I have a suburban kitchen. Fantasy whispers, "Put the dragon *in* the suburban kitchen if you want, I'll still love you in the morning."

I am a fantasy writer. I have learned my lesson, and I embrace it.

The Fanloric Cycle

So folks have been talking about fan fiction again.

It seems like every few years, a big name author will holler something about how evil, heinous, and morally wrong fan fiction and fan fiction writers are, and then the Internet gets all upset and shocked, and then the author is shocked that people could get so upset. After all, all they did was massively insult a large portion of their most loyal fanbase. Why should anyone make a *thing* about it?

And I think: how many times are we going to go through this? Because the last time I posted about my stance on fan fiction, it was during another one of these pistols-at-dawn Internet brawls. Of course, then I'd barely started publishing, so it's probably time for an update anyway.

This round of nonsense is mostly up to Diana Gabaldon and George R.R. Martin posting about how they don't understand the impulse to write fan fiction and think it's dirty and wrong in many legal and moral ways, ~~and also fanficcers killed Lovecraft and made him cry~~.

What gets me in this conversation is the privilege involved. You're talking about hugely successful writers who are so successful that they do not have to be concerned with offending their most loyal and invested fans - and make no mistake, kids. The people who write fanfic in your worlds are among your biggest fans. They have assistants to sort through their blog comments so that they don't have to deal with the fallout of what they say, and shut down comments after 400 because it's not a constructive conversation (which - when is it ever, on a blog, but rarely? And if you're a bestselling writer, you have to know people want to talk in your space) anymore. They had to have it pointed out to them that people might write fan fiction out of love. They go on and on about how they would never write fanfic, but waste no space on empathy for others who might. These are writers who are really probably never going to be hurt by fan fiction, who can't even be hurt by kissing off a nice slice of their paying audience. That's even if you make the argument that fan fiction can hurt people, that fanfic writers are just waiting to pounce on their favorite author and sue them to bits.

That said, y'all, don't prove me wrong on this score. I'm very touchy feely with my fandom, in part because they've never done me wrong or hurt me in any way. This is an awesome balance. I hope it stays that way forever.

For most of us, fan fiction is a non-issue. Even for midlist writers. We will never be popular enough for people to play in our worlds with any frequency. The problem for us is getting people to read and care about our books that much in the first place. I have never heard a midlist or small press writer shriek about fanfic the way bestsellers do. So much ire spent over something that ultimately helps books, keeps the conversation going past the long tail of marketing, keeps them alive and loved - I've never understood it. Quashing fan activity is not only self-sabotaging, but unkind. I have always been delighted when told there was a piece of fanfic inspired by a book of mine floating about. I don't read it for legal reasons, but I'm thrilled to know it's there. Someone cared. Someone loved it enough to spend their free time writing about it for free. My rule has always been: don't make money off it and we're cool. Writers require fans in order to keep living and working - it behooves us not to call them names or accuse them of incredibly awful crimes that are not remotely comparable to writing a little story about Buffy and Spike. (I do think this is partly a sex issue - authors seem to get most upset when they discover slash fic, to which I say: welcome to the Internet. How did you avoid it so far?)

Is it a legal grey area? There has never been a test case. Of course it is. But look. It would be a bit shit of me to holler about fan fiction being evil when I've made a name for myself at least in part by retelling fairy tales. I learned to write short fiction partly by wearing the narrative bones of fairy tales and then re-breaking them in interesting ways. And I can't say: *I got mine, now no touching.*

It is part of the human activity of storytelling to retell, misremember, breakup and tell backwards, peek into the crannies and tell the other stories (thank you Euripides), wonder what might have been, what could be, and tell the same stories over and over, but tell them slant. I feel that trying to destroy that impulse is not only hopeless but cruel. I love my characters and worlds no less than any other writer. They are, as has been said over and over, my children. But with every child there comes a time when they are grown and out in the world, free to smoke in alleys and consort with boys of poor reputation, get in trouble on their own and probably screw around a lot. And you have to let them go. My characters and worlds are not wholly mine in the spiritual sense, even if they are in a legal sense. Reading is an active sport, and we create books together, in the space between my words and your heart. I put those people into the world, into the sphere of collective imagination. How can I possibly begrduge others playing with them? *The whole point of publishing them was for others to love them.*

I believe in planet remix. In culture as a vibrant and changing thing. I do not believe fanfic violates that, but encourages it. Yes, much fanfic is bad. I've got news for you. Most published fiction is bad, too. Life goes on.

In the end, I have an important secret to tell you. Huddle up.

This argument is already over. It is a generational one. You've got a whole host of authors coming into their own who grew up with fanfic as a fact of life, or even committed it themselves. Who have been messing about with creative commons since forever. A whole generation who sees fanfic as, not a nuisance, but a mark of success, a benchmark - if someone wrote fanfic about my book, then I've really made it. A certain generation of authors will always hate and fear fanfic, and every once in awhile the Internet will get its hackles up and have a conversation about it. But that will happen less and less as years go by. You can't stop this beat, my friends. It's too old, and too basic.

Little e, Big B: Books and EBooks and Love and War

I'm sick to death of talking about ebooks.

In the current economic and publishing climate, that is a shocking thing to say. Posts about epublishing regularly get the most comments and pingbacks, I'm constantly asked to give talks about my own experiments in that arena, and I usually agree to do them. It is the topic of conversation among authors, agents and publishers alike. How we're going to adapt, how it will change the publishing environment, how, most importantly, to make money with ebooks.

But I've had it. Because something seems to get lost all the time in these endless conversational loops that make me want to embed something in Data's wrist so that I know how to break the cycle.

And that something is, you know, *books*.

My interest in ebooks is a tiny percentage of my interest in books. I didn't dream of being a writer so I could spend my time discussing file formats and what Author X (even if X = me) did to sell a whole bunch of copies. Maybe it's stupid and romantic, but I got into this because I loved books. Because stories were the most important things in the world to me, and I had so many of them to tell. Don't get me wrong, there are vital and important things to talk about with regards to ebooks, and it *is* changing the industry. But when we discuss writing these days, we almost always end up talking about self-publishing and ebooks. And then any other conversation is over.

I and you and everyone has heard a lot about Amanda Hocking in the last year. But no one has ever said to me: *Amanda Hocking's books moved me and spoke to my life, I love them and I read them over and over because they mean so much to me.* They say: *Amanda Hocking sold a million ebooks.* Frankly, I couldn't tell you one of her titles without Googling if you paid me. And this gets repeated over and over. It doesn't seem to matter what's *in* the ebook as much as that it's an ebook. I hear about so-and-so and how they charge 99 cents for their ebooks and make money hand over fist. And that's the topic for an hour in some con bar, and it might not even get mentioned what the book in question is *about*.

I understand that we're all just trying to get by in an industry that was always brutally tough. But remember how when we were all kids and wanted to be writers and a big part of that was sitting around with other bookish people and talking about literature? Yeah, me too. Nowhere in there was a deep longing to talk about epub vs mobi until I can't remember which one makes techno music.

So many blog posts list reasons people want to be writers, and precious few of them have anything to do with "I want to tell stories." They are, instead, status and financially-related reasons. And the sad thing is I believe they're probably right about those reasons, for a lot of people who cheer Amazon and sneer at us "dinosaurs." (Though now that Amazon is breaking into the traditional publishing business, I suspect things will get dicey in Whoville.) Being a Writer has tremendous cultural cache, and it's part of why everyone and their cat wants to be one.

But it seems to me that ebooks are now a subject almost wholly unrelated to books. It's about money and it's about "the industry" and it's about form, but not content. And not infrequently, it's about scoring status points by being more plugged in to the new system than thou. And the great conversation has started to accrue a kind of inertia - someone says the Kindle is the future and "trad" publishing is dead, someone else defends traditional publishing and points out Amazon's robber baron tactics, someone else brings up Smashwords and other indie options, someone else sides with Apple. So-and-so sold a million ebooks. So-and-so turned down a print contract to self-publish. So on and so forth.

Now, obviously, I have been experimenting with publishing on the Internet for a long time. This may be coloring my experience, because I am asked to talk about the brave new world of ebooks far more often than if I had never written serial novels online or started mailing wax-sealed stories to people around the world out of my dining room. But the fact is, I would, a thousand times over, rather talk about what I wrote than how I published it. And I feel like stories - you know, those things we're all fighting for? - are getting lost in the rush to be the one who knows the score, who says the definitive thing about the new tech, or the one who needs the knowledge to be able to launch their own million ebooks empire. Honestly, you'd think there was a prize for the first one to call time of death on traditional publishing, given how popular that headline has become.

It's a land rush right now. I get it. Boy, do I get it. I'm sure that back in the day, every music conference was obsessively buzzing about mp3s. But if you put a penny in a jar for every article you read about ebooks, and took one out for every book review or book discussion you read, I'm willing to bet, for most of us, the jar would never go dry. And I'm guilty of that, too.

So I guess this is a call to arms. I do that from time to time. It's a habit left over from college. We don't have to stop talking about ebooks - that's putting one's finger in a dyke that has already blown. But let's talk about books. Let's allow the fact that our obsession over ebooks stems from a deep and abiding love of *books* shine through. Let's take just a cup or two of that excitement about our Star Trek Future!Tablets and use it to get geekyhappythrilled about the actual stories it lets us read with ease. No more namechecking "hot" things we haven't even looked at because they came in a new business package. When we talk about an electronic publishing success, let's try *reading the books*, and then talking about them. We might even learn something about writing and publishing and commercial appeal, something about telling stories, that we couldn't learn from a hundred tech blogs. That may sound naive, but after being an editor for 18 months, I can tell you that even the worst derivative vampire love triangle tale can be what the kids call a "teaching moment" if you let it. And I think we have forgotten to let stories teach us as much as trends do.

Maybe this isn't a problem for you. Maybe you post every day on GoodReads and tweet about books and giddily talk to your friends about them all the time. Maybe for every post about ebook tech, you post two book reviews. Maybe you read every ebook you post about. If so, you are my hero. No joke, my hero. Like Superman, but with books. But it's been a problem for me. I'm as guilty as anyone else. And I want to be better.

Books are not going away. That much is abundantly clear. There is an incredible hunger for stories out there. And eventually the tech will reach a plateau, until the next revolution. I want to focus on the food that sates that hunger, not the plate it comes on. *Read* the books, and then *talk* about them. Read the *books*, and then talk about *them*.

Now, if you'll excuse me, I'm going to go read one of Amanda Hocking's books. I think I owe her that.

One Art, Please. I Have 99 Cents.

There's a philosophical notion floating around the self-publishing world that the proper price of a novel is 99 cents. After all, songs are 99 cents. Why are novels $15? The train of thought holds that it's an issue of time invested; some novels are written in a week; some songs take years. It's all art, right?

Whoa. Let's back that truck up.

Here's the thing - the argument here is not that novels are somehow higher art than music, no one makes that argument. And a three-minute song with pro mastering and recording probably does take a lot longer than people think, likely as long as it takes *fast* writers to create a novel. Not the point - the hours that go into something are not printed on the label.

The point is that the unit value of "song" is not the same as the unit value of "novel." The comparison is more song :: short story or song :: chapter, and *album* :: novel.

Get thee to iTunes. Most albums? Are still about $10 to $15.

A song is a part of a whole. A novel is a whole. They do not equate. Sure, there are singles, but most people still put out albums, not 14 singles all in a row. It takes three minutes on average to listen to a song. It takes hours, and often days or weeks, to read and enjoy a novel. The entertainment output is enormous. It takes longer to read a novel than to play some video games - and if you want to talk about price gouging, let's break out my XBox, shall we? Now, of course, one listens to songs more than once, and so you might end up with several hours' worth of pleasure out of a single song. Many people also read novels more than once, and you can never tell when you click the buy button if this book/song will be one you love forever and read/listen to over and over, or one you get bored with and forget about after a week.

Ultimately, I'm a little tired of people telling me my work isn't worth very much. That we should accept Apple - *Apple!* - price points without hesitation or consideration, that all units are the same units, all art is the same art. Obviously, sculpture, paintings, murals, and jewelry should also all cost 99 cents each. Actors should only get paid 99 cents per performance. Dancers should only get 99 cents per dance. Architects should get 99 cents per building. Concerts should also charge 99 cents admission. It's all art - the units are all interchangeable, and should all be tied to iTunes pricing.

This is madness, to me.

Because of the 99 cents model on iTunes (and piracy), most musicians who are not the Black Eyed Peas or some such have moved to a donations model to support themselves and continue to make albums. Writers do this too - we all have tip jars, but far fewer people throw in because writing in general gets a bit shat upon as an art form. (And the fact that it takes longer to consume means many people just download a file and never look at it again. Don't think your piracy figures equate to actual readers.) Anyone can do it, obviously. They're all greedy hacks. That's why Amazon users figure ebooks should be free. You're not doing anything special, how dare you ask for money for it? That's like *begging*.

Do I think ebooks are priced too high? Probably. I think the price should be more like a mass market paperback - which is not 99 cents, you'll notice.

You pay 5.99 for a mocha, dude. Why would you not pay it for a book?

Moreover, why would anyone insist that everyone charge the same for their books, that the "market" settle out to conform to Apple's idea of pricing circa 2001? What that's actually saying is: no one should make more than a little bit of money from writing. It's a hobby, not a job anyone needs to be compensated for. You *need* that skilled barista to make your fancy mocha, but a writer? Unless the idea is that publishers would still pay advances as they do now, but only charge 99 cents for the ebooks. Which does not compute. Or that publishers should vanish altogether, which point we have already discussed ad nauseam. Of course even at 99 cents, some people will be successful, but that number will be even smaller than it is now.

No one benefits from a field that is bled dry of talent and especially risk-taking talent so that downloads can be brought down to 99 cents. I am not cool with this, and you shouldn't be either. I will happily overpay for every ebook if it means writers get to eat and feed their families. I overpay for shit all the time without making righteous judgments about what it "should" cost in some impossibly ideal world where everyone has insurance and no one is hungry and everything in the entire universe costs 99 cents.

Work is Never Over:
On Publishing and Its Many Faces

There are a blistering array of publishing options currently fighting it out Pon Farr style in the contemporary world of letters. I sometimes feel that with every blog post on self-publishing, we draw closer to some millionth-customer trumpeting confetti-strewn alarum announcing *the Internet has had enough, no further commentary is necessary. Keep calm and publish however you want.*

Wishful thinking.

But it's true that I've published with the Big Six and I've published on my own damn website, I started out in the small and micro press world and I've experimented with all the methods of getting my words into people's heads that seemed to make sense to me, so I do have A Perspective. I've talked before about my thoughts on the writing life in this age of uncertainty, innovation, and hyperbole - for never was there a thinkpiece on why traditional publishing still has a whole lot to offer for those of us who never had any ambition to start a small press that only publishes one author that was not answered by gnashing of polearms and delighted furor insisting that Kindle will save us all, publishing itself is dead, or in some charming cases, that taking money from a publishing company in order to write a novel is akin to being a house slave in the American South.

I've also had incredibly negative publishing experiences and incredibly positive ones. I've had big giant presses treat me badly and drop my books down a Well of Forgetting that I'm convinced exists in the center of New York. I've had big giant presses stick by me and treat me like family. I've had teeny presses put out wonderful books and behave with kindness and professionalism; I've had teeny presses treat me like something to scrape off their shoe when no one is looking. I've had self-published projects that won major literary awards and literally made my name and ones that no one gave much of a crap about. You'll notice that it doesn't matter much what method was used to bring a book into the world - it can go poorly and it can go well in each and every camp.

Much of the blaggering about How to Publish Without Those Foul, Cackling Warlock-Publishers relies on the idea, which most aspiring writers have, though the smart ones keep it on the down-low, that there is some kind of magic Success Wand that can cast Accio Everything I've Ever Wanted over them and make them sell a million ebooks just like Amanda Hocking. No one would ever admit that they think this wand exists - they pay lip service to the idea that writing is hard work and you never know what will get traction in the market - and yet I get several emails a week asking me to share the secret of how I "made" *The Girl Who Circumnavigated Fairyland* such a hit.

At the moment, the Success Wand is the Kindle. Why, it's easy! Everyone is doing it! Nothing could ever possibly go wrong! Why would you trust your work, the substance of your soul, to a greedy, Machiavellian, rapacious corporation that only wants to edit, package, and sell your book use you and screw you and when you could instead trust it to a different greedy, Machiavellian, rapacious corporation who won't do any of those things before using you and screwing you?

And you know, funny thing, that corporation just yanked thousands of ebooks because it wants to dictate contract terms to the second-biggest independent distributor in the US instead of negotiating like a normal fucking business whose official moral stance doesn't include: be a schoolyard bully and swing your weight around because no one can stop you (this year).

I know it's super boring to say: e-publishing doesn't change the fact that writing is hard work, editing is hard work, finding and legitimately paying for *good* art and cover design is hard, copyediting is hard, marketing is hard, and it all costs money and takes a huge amount of time. I want to be a writer, not a small press - and that's been said before oh so many times, including by Our Host, but it's true. I barely have time as it is to keep writing books while handling the business of writing. I have no interest in taking on six other jobs. Yes, quicky formatting and slapping a stock image/stealing something from Google Images and hoping for the best on a book and uploading it to Amazon does not take very much work. But those methods do not fill me with assurance that the work itself has been crafted with skill, patience, or deep knowledge and feeling. There is a reason for the traditional publishing process. Yes, they screw up sometimes. Yes, they publish bad books. Yes, they can and hopefully will learn to speed up their cycles and administer erights in a fair way and adapt to a changing world.

But if they were so useless now that we live in the Publishing Singularity, Amazon wouldn't be setting up shop as a print publisher, cherry-picking already successful authors, and doing everything New York gets hated on for while insisting on exclusive contracts, listing books early, screwing bookstores, distributors, authors, and trying to replace an entire industry with itself like some kind of capitalist Abzorbaloff.

Honestly, it's not so much that they do these things - that's what corporations do, and getting mad at them for acting like robber barons is like getting mad at rain. What frustrates me is the geek insistence that they are our friends, not only friends but savior and great democratizer, that they are more fair than other publishers despite their propensity for pulling books and the fact that the juicy royalty rate can change at any time and most probably will, given that this is how robber barons work: lower prices and operate at a loss until no one else can compete with your deep pockets, then jack them up again when you've clear cut your industry and left only yourself standing. I mean, it's a classic.

Ebooks are most definitely the future, and they are very nearly the present. I don't think we'll stop print runs any time soon - when millions of copies of a product still sell, it's a little early to crow over the death knell of their manufacturers. But I don't see why I should put on my frilly come-hither dress for robber barons and count myself on their side. Amazon is and should be seen by everyone who lists their books with them not as a savior but as a brute beast that you can strap yourself to for the present, but never forget that they can trample you, and you may want to leave a knot or two lose for a quick escape. No one ever loved and feared iUniverse this way. Self-publishing has always been hailed as the great equalizer, and it has always had these exact drawbacks: uneven quality, overweening quantity, low profit margins for authors, and poor packaging. Only one of those - the profit issue - is helped by the current system.

But enough about Amazon. Part of my issue with the whole dialogue is that they dominate every conversation, and the whole part where we write books and love them and people care about those books gets lost, because it's all about the format, it's all about being more tech savvy that the next author, all about selling - when really, it's not any more likely to sell big numbers than before. Where Kindle shines is in its ability to sell back-catalogue books for authors who've had some print publishing. New Kindle-only authors are as unlikely as ever to make a big splash, though of course it happens, just like the *NYT* list happens, just like lightning happens. And now, it's probable that any Kindle stars will be snapped up by Amazon's print arm anyway.

So yeah, enough. We all have to work with them. They have a use. But they are not quite the neutral tool for forging the new world that so many seem to think they are.

But what I was asked was: how did it work for me? No one wants to hear there is no secret, it's luck, it's writing something people respond to, it's effort and time and work. *So boring.*

So here's some data points. In seven and a half years in the game, I have published five novels with indie presses, one with a micropress, six with New York presses (Bantam, Tor, and Feiwel and Friends), and two serial novels. Two collections with indie presses, five poetry collections with micro or small presses, a standalone hardback novella with a regional science fiction association, and one collection self-published via Kindle and Lulu.

I'm sure there are ways and means of publishing I have not tried. But I've done most of it at least once. In every single instance, I have busted my ass marketing and trying to get those books in front of people, made all the more difficult by the fact that I don't really write easily-digestible thrillers. I have toured on my own dime, run ARGs, made book trailers (one of which got over two million hits, one of which didn't manage to top 2000), blogged unceasingly, done tie-in musical albums, thrown masked balls, anything I could think of. I have been nominated for awards, won and lost them, in fairly equal measure between traditionally published material and online publications, as far as anyone can tell *Fairyland* was the first self-published book to win a major literary award before appearing in print in any fashion. But I didn't get nominated for the Nebula until I did a standalone limited edition novella with the WSFA as part of my obligations as the GOH for a small regional convention.

The point of that little infodump is to say: everything is always and forever unpredictable. I had no idea that the serial novel I put on my website in 2009 to pay my rent would become my breakout book. I had no idea my deeply strange surrealist sex novel would get me my first Hugo nomination - I wouldn't have bet a dollar on that. Is "the secret" to publish with Tor or Orbit or Bantam or DAW? Is it to put a children's book on your website and not even bother to list it in the Kindle marketplace because that's a lot of work (actual reason for *Fairyland* not serializing on the Kindle)? Is it to publish with WSFA? No, because those were all very specific circumstances, and if you ask any writer, you will find that very specific circumstances, impossible to manufacture, predict, and often repeat, govern just about every success story. And I've easily had as many failures as successes, all governed by equally specific and unrepeatable circumstances.

You simply cannot know what, when you are a working writer, will take off and what will flop. You do not know it anymore now that ebooks are on the rise than you did before. The ebook marketplace is the slushpile, and it is just as long a shot to be plucked out of it as it ever was. You cannot know when someone with a lot of influence will read and like your book, or when a juried award will pick yours out of low-middling performance obscurity and make your name, you cannot know if the cover of your book will sell it to people who've never heard of you and don't even like fantasy. It's not that you have no control over it. It is gameable, but chaotic. The system is not rigged, but it is slanted - publishers can put a tremendous amount of energy behind a book to make it a success and it can work most of the time, but it fails, too. And there is very little you can do to determine whether your book is chosen for that infusion of life or not, whether the thousands of Kindle-available books will part like a sea to reveal your perfect pearl of a novel to the millions of readers looking for a 99 cent fix.

Art, it turns out, is hard.

So we wrap around to a point I made at the beginning of that massive four-part post about writing advice. Since you don't know, and likely are not in a position to game it with much skill, you might as well write what you love, write what you believe in, and use every trick to get it out there. Start with the big presses because they are still the best path to growing as a writer (you will be edited and this is not a bad thing, it's not cramping your pure vision, it's not violating you as an auteur) and making your book available in multiple venues (not locking you into exclusivity with one website or bookstore). If it doesn't work, write harder, write better, become more awesome at it. Then try again. Try smaller presses. Get an agent - or don't, I sold four novels before I got one. But I couldn't live without mine now. If you still can't sell, hit the e-market, Kindle, Smashwords, your own site, give it away for free in hopes of going viral or charge what you think the market will bear.

Hire someone to edit you, hire someone to copyedit you, hire an artist/designer or buy good art legitimately, maybe learn to design yourself, but always have people to tell you if your design sucks. Be creative, advertise with content: for every bit of advertisement, supply an equal bit of interesting content so people don't get irritated. Do the best you can, and then do it again. Pay them money, because if you think writing should earn money, if you think it's a job that you should be compensated for, then what editors and designers do should also earn payment, is also deserving a slice of the riches you hope to pull in from Amazon's royalty rate. At least barter. At least, if you're going to make yourself into a small press, behave with the professionalism toward your own work that a press would.

There is no one answer. Do it all. Try everything. Be canny and aware. Protect yourself and don't trust any company to have your full interests at heart - *even if they do*, the company itself can fail, as so many did in late 2008, which, combined with other companies failing and laying off my husband, is what forced me to start serializing a weird kid's book to begin with, which turned out to be the best thing I ever did for my career.

Be a hybrid, leave no tool unused.

We are in a transitional state in this industry. No one knows how it will shake out. Greater forces than we stalwart authors are at work. All you can do is be like unto Boxer: work harder. Decide what it is you want. Do you want to Be a Writer? Or do you want to write? Is it not good enough if you're not on the NYT list? Or enough that one person somewhere was touched by your book? If you can do the work, some level of success is available to you. There are many paths to it, and no one of them are easy, but the raw fact is that the world wants good books, and if you can make them, it is very likely that you will find a way to one of those levels. Beyond that, there is luck and there is brutal bloodyminded drive and stubbornness and there is work. Work, as the Daft Punk kids say, is never over.

And no matter what new thing is being waved about as a Success Wand for the new era, there is no shortcut around that work.

Operating Narrative Machinery

I've been teaching a lot of late, and thus having to think more about that old question: *do you have any advice for young/aspiring writers?* Since I'm still usually the youngest person on any given panel and not too long ago I couldn't sell a book to save my life, in many ways I still see myself as a young/aspiring writer. I wrote my first book when I was 22; it came out when I was 25. And I'll tell you, when it came out? I knew jackshit about writing. I did it because I wanted to and because I didn't know I couldn't. And I hit the ground running. But the result is that I'm kind of like a sitcom kid - I grew up in front of everyone. All my (ongoing) efforts to figure out life, the universe, and fiction have happened on paper, widely published, in more or less equal measure torn apart and loved. It's a harrowing, amazing, nailbiting way to spend your twenties.

You can find lists of rules for writers and advice and top ten dos and don'ts just about anywhere you care to look online. They're mostly of a kind: write what you love, follow submission guidelines, don't quit. Market yourself aggressively but not too aggressively. Write every day. There, I've saved you at least the cost of two books on writing. I've always been uncomfortable with telling people how to do these things we do, in part because I don't really see myself as an authority - why would anyone want to do it my way? And in part because good writing is a moving target, and what's more, no one agrees on where the target lies. But it is Friday and I am almost over my cold and I have students this weekend, so I'm going to drop some knowledge - which you should pick up, brush off, squint at dubiously, and only take home with you if you really like it and are willing to feed it, walk it, and pick up after it. Since I don't believe in soundbites and even two entries on the list is bordering on the epic, this is going to take a little while, so I'm splitting up the entries over the weekend and hopefully some of you won't vanish into the pre-Valentine's Day thrill ride.

Let's all repeat the holy refrain: Your Mileage May Vary. I am assuming here a level of desire to write interesting, chewy, risky fiction. Those who aren't into that sort of thing will find many other authors to guide them on their way. I can only attest to what I've learned, I can't mama bear every kind of writer there is.

Readysetgo.

1. Write What You Love

Aha! I have suckered you in and hit you with a cliche. The lessons here are two - cliche is horrible and disappointing! When you open a book that looks like it will shatter your heart and put you back together again a new human and what you find inside is instead some lukewarm frittata of D&D, white alpha male triumphalism, bad robots, and/or the redeeming/world-saving/death-defying/technology exploding (looking at you, *Doctor Who*) power of monogamous, child-producing heterosexual lurve, it is like unto whipping off one of those fancy rich-person silver dinner-domes to reveal something stale and rotten and beyond the veil of expiration dates within.

And also, write what you love.

Cliches come from somewhere, and they do have power if you're willing to get in there and examine them. The fact is, you might as well write the weird shit that ties you up in knots you're so into it, because the landfills are full of derivative books and experiments alike. You can write something along the exact formula of the most recent mega-hit and it can absolutely fail. You can write yet another steampunk zombie or epic RISK-style fantasy and have it disappears though it never was. You can write a pastiche of early twentieth-century children's fiction with polyamorous witches and too many big words or a multigenerational econopunk Singularity saga with uploaded lobsters and have it be a huge hit. You cannot know. Publishing (and writers) still move slowly enough that you cannot predict the next trend, so you might as well dork out over the things that thrill you down to your toes. And it's true that there are people who are excited by genres and tropes that others find distasteful. That's why we publish more than one book a year. There are even people who are *super electrified* by writing about a farmboy who finds out he's the secret heir to the Magicdragonsparklefire Kingdom. And that's ok. (I mean, it's ok like it's ok that you still live with your parents at age 38. It's not ideal, but rent's cheap and there's room for all your stuff. Life is hard and everyone's pulling for you to sort it out, buddy.) It means that those farmboys have people to shepherd them on their way to the Throne of Ultimate Power. I don't have to pay them any mind.

A comment on one of my previous posts just keeps going around and around in my head. It espoused the idea that "hard" SF is more difficult to perform, more rigorous, as fantasy does not require a PhD or at least working knowledge of physics. I've heard this so often, I can sing along with the chorus. I've even, when I first started writing science fiction, said it myself. But the fact is, very few people go out and get a PhD in physics just to write SF. People write what they know about, they write what excites them (which is a better measure than love, anyway). People who already have PhDs in physics are more likely to write SF than fantasy - and would find it much harder to write a moving, tech-free fairy tale than to riff on the stuff that gets them going in the morning. The body of knowledge required to write awesome, paradigm-shifting fantasy is easily equal to SF. Just ask Tolkien, who could hog-tie you into a Christmas bow with his doctorates. We find it difficult to write about things we haven't spent half our lives studying. What is new is strange and scary.

So yes, write what you love - but it's also good to stretch out and try something outside your idiom. I learned a tremendous amount about myself as a

writer and a human when I started making inroads into SF and horror as well
as fantasy. What is new is good for you, wherever you start out. So write what
you love - but also write what you fear.

2. Cliche Poisons the Soul

So you may have noticed I have this thing about cliche. I hate it, and wish to
stamp it out wherever I find it. This comes directly from my training as a poet.
Any formal training I have in writing is in poetry (this is... not shocking for those
who have read my work) and in that august field one learns to harbor a horror
of cliche as intense as a horror of communicable disease.

In fact, cliche is at its core a communicable disease. The polite way of calling
out the beast is to call it "received language." It's more than language, though.
It's anything that you just barfed up onto the page without thinking about it.
Sure, everyone on that planet obviously has the same religion. Yep, her skin sure
is milky/chocolate/cinnamon colored. I'll bet her (non-white) eyes are almond-
shaped, too! No reason this poorly-sketched female character shouldn't die horribly in some sexualized fashion simply to motivate the male hero - sounds
awesome! This is the entire reason we have TV Tropes.

It's also part of the reason that our genre can't have nice things. We love our
cliches *so hard*. Our received plots get put on pedestals and regular manifestos
appear exhorting us all to get rid of all this new-fangled stylistic/feminist/wib-
bleywobbley/deconstructive/non-Golden Age stuff and rewrite Asimov 'til we all
choke and die.

And the hard thing is that sometimes cliche can be a useful tool. It is a fairly
awesome thing to lay out and examine a cliched concept or character in a meta-
sense, to see why it got so hot everyone wanted to date it in the first place. To
take it apart and turn it against itself. I love that shit. The danger there is coming
off as too cute and knowing and ironic, too good for your home, so to speak.
But it can be done beautifully and well, because cliche is part of how we shorthand our entire culture, and if you can step back enough to use it instead of it
using you, it can be a monstrous tool in your belt. And looking at the cliches of
cultures other than your own can teach you a staggering amount about how they
see the world. If you're creating an alien or magical or alternate world, the cliches of that world should not be those of the West in the twenty-first century.
An understanding of cliche on the anthopological level is a high-level spell. Cast
with care. (And pretty much the only way to tune up your Cliche-Detecting
Engine is to read constantly, in every genre, all the time.)

But for the most part, it's just insidious and ugly and boring. If you're writing
is the same as everyone else's, there's no reason not to read literally anyone else.
A huge part of the editing process for me is to put on my Cliche Riot Police gear
and go hunting through my book, on the micro (sentence) and macro (plot,

character) level, looking for received crap to zap into some kind of foul Ghostbusters-style containment device for future study.

In the end, as a writer, you are a TARDIS. You are bigger on the inside. And constantly inviting wide-eyed young things to see the insides of you, to come with you to places extraordinary and terrible, to trust you to give them a story worth leaving the real world behind. It's an awful, intimate thing. Black magic for true. I genuinely believe that there is no one whose insides are nothing but pale retreads of other books, movies, TV and games. We use those things as armor so that we don't have to bring out the scary, sincere, bombastic, complicated, desperate, ugly, unkind, astonishing, bizarre, gorgeous, sometimes weak and broken parts of ourselves. How much easier to fall back on that poor fucking kid living the monomyth than to put ourselves on the line in our books. Cliche is tempting and warm and comfortable - and great books are rarely comfortable. And hey, maybe you and I never write a great book. But it's better, I have to believe it's always better, to try for great than to settle for more of the same.

3. People Are Going to Shit All Over You

Oh, yes they are. It really doesn't matter if you try to do something different or you just want to rescue the princess in the tower. It'll start with your teachers, in college or high school or workshops. You are going to have to hear, more than once, more than ten times, that not only does your work suck, but it betrays some signal flaw within yourself, and you as a person are terrible for having written this thing. This is true, basically, no matter what you write. It is especially true if you are trying something off the beaten path, whether that beaten path is one of bestsellers or your teacher's own predilections. I have personally had verse and chorus of "Nothing" from *A Chorus Line* spewed at me from numerous teachers. For those of you not musically inclined, it goes something like: you're bad at this, you'll never amount to anything, give up and work at a gas station and leave this to the real artists. One professor literally threw up his hands at our final conference and said "You're just going to do whatever you want no matter what I say so there's no point in even trying to teach you about good writing."

We all have stories like that, I suspect. Most particularly those of us who write SFF, which makes no friends in universities. The best part is, it doesn't stop there! Once you're published, new and exciting people will appear to tell you how bad your work is, even if you are popular and/or critically acclaimed. And it will get personal, especially if you are throwing down with your whole being, laying your kinks and history on the page like a sacrifice. If you're a woman, or other-than-white, or queer, it will probably, at some point, get *really* personal. Many readers have a huge problem separating the work from the creator. The mountain of crap I got for writing *Palimpsest*, both in public venues and in private emails, would make you crawl under the table with a bottle of fuck-you whiskey. I not only wrote a bad book, but I am sexually disturbed (I either hate sex or like it way too much, depending on who you ask) and politically suspect. Give up and work in a gas station. Name a book you think is universally liked and I will find someone saying it is a sin against man, decency, and the dictionary. People get very invested in books, which is the whole point of writing books. I have myself gotten upset to tears over books and have said so online. I try not to do that unless at great need now. I know too much.

It's easy to say: *you must develop grace about this*. I doubt anyone actually has grace about it. We all get mad or sad or hit the bar and rage against it all. It takes a really long time, or a really good Internet filter, to be ok with how much some people will not like your work and by extension you. I'm not saying get grace at the bargain virtue store.

But you can *fake* grace.

Do not respond to online wars about your book unless you can do so with a cool head - and even then, have someone else look over your response and gauge the probably fallout before clicking "post." Know that once a book is published it no longer belongs entirely to you. Readers will engage with it and take it apart if you are very lucky. Let them do that - it's their right as readers. If someone says your book is racist or sexist or homophobic or fatphobic or cruel, try to listen and see if there's something you can do better - because the nature of prejudice is that most people don't know they have it. Scream into your beer with your real life friends or over email. Fake the grace not to do it in public. Some takedowns are because people are dicks and want to shred things they don't understand. Some are because there's really a problem. And we as the authors of the text are way too close to it to be the ones deciding which is which.

And know that someone, always, will not like your work. Those voices sound louder than the ones who love it sometimes, because we are human and hurt easily. Because these books are pieces of our hearts bound in glue and card-stock. If you can't fake grace, just don't read your reviews. Reviews are a brutal kind of crack: when they're good, you feel you can conquer the world and everything is fine. When they aren't, it's a painful come down from the level of ego it took to write a book in the first place. All these things are normal. A mask of grace will get you further than Hulking out on every blog that reminds you of how much painful, painful rejection and misery comes stapled to the contract.

Carrie's mom was right: they're all going to laugh at you. Bucket of blood is not actually the answer.

4. You Will Never Be As Good As You Want To Be

And that's a good thing. There's always some data loss between the perfect book that existed in your head before you screwed it all up by writing it down and the final, actual book that heads out into the world. (Peter Straub's *In the Night Room* is possibly the best literary treatment of this sad fact that I've ever seen.)

At least for me, every single book I've ever written (12 so far) has seemed so big and monstrous when it only existed inside me that I could not even imagine, at first, how to begin writing it. I have torn my hair out in stages over every book, and with every book there were moments when I thought I'd never finish it, or worse, that I was simply not good enough yet to pull it off (possibly actually true). I genuinely believe that variously-attributed quote: "You never learn how to write a novel, you only learn how to write this novel." I have felt, every time, like I was starting over as a beginner.

You learn to live in that space between the perfect and the real. Walking that fence keeps you hungry, keeps you turning over the things you're obsessed with until, like the rock tumblers we geologically inclined children loved, eventually those concepts begin to gleam with clarity and color. But they will never be perfect. They will always have lumps and pockmarks. That's why working writers write for their whole lives, chasing that book that says it the way you meant it, a grail that is always in the next castle. We are Lancelots, not Galahads. And it's almost worse if you do come close and write something incredibly good, because that next castle can become terrifying, paralyzing. Doing it again can feel impossible. This is another high-level writer spell I didn't get until I had a big hit: it's far easier to say *fuck the haters, I'm gonna knock out the next one like a motherfucking prizefighter* than to whisper *everyone loved this, and I don't remember how I did it.*

The point is, the race is long. It is never about only one book, unless you get well and truly paralyzed and only ever write one. What keeps me going in the long dark deadlines of my soul when I think my old professor was right is the hope that someday I will write something as good as I hoped it would be when the idea first landed in my brain. I won't; the rabbit races forever in front of me. But sometimes, just sometimes, I can smell it as I run.

5. Use Your Voice

This one comes in two parts.

You know how everyone says all the stories have already been told? (Aristotle did, but also probably your flatmate.) It's totally true.

I've never understood why that means we shouldn't write anything else ever. There are a limited number of stories when you boil it down to Event A + Event

B = Narrative C. But that's never been the whole of literature. Yes, indeed, your plot is basically Beowulf/Arabian Nights/Antigone. So? What makes the difference is voice. Every story has been told, but you have not told every story. What your peculiar experience brings to a narrative is what makes it new. Human skeletons come in a certain more or less fixed configuration, but we all look completely different. The musculature and skin are as important as the bones. (Or: style is content, as the man said.)

This may seem to fly in the face of the No Cliche Stinkeye I have already cast. I poked fun at the monomyth because it's so easily recognizable as a Thing That Has Been Done. But you can even make the monomyth fresh - it just takes a lot of work and awareness. And I think awareness is the key. Examining the tools and materials you're working with, asking yourself what is necessary and what is simply easy, what is your own and what you borrowed. Asking yourself repeatedly why you are writing what you're writing, is it still what you want to be writing, has it become something else, something more or less interesting than when you started out? Being willing to take it apart again and start over. And most of all, most especially if you are working with well-worn tropes or retellings or engaging vigorously with the Great Conversation, be that the science fictional one, the critical one, or the one you've been having with your friends for the last ten years, does this thing you end up with look and sound like you? How have you added to or subtracted from the model you started with?

Follow your voice is a common bit of teacherly advice. And yeah, it's true, sort of. I think that in the beginning, most of us try on the voices of other writers, because we love them, because they resonate with us, because we want to see what fits and what doesn't. You're Sylvia Plath for a year, then you're Ursula Le Guin, then you're Charles Stross, then you're Jane Austen, then you're Homer for awhile. Eventually you come out with a technicolor dreamcoat of all the bits of voice and technique and style you've loved, minus what you don't, and stitched together with what is uniquely yourself, and that's what we call a voice. When you're just starting out it's ok to wear Jane's dress and Kafka's shoes. Hopefully, you outgrow it and keep growing into and out of things your whole life. This is part - but only part - of why it is not possible to be a writer without being a reader. Follow all the voices. See where they lead. And use it. All the tricks, all the backflips and hat-dwelling rabbits you know.

The second part is a more technical thing: read your stuff aloud.

Not just to yourself, preferably, but to someone who can react in ways subtle and gross. But if it's just to your cat, it's still the best tool I know for editing. You learn immediately what dialogue does and doesn't work, what flows and what judders, what beats you're hitting and what you're missing. (You also clean up your spelling real nice.) If you have another person to listen, you can see when they get bored, when they get excited, when they don't understand. I was in theatre for the first major portion of my life, and my parents were, too. I can preach this like the gospel. Stories were performed once upon a time, and you can see your work plainly, nakedly, fully only if you speak it aloud. You will also figure out what Your Voice really is, the natural cadences of your own accent/dialect, your sense of speech and rhythm, and how to invert or play into those hidden tics.

Not for nothing are the first verbs of the *Iliad* and the *Odyssey* Speak and Sing.

6. Hurt

It's really hard to give technical advice in writing. Every kind of writing, every trick and tactic can be both poorly done and well done, and many won't agree on which example is crap and which is an exemplar of the craft. What works for me may not work for you, and hell, maybe it doesn't even work for me, I just like it and can't stop, like a second piece of cake. A whole lot of people dig invisible prose; I am allergic to it like a freaking peanut in a preschool lunchroom. I like reading it fine, but writing it isn't interesting to me - and that's a salient point, too. What you enjoy reading may not have anything to do with what you enjoy writing. I like eating French pastries. Making one would frustrate me to tears, what with all the layers and butter-brushing. (It's possible I haven't had lunch yet, as I notice now-made three food analogies in one paragraph.)

But I had to give a talk on "the craft" at a recent book festival (which always puts me in mind of the movie about the angry girl witches, and honestly writing is not entirely unlike ceremonial magic with added angst so it's fairly apt) and I came up with a couple of things that were actually useful to me in terms of how I think about the individual moving parts of a novel.

I want to say I was asked to discuss this first thing, because it's a phrase that's often used - how to create sympathetic characters. But I'm not sure "sympathetic" is the dominant consideration when it comes to characters. Sometimes you want a character the audience can relate to, feel compassionate toward, in whom they can recognize themselves. Sometimes you don't. And the thing about characters is that the girl I want to hang out with and see myself in an want on my team in the apocalypse is not necessarily the girl that you want to have a beer with and see emerge victorious over a laser-dragon. Writers take character notes from the people they know and the social interactions they've been part of and we're all drastically different people, so the things we think make for sympathy often do not translate. And half the time, SFF characters are non-human, posthuman, augmented human, inhuman, or off the neurotypical spectrum, so the question of sympathy with such entities - the extent to which sympathy must come from similarity, the emotional relationship you want your audience to have with such characters - is extremely complicated. This doesn't even get into the weird and swampy territory of how often readers prefer to sympathize only with characters that share some or all of their demographic identities.

What I think we all do aim for is *interesting* characters. I want a character to fascinate me, whether I sympathize with them emotionally or not. So here's my little formula for creating an interesting character - and it happens to be a pretty good emotional cheat for making a sympathetic one as well. It also has five helpful points, and everyone knows bullet points mean it's the truth.

Take one (1) unformed character, be they protagonist, antagonist, comic relief, or BFF.

- Give them something to want.
- Give them something to hide.
- Give them something to fear.
- Give them something to obsess over.
- Then hurt them.

These are basic things and they're meant to be. People who want things passionately are more interesting than those who don't (usually). People who have obsessions, be they sixteenth-century cosmetics or an ex-girlfriend, show who they are by how they deal with their compulsions. People who fear nothing are cartoons and people who hide things instantly set up a mystery that the brain starts to puzzle over.

And the easiest way possible to get a reader to care about a character is to hurt that character, especially unfairly, especially when it's many against one or when they are humiliated and forced to suffer social castigation. Especially us geeks, who have often been the victim of this, we tend to want to protect the hurt unless they are truly vile. Spike was fun, but he became loved when we saw his humiliation. Rory on *Doctor Who* is a great example - he's a pretty milquetoast character, but he's been humiliated by Amy, abandoned, put down, and actually killed so often he's become utterly beloved, mostly because the audience wants to comfort him. At least for me, Bond became more interesting when we actually saw him suffer pain, both physical and emotional, in *Casino Royale*, rather than just being slick and untouchable.

A good way to get a handle on this is to (shudder) watch reality TV. The editing is pretty brilliant on the marquee shows like *Survivor* - they can make you hate or love someone incredibly fast. Take notes. Most of this appeals to primate psychology - either protect the weak or destroy it with your friends - and that's a powerful thing.

This can go bad - the number of female characters who are raped in fiction for little reason other than to give them a "dark" past, to upset the main male character and somehow rather grossly give *him* depth, or because hurting a character can be a source of pleasure for a reader is, well, depressing. I think avoiding the yuck of that should probably be a codicil to the five point plan, so here it is:

- *Do not operate narrative machinery while being an asshole.*

Don't rape your female characters because you can't think of anything else interesting that might happen to a woman, don't kill your gays because obviously all gay love must end in death in order to set the universe to rights, don't send a white savior to teach non-whites how to be civilized just because you think that's how it works in the real world, don't gleefully leap into historical settings because you think can be safely racist and sexist there just because reading an actual history book is hard.

It's good to remember that we are operating a huge machine when we write a book. It is an interface between two humans, author and reader. That machine can accomplish great tasks - it can also bite off fingers and crush its operators under it's own weight. Operating while under the influence of ignorance, laziness, cruelty, or carelessness not recommended.

7. What Everyone Knows

As a sort of freelance folklorist, I am enormously interested in the stories cultures tell about themselves. In genre fiction, this is called worldbuilding.

Any piece of history or genealogy or backstory that might infill a fictional world is a story that world tells to itself about itself. It's not necessarily fact. For example, as I mentioned above, a lot of people love medieval settings *in part* because they got the idea that it was a paradise for white strong men. Women had no power, everyone had the same religion, the West was the prime cultural force in the world, gays were on the Extreme Down Low, and everyone who mattered was a warrior poet. The world was your Ren Faire!

This is a story Western post-Renaissance culture tells about itself to itself. It is not fact. Any list of facts about that era would have to include Eleanor of Acquitane, Margery Kempe, Julian of Norwich, Empress Theodora, Anna Comnenus, Joan of Arc, the flowering of Islamic culture, Byzantine culture, China, India, Kievan Rus, and the Great Schism, all of which fly in the face of that picture.

But the reasons for telling that story about the medieval world are very revealing and have a lot to do with the Renaissance's Crisis of Needing to Be the Awesomest. They always are. And when I think about my own fictional cultures and worlds, one of the things I consider is who is telling the story of *this* history I am choosing to side with in my narrative, telling it to whom, and why.

126

There's a shorthand to this. To me, the most interesting question, *whether the answers are true or not*, about a culture is: *what does everyone know?*

For example, in America, everyone knows we're the best. Everyone knows childhood is a time of innocence and fun. Everyone knows killing people is bad. Everyone knows the economy will get better. Everyone knows what a real family looks like. Everyone knows motherhood is wonderful. In conservative culture, everyone knows life was better in the 50s. In liberal culture, everyone knows the 60s was where it was at. Everyone knows what the Dark Ages were like.

A quick way of figuring out whether something falls into the cognitive hole of What Everyone Knows? Ask yourself what statement would get the most outcry within a given (large or small) group. What you cannot say in that group, even if you think it. The things you can say, which would cause only responses of *fuck yeah! Agreed!*: that's What Everyone Knows.

The thing about What Everyone Knows is it's only sometimes factual - I hesitate to say "almost never" but that's probably closer. But it's *true*, in the sense that people comport their lives according to their belief in it, teach it to others, and get upset when What Some Other Group knows comes into conflict with it. Most stories, at their core, involve someone finding out that What Everyone Knows is or is not true, and what they do with that information.

So when writing, it pays to ask yourself What Everyone In This Story Knows. Buggers are the enemy. Winter is coming. The Doctor will save us. There is nothing unusual about our family. Magic is/isn't real. The King/Queen is bad/good. You can/can't fight the Man. They only come out at night.

In fact, when you don't ask this question explicitly, you fall into communicating What You Know as though it's What Everyone Knows. Women aren't as good as men. There is such a thing as a rightful ruler. Beautiful people are better than ugly people, or vice versa. Technology is always good, or always bad. God is real or God is dead, humanity is specially good or specially crap, people with British or Russian or Arab accents are automatically suspicious, one gender expressing traits of another is gross or funny or punishable, robots will destroy us or robots will save us. And even from this list you can probably tell a little of What I Know, which may or may not jive with What You Know. We all communicate the stories of our culture, whether that culture is a country, a planet, a family, or a fandom, in most of the things that we say and do. That is why folklore is awesome and necessary for understanding human groups.

8. A Ratio of Tradition to Experiment

This one, honestly, has taken me a long time to learn. When I started out writing fiction, I was 22 and I had a degree in (ancient, non-English) literature goddammit so *fuck your sensibilities, eat awesome.*

If you look at my books then and my books now, you can see that they're the same writer, sure. We all have our kinks and tics and themes that we just cannot let go of. But I've become, by leaps and bounds, more accessible. My 22-year-old self thinks that kind of sucks, because it is compromise and *we do not compromise on teh artz*. But my slightly more grown-up self knows that eventually it's not completely about what the author thinks (Knows) is awesome, but also about what the reader is willing to put up with to get that awesome.

So my rule of thumb is that given Plot, Structure, and Style, one of them has to tap out and play for Team Mundane. The reader needs something to hold on to while the author experiments with something that excites them: a linear, straightforward structure, unvarnished, solid prose, a plot that lines up with their cultural expectations of narrative. Most really good books pick one of those things to go wild with. Books that pick two are called avant-garde, and those that don't call any quarter for readers without obscure degrees are more often than not called remaindered. Look at *House of Leaves*, which has a structure like *good grief, Charlie Pomo*, but the sentence-level prose style is pretty workaday in 2/3 of the book, with only the occasional Truant/grad school thesis sections and the poetry, which is not part of the main body of narrative, going off the farm. The plot is a pretty standard haunted house story, with a literary fetch quest stapled onto it. And even *those* numbers are too much for a lot of readers to dance with.

There is a generous explanation in here, I think, as to why most hard SF, as rule, doesn't trouble itself too much with silly things like characters and feelings. (I'm going to be generous and not poke the cultural argument on this score.) When hard, technical science and technological ideas, which require much explanation and exploration, are in the position of being The Experiment, the thing that makes the story different and interesting, it probably helps to ground the reader with characters and motivations that don't *also* require them to question What They Know and puzzle out and work hard to understand. So perhaps also given Character, Idea, and World, the regular:funky ratio of 1:2 (avant-garde) and 2:1 (quality commercial) might still hold, but I haven't thought about that quite as much, so I won't bet my speaking fee on it.

If you don't care whether a large number of people read your stuff, then hey, knock yourself out. Go for batshit 0:3 or slush pile 3:0. I didn't care about The Market when my literary principles lived in ALLCAPSTOWN. I'm still proud of what I wrote there. But most people who read lists of writing advice want to be widely published and/or read, and to do that you have to pick one, maybe even two if you don't get called out for being "too hard" with every single damn book, and make them the designated driver, who can behave responsibly and according to expectations while the kids in the party bus are guzzling neon cocktails, dancing the space tango, and deconstructing gravity.

9. Authorial Credit

My mental processes about writing tend to flip back and forth from the idealistic to the extremely hard-headed and sensible. I both love writing with all my being, and reading too - a friend (not even an author friend) posted recently that nothing else in the world mattered but reading and writing and while I can pick holes in that as well as you can, part of me, the idealistic part, thinks there is a crazy truth in that, that stories are such a core part of being human that a massive portion of our activity on planet earth is telling and hearing them, whether or not that means getting in the publication game or the old porch-yarn here's a pot of butter for me and a tale for you magic.

I think a lot about the relationship between the reader and the writer. Because it's a weird, intimate thing between two people who are probably not going to meet. Text is fluid - there is no one book, there is the book the reader and the writer make together, and that book changes subtly for every reader because every reader is rolling up to the table with a whole different set of expectations and experiences and desires. Once you finish a book, it no longer quite belongs to you in a spiritual sense, at least not as it did when it only lived in your head. It has become part of other people's heads, and mutated there. I've heard a lot of teachers say that you should write for yourself and not an audience, and while it's true that you shouldn't pander to an audience's expectations (you can never satisfy them) to the exclusion of your own sensibilities and enjoyment, to me writing is hugely about the audience. Maybe it's my theatrical upbringing. Playing to an empty house is a fundamentally different act. And not as much fun.

So I have a number of different metaphors for that relationship. Possibly the one that gets remembered the most, which I said to a crowded room at Readercon not quite realizing the reaction it would get, is that it's a D/s relationship, and it's my book, so I'm the top. Meaning: I am creating a scene and guiding the reader through it, hoping not to screw up, to satisfy their needs, to deliver the goods with authority and power, and if they don't want to play anymore, well, safewording = closing the book.

That's the idealistic/romantic part of me, that sees the weird kind of love, that is not like anything else we call love but English is very word-poor in some areas, that happens between writers and their audience. The hard-headed part thinks of the relationship as a creditor and a debtor. (I am quite sure this is influenced by my time as an editor, when I was very interested in the point where I could tell a story was worth reading or never would be.) The reader extends a certain amount of credit to the author - let's say 50 pages worth. And if the author can pay off that credit, then that earns them more credit.

I think this proceeds very quickly: the first line earns you the first paragraph, the first paragraph earns you the first page, the first page will probably get you the whole first chapter, the first chapter will get you to Chapter Three, and if a reader gets to Chapter Three and is still invested, they'll probably give you half the book if it's very long and the whole book if it's not.

That's kind of a brutal calculus, because a lot of readers will forgive a crappy first line or first paragraph, maybe they're not here for the prose stylings or they just have a lot of patience, and SFF readers tend to. But I think it's a good idea to write as though all your readers are your most cutthroat readers - they don't have the time for bad books and the Internet has trashed their attention span and they have kids and jobs and a hundred other things so the time spent with this book has to count against all of that. That first part of the book is so vital, because it spikes your reader credit score.

And if they liked one book of yours, it fascinates me how that credit stretches or doesn't. As a reader, if I loved one book by an author, I'm likely to read through at least two, maybe three more that I don't like at all before I give up on them, and even more if I hear that they've taken off in a new direction or I have reason to think they're over whatever I didn't like. So it goes from flipping over pretty fast - line, paragraph, page, chapter - to going quite slow, whole books that I just credit as being awesome because of another book I loved. Those new books have to actively not pay their bills for awhile before I cut my losses.

On the other hand, if I hate a book by an author, I'm not likely to pick up another one. They blew their credit with me already. It does happen, I can think of two major authors off the top of my head where I made a big stinkface on our first go only to fall in love with a later work.

So how does this apply practically? Well, you have to establish your credit. Those first lines and first pages really do matter - Ezra Pound cut the first 250 lines of "The Waste Land" - and the line he told Tom to start with is one of the most famous in the English language. Look at your beginning. Cut until you hit something you can't sacrifice, or is too awesome to lose. Consider where you're starting your story, if you've buried the lede and not given the reader something else - an interesting voice or idea or something - to pull them through. Hell, I had no idea what *Snow Crash* was about from the first page, but I'll be damned if I wasn't sold on reading the whole thing after one damned paragraph. That isn't always what you can pull off - but it should be the goal.

10. Radical Sincerity

So look. Here's the thing about writing. Some people think it's magical, some people think it's a job. I think it's a magical job. It's a job in that I have to go to it every day, and sit at a computer, and enter data. It's hard and I'm not always inspired and sometimes I really just want to play video games and eat cake and never think about narrative structure again. And sometimes it's not even the fun part of making things up, but the copyediting and admin and correspondence and total breakdown level exhaustion after months on tour. It is more than a full time job, and even though it is an amazing job, there is nothing particularly mystical about being a writer over, say, being a programmer.

But on the other hand, it is kind of magical. Like trauma, I'm convinced there's some chemical release that erases the knowledge of how I ever managed to write a book as soon as I've finished it. Things just drop into your head without warning and the story seems to take on its own life. For me it's a combination of playing a complex game, casting a spell, and solving a puzzle in which many pieces fit correctly but only one makes the right picture. We all come up with metaphors about writing and compare it to other tasks because even as writers we're constantly trying to understand it. We talk about muses and characters sprinting off on their own recognizance and channeling inspiration (ok, other people do; I get hives when those conversations spring up), because a lot of times we don't have a good explanation for where ideas come from, or why the story needed to go in just that way, or why on Tuesday nothing happened and at least one eyeball actually wept blood while staring at a blank screen and on Wednesday a whole story just fell out and was amazing. Why stuff that seemed phenomenally, brain-sizzlingly awesome last night is crap this morning, and what seemed like cold garbage when you finished writing it is actually pretty good when you make your editing pass. It's all weird stuff, and like most groups who suffer from low personal power and random reinforcement, we get superstitious and start churning out odd folklore.

And then you slap down your most personal obsessions and best guesses and terrors and longings and it gets mass-reproduced and a whole bunch of people (hopefully) read it and then you have to look them in the eye at readings and signings and conventions and try to black out what they know about your past, your future, how you want the world to be and what you love so that you can have a normal conversation, so that you can try to be the better self that sometimes, on really good days, goes into the work. It's not exactly normal, this thing we do. But there is a reason that so many people want to do it, and that reason is because it is awesome. Sometimes I realize the awful truth that being a writer is exactly as amazing and magical as I thought it would be when I was a kid and that's really a bit terrifying.

Almost every writer I know has at one time or another said they felt they were Doing It Wrong and there had to be an easier/faster/slower/better/less stressful/better tasting way to write a book. Not just the standard long dark teatime of the middle third of the novel where we pretty much all think we're terrible at this and should be strung up for the imposters we are, but that the method by which we accomplish books is the wrong one.

The truth is, if there's a finished book at the end of it, it's the right way to write a book. I say that having just stayed up all night for the second time this week to finish something, which I always tell myself is stupid, and I am stupid, and I am not in college and why couldn't I do it during the day like a non-vampire? But it's never been a realistic expectation of myself not to write things the way I have always written them, which is to say all in one go, usually late at night, pushing through because if I don't stop I can't doubt myself. It's part of who I am as a writer, and however you write is part of who you are, too.

I don't really think I'm any kind of expert at this, which is a scary thing to say on the Internet where No One Is Wrong. I think there has to be an easier and better way to write a book than I do, too. When interviewers ask me for advice for young writers I usually punt and say: read everything. And that's completely true, you do have to read everything, as much as possible, to even hope to take a swing at writing, and if that sounds like too much work you probably should take up another hobby. But it's also an easy answer, because all the other ones are hard and often contradictory, like avoid cliche but also give your reader something familiar to stand on. Be radically sincere. Be in love with the world because the world is this amazing place, the present and past no less than the future and you live in it and your job is to translate it and rephrase it and turn it on its head so that other people can see it the way you do, the way it might be, or almost was, or never could be but still, somehow, is true. Don't hold anything back because you never know when you'll get another contract, but at the same time cultivate calm, and realize that you probably will if you got the first one, and don't throw the kitchen sink at it. You must be at least this passionate and driven and obsessive and committed and joyful about the minutia of literature to ride this ride. Write as fast as you can because someday you'll die and if you didn't tell all the stories you had in you it will hurt. (No one believes me when I say this is the exact and honest reason that I have written so many books while being so young. I tell them: *I'm going to die soon. I have to write faster. I only have 50 years or so left if I'm lucky. That's not enough time.* They laugh, and I'm not joking.)

I don't know, wear sunscreen.

Mars Needs Women

Gender, Race, and Storytelling

Dorothy Sayers Explains It All

"Let us accept the idea that women should stick to their own jobs - the jobs they did so well in the good old days before they started talking about votes and women's rights. Let us return to the Middle Ages and ask what we should get then in return for certain political and educational privileges which we should have to abandon.

It is a formidable list of jobs: the whole of the spinning industry, the whole of the dyeing industry, the whole of the weaving industry. The whole catering industry and... the whole of the nation's brewing and distilling. All the preserving, pickling, and bottling industry, all the bacon-curing. And (since in those days a man was often absent from home for months together on war or business) a very large share in the management of landed estates. Here are the women's jobs - and what has become of them? They are all being handled by men. It is all very well to say that woman's place is the home - but modern civilisation has taken all these pleasant and profitable activities out of the home, where the women looked after them, and handed them over to big industry to be directed and organised by men at the head of large factories. ...

The fact remains that the home contains much less of interesting activity than it used to contain... It is perfectly idiotic to take away women's traditional occupations and then complain because she looks for new ones. Every woman is a human being - one cannot repeat that too often - and a human being must have occupation."

—Dorothy Sayers, *19freaking47*

This is a very true thing. Being a "homemaker" these days involves raising children (or not) and keeping the house reasonably, but not even particularly immaculately, clean. If you want immaculate, you hire someone. My mother in law, a Russian woman who practically has Work Ethic tattooed on her back in prison font, told me to hire a maid, because no one could expect one person to clean a house this big (it's not obscenely big). It's considered cool enough for men to cook (easily the most fun and creative of household chores - and probably not coincidentally the one which actually produces a tangible thing, rather than the vague "cleanliness" or "non-psychotic child development") that home-making might not even include cooking every day of the week.

I wonder if this is part of the reason there has been such a revival of cottage industry home crafts in recent years. I mean, without even thinking, I can name someone I know who knits, spins and/or dyes fiber, makes beer at home, pickles things, preserves things, grows their own food, makes wine, cures their own meat, raises chickens or ducks or goats or horses, makes their own butter, jam and/or bread, quilts, makes jewelry (practically everyone I know makes jewelry) or clothes, and bakes from scratch. Hell, I do most of those things and I am not by any stretch a homemaker. But we've lost the home tasks which provided the most creative output and enjoyment (no one liked washing laundry with lye, no matter how idyllic scrubbing linens in the river looks in movies, but knitting is damned pleasant, and food activities have their peculiar joys, even when they are tedious and strenuous, like pickling and preserving) and yet we still have to spend a lot of time at home, and still have this cultural meme of "home = woman" which leads to not teaching sons to do even the child and cleanliness things, and teaching them also that someone, eventually, *will do those things for them*. I wonder if we're just trying to get those parts that provided connection and community and occupation back somehow. Even parenting has become a kind of competitive performance art not wholly related to how we ourselves were raised. The thing is, almost (I said *almost*, do not get offended if you are a homemaking superman) everyone I can think of who does those things, with the exception of beermaking, because duh, is a woman. I think I know one man who knits the way I and my female friends do, which is to say obsessively. Most of this revival is feminine, and I don't quite know why, except that we're all unemployed or non-traditionally employed, and these things do provide a high level of tangible occupational satisfaction.

Because let's be honest here. I don't know very many people of my generation who can afford to "just stay at home." They do it when they can't find work or cinch their belts for the first years when child development is so important, but I can't really think of anyone starting to have their babies now who can just blithely kick it housewife style.

Of course, men also used to be expected to know a whole lot of home-things, too. Like how to fix anything that goes wrong with household machines, care for livestock, and literally build more house - and the build more house bit was often a hobby. Even one generation back, I see men on this island whose idea of a rocking awesome weekend is to build something out of wood and glass that adds to the beauty and utility of their home. We don't teach that anymore either. There's always someone to hire to do it. What I am capable of doing in that field is purely due to my own streak of *I Will Do Boy Things Fuck You* and not anything I've been taught - but more interestingly, my husband is fairly competent at fixing (better at computers than ovens) and can assist at building, but his father can do more or less everything. That's how I think it happens - each generation needs these skills less, so learns maybe half of what their parents knew, and pretty soon no one knows how to do shit our great-grandparents considered basic.

I'm not singing the modern world sucks rag. I really like my technology. Of course, I still get it from all corners that I should be buckling down and having a baby, as though my career is just faffing about and killing time. If the house is awry that's on me, not my husband - who is a good post-feminist boy and does all kinds of cleaning and cooking! But external judgment will always be on me, no matter how many books are on the shelf with my name on them. I became so much more socially acceptable when I wrote a book for children. And though I bake like a mofo and cook and preserve and pickle, I've never touched a grill in my life, for lo, that is sacred Man Territory. I am the very model of a modern pomo feminist, yet oh, how my life is still strewn with this crap. Let's set aside for a moment the issues of sexism in my industry, and how I so rarely read a book or watch a TV show where a woman has an internal life, a job outside the home, a friend, desires or ambitions. (I just saw someone list off the best shows evar, and none of them had any interest in women's stories or passed the Bechdel test, rather, they were all the sorts of shows that get described to me as being "interesting in masculinity" which apparently means no chicks plz.)

I find the very simple question at the beginning of the quote fascinating, because I've never heard it asked. If we, as conservatives would have us do, give up all those pesky votes and rights and bodily autonomy and needs to be recognized as human, what do we get in return? Because "the home" is kind of a shitty answer. It's always been a brutal gig to be asked to be intelligent and creative and engaged enough to raise a highly successful child, yet to be satisfied with only that, forever, along with some cleaning and cooking. But the home as they seem to conceive it no longer exists. The home is a place now, not an industry.

I saw a comedian the other day talking about how little girls never get to be kids. (For values of our current "to be a child is to be carefree, work-free, trauma-free and innocent" meme.) A baby boy's toys are trucks, spaceships, guns, robots. A baby girl's is another baby girl to take care of. The comedian looked up plaintively to the spotlight and said: "But I just got here."

Quite so. And this got a little long. But the gender stuff is still spicing the soup and it's gross and weird and ugly and even moreso on the Internet where no one has to look a woman in the eye when they tell her to shut up. I wish we were doing a little better. A little better than the commentary of 1947. Than the gender politics of early-90s *Star Trek*, which looks so quaint now, not actually worshiping full-tilt at the font of overweening masculinity. (As the new movie does, as *Mad Men* does even while caring a great deal about women - if you think that show would have succeeded without Don Draper set up for a long while as a good old days ubermensch for men to adore and emulate, think again, while you're trying on that Banana Republic Sterling Cooper suit. Which doesn't even get into a whole new genre of film and TV set in historical tiemz, so that we can ogle ladies being treated badly without feeling bad about it, because accuracy! Please do not pay attention to anyone named Eleanor in either the twelfth or twentieth centuries.) I wish the quote that made me ramble on forever didn't strike me the way it did, because my culture considers those issues asked and answered, even while it tells me to have a kid, stay at home as much as I can, be thin and pretty all the time, don't have an abortion ever, stop complaining, take less money, it's only logical as you're weaker and will probably just have a baby anyway, but don't call yourself a feminist, and that it's scientifically proven that my voice doesn't command as much attention as a man (harmonics! not cultural, just *fact*) and that my orgasms are evolutionarily useless.

You can keep your flying cars and jetpacks - I was promised a future where my gender would not define me. And yet.

The Story of Us

Do you know why we get so upset about whether or not there are depictions of women, people of color, gays, lesbians, transgendered, and humans of all sizes and kinds in genre fiction? Because it seems a bit of a small issue, what SFF writers choose to write about as opposed to equal pay, equal rights, and protection from rape, right? Yet we all seem get so very upset when this subject is brought up, when *Dollhouse* makes rape so neat and pretty, when *CSI* punishes women for living every week, when space opera has blue and green but no black. The straight, white males of the Internet get their hackles up, because it isn't a big deal to them, and they can't understand why it's *this* big a deal to us. It sucks, sure, but why the rage? Why does this cut us so deeply? Why are we criticizing what they have poured blood and love into, the works of their lives?

I have a theory. The reason, I think, is subtle, and doesn't usually get brought to light.

Why do we need stories? In the greater human sense, not in the bestseller, ZOMG Alan Moore is awesome sense. Storytelling is an essential human activity, a paleolithic one, hardwired into us. It's the campfire and the tribal circle, the shaman and the nomad. And while you could argue many motivations for this ritual act, I want to focus on one. One especially applicable to folklore, fairy tales, mythology - and therefore to fantasy and science fiction.

Stories teach us how to survive. They tell us that our lives can be transcendent, that we can overcome almost anything, no matter how strange, that we can go into the black wood and come out again, that the witch can be burned up in her own oven, that we can find someone who fits a shoe, that the youngest, unloved child will find their way in the world, that those who suffer can become strong, can escape, can find their way into comfort and joy again. That there are secrets, and they are always worth discovering, that there are more and different creatures in the world than we can ever imagine, and not all want to eat us. Stories teach us how to win through, how to persevere, how to *live.*

As a child of abuse, fairy tales kept me going when I was a girl. Because Gretel could kill the witch, because Snow White could come back from death, because Rapunzel could live even in the desert - then, well, I could too. I could dry my tears and clean up the blood and keep living. This is what stories do. They say: *you are worthy of the world, no less than these heroes.*

And when we see story after story that has no one like us in it, a book entirely without women, a TV show where white people speak Chinese but there are no Asians visible, a movie set in California without Hispanics, image after image of a world where everyone is straight, and when *we are told that it's no big deal,* really, there is no race in future societies, that it's not anyone's fault if all the characters are white, that's just how they *are*, in the pure authorial mind, that we have no sense of humor, that we are ganging up on people because we speak our minds, this is what we hear:

You do not have a right to live. There are no stories for you, to teach you how to survive, because the world would prefer you didn't. You don't get to be human, to understand your suffering or move beyond it. In the perfect future society, you do not exist. We who are colorblind, genderblind, sexualityblind would prefer not to see you even now. In the world we make in our heads, you have been obliterated - even better, you never were. You are incapable of transcendence. You are not worthy of the most essential of human behavior. If you are lucky, we will let you into our stories, and you can learn to be a whore, or someone's mother, or someone's slave, or someone's prey. That is all you are, so pay attention: this is what we want to teach you to be.

And when our protests are drowned out by a privileged few who insist that their stories are even more difficult than ours, even more hurtful, in fact just *like* ours but *better* because someone who looks like them is telling them, that *their* voices *must* be heard, that we are wrong to even bring up the subject, when they try to punish people for speaking out, when they tell us over and over that when *they* are done speaking, when *they* are done telling their stories to all the people who look just like them, so that people who look like them can learn to survive and be strong, maybe we can have the mic for a minute while the janitors who look like us are cleaning up, what they are saying is not literary theory.

It is eugenics.

That is what this is about. Evolution. Only those who look a certain way, act a certain way, fuck a certain way are allowed to have the blueprint, to have any guide on a path grace, peace, love in their lives. Everyone else can just lay down and die. It is almost never a virtue to silence another soul, by shouting them down, by shutting them out, by derision, by omission. Even the worst soul has the right to tell its tale. And we are not the worst souls.

Stories are important. Stories, in fact, are life. They are what is left of our unique experience in this world. They speak - no. They *scream*. And when an author sits down and constructs a completely imaginary world in their heads, if people like me, people like us, do not exist in it, or exist only to be ridden like animals or raped or murdered or humiliated or destroyed so that an audience can achieve catharsis via symbolic *annihilation of our lives, bodies, and souls*, well, certainly, we can sit down and look at the floor and say: *yes, you're right, that is what we deserve.*

Or we can stand up. We can scream back. We can band together. We can demand our right to exist, to take part in humanity, to learn, to grow, to evolve, to self-examine. We can tell our stories, to anyone who will listen, to the campfire, to our lovers, to coffee shops, to strangers, to publishers' skyscrapers in New York, to the heavens, to the earth. Yes, you're fucking well right we can.

An Open Letter to Certain Segments of the Science Fictional Universe

Please, please stop.

You are showing your ass in public. I cannot overstate the aptness of this metaphor. This kind of behavior is exactly the same thing as running out in the town square, dropping your pants, and slapping your pustule-laden ass while babbling about the end times.

The Internet is the public sphere. It is not a private salon where only your friends will hear you and forgive you because they know you're a really nice guy at heart. Apologies to all, but fuck Usenet. That ship has sailed. This is becoming embarrassing for everyone. Why it's always people in my genre that feel the need to jump up and holler I have no idea, but seriously, knock it the fuck off. I'm not going to try to talk y'all into, you know, not thinking stupid things, because I think we all know that's a lifetime's work and the truth is everyone involved has better things to do. Allow me, instead, to appeal to a baser, more primitive instinct than the basic fucking sense of decency that might lead you to not shit all over anyone different from you.

You are hurting yourselves.

It's a pretty simple equation, really. Limited lifespan divided by number of books it's possible to consume due to vagaries of money and mortality equals *I am not buying your books if you behave like a fuckmuppet in public.*

Oh, but it should be about the art, shouldn't it? We should separate the art from the artist.

Allow me to be frank.

I *might* be willing to do that kind of forgiveness for genius-level work. I can get through Aristotle and Euripides even if they aren't so hot with the chicks. Ditto Tolkien, Eliot, Henry Miller. I can stomach a little Lovecraft, even. I can just barely almost start thinking about *Ender's Game* and *Wyrms* because he wasn't spouting that shit when I read them. Hell, I'll even throw in Mark Helprin's *Winter's Tale*, (author is a neocon copyright illiterate sack of hubris), but *Winter's Tale* is the *bargain basement lowest denominator level of genius* I require before I even start trying to overlook your ass in my public.

For your derivative hacktastic doorstopper fantasy? Not a chance. You guys? Are no *Winter's Tale*. Y'all aren't even *Wyrms*.

It takes work and energy above and beyond the reading of the book for me to get over authorial fuckmuppetry. I am not sitting down to that task for pastel-covered, _____ of Made Up Word _____, sloppy Joseph Campbell blowjob extruded product. Especially since that product is likely colored by the personal beliefs of the authors, which are, in general, ugly and cruel.

Guys, learn this rule. Love it. Embrace it.

Every time you bloviate offensively on the Internet, a reader swears off your work for life.

It is so easy to lose readers. A cranky day at a con will do it. A single bad book will do it. Insulting an entire swath of readers, calling them evil and immoral, or shouting their concerns down and swearing at them? Especially when SFF readership has rather a lot of the sort of readers you're likely to insult with this kind of nonsense? Will do it so incredibly efficiently, it'll make Bookscan spin. Especially if you happen to be a midlist or indie writer, and can't weather decreased sales with a shrug and a grin.

Not to mention? If you really, in your heart of hearts, think there is a homosexual agenda, a PC army, a feminist conspiracy - *why do you feel so comfortable and gleeful spewing bile about them in public?* I assure you, the easiest way to determine who has power in a culture and who does not is to look at who feels safe to speak freely, and who does not. The homosexual/feminist/PC agenda? I'll give it to you in one sentence:

We would like to be treated as humans.

That's it. That's all. And that does not actually impinge on your right to be treated as same.

Some days I feel like the Internet is a possessing demon, and when people I thought were on my team start slashing at me and mine with claws out, teeth bared, it was just their turn to be possessed. It's easier than dealing with the idea that I've misjudged people so badly. That I pass enough to earn the basic minimum of human treatment in person, but that thin veneer of passing is all that protects me from their dark, ugly internal drives, their fear, their rage. I don't want my "office" to be peopled with dangerously unfiltered folk who hate people like me, and only hug me when we meet because for a moment, I looked like them.

But I am digressing. I said I wouldn't try to change your minds. It's pointless. All I'm saying is that when given an opportunity to spend my $10 on a book by someone who hasn't personally insulted me and my friends, and someone who has? It's an easy choice. It's a predictable choice. And fortunately, not a one of you is making it any harder by writing such heartbreaking works of genius that I have to second guess that choice, even a little bit.

So, uh, thanks, I guess.

Life With and Without Animated Ducks:
The Future is Gender Distributed

You know that wonderfully, wryly apt Gibson line: "The future is here, it's just not evenly distributed"?

I came across an article a few days ago, detailing several self-cleaning fabric technologies, some chemical, some using nanotech. Some safer than others. It is pretty damned awesome. And it made me think of one of the particular vectors of uneven distribution. Bear with me for a minute, this is going to seem like a tangent, but it's not.

In a former life, I lived in Japan for several years, in Yokosuka, which is just south of Yokohama, about two hours by train east of Tokyo. Now, this was in the early naughts, so I'm willing to entertain the notion that it's all completely changed by now and what I'm about to say no longer applies. Nevertheless, moving there was challenging on multiple levels - personally, in terms of severe isolation; professionally, since I started publishing in America while living there and was far too broke to fly back to go to conventions or give readings.

But also, technologically.

Japan in those days, and possibly now, was technologically schizophrenic. On the one hand, no one in the US was texting regularly yet, and our cell phones, both in the way of payment plans and the object themselves, were sad little things compared to what I could get in Japan. My phone would show me a little animated duck every morning, wearing a kimono. The duck would bow and say hello. If it was a holiday, my duck would be tricked out in a fabulous holiday-appropriate outfit and would wiggle its feathered butt, smile, and quack out a little greeting wishing me a Happy Boys' Day or O-Bon. I did not download the duck, it was just part of the phone. The toilets were deservedly notorious. If I went to the mall, I could be treated to a heated-seat toiled with more options than my phone, which would sing me a little song when I used it. I had so many gadgets to heat various parts of my body individually, and a vending machine every 100 feet in my neighborhood that would dispense warm cans of coffee or cold ones, whichever the weather required.

Outside my house, the world was full of singing, bowing, wiggling, hot and cold running futuretech.

Inside my house was a different story.

Because I was then the wife of an American naval officer (I told you, a former life), we were given a washer and dryer by the Navy. It was a Japanese model, but it did not sing, it did not have many options at all, and it certainly did not have an animated duck that wished me a Happy Emperor's Birthday in a sudsy kimono. Eventually, as I got to know my neighbors, I realized that duck or not, the mere fact of owning a washing machine was unusual - having a dryer made me unique in the neighborhood. Everyone hung their wash out to dry, and most of the wives, the majority of whom stayed home, washed clothes by hand. Dishwashers were unheard of, there were no garbage disposals (instead you use a fine mesh bag inserted into a small bucket-sieve in the sink), and central heating or air conditioning was simply not done. Where I lived, there was no insulation in the houses. The walls were raw, exposed concrete; any heat or cool air escaped out of the walls the moment you turned the wall-mounted swamp heaters/coolers off. (It does, however, make a horrible kind of sense that so many of the houses in that part of Japan are 60 years old and quickly made of questionable materials, as the US bombed most major cities into rubble, and that goes double for a military town like Yokosuka.)

The electrical systems in our neck of the woods were such that you could only have one wall-mounted heater/cooler on at a time without blowing the breaker. Mildew was a huge problem because of the concrete walls and tatami floors, which look nice in movies but have to be replaced often in the humid climate as they slowly rot. The conventional wisdom on the temperature issue was that it was too expensive to heat a whole house. And yet, I have never spent so much money on heat as the winters I spent in Japan - and I moved during the California energy crisis. I owned gloves that could heat my hands and a table with heaters embedded underneath to heat my legs, heated footpads and kerosene heaters, all of which were considered the efficient way to go, but were vastly expensive items that sucked up electricity like elephants having a water fight. I spent a fortune to huddle in the dark next to a space heater I am still convinced gave off actively carcinogenic. (Even from several feet away, it left a red impression of its netted grate on my legs once I turned it off; if my dog lay near it, her whole face swelled up until she couldn't see. Not a good sign.) I could go on. (The toilet in my house, by the way, did not have buttons or lights, however the mall model impressed.)

This may sound like bitching, and of course in some sense it is. But it began to occur to me that the tech I was using was incredibly gendered. In the "male" sphere, of professional operations, offices, corporations, pop culture, businesses, the available technology was extremely high-level, better than anywhere I'd yet lived. In the "female" sphere, the home, domestic duties, daily chores, cleaning, heating, anything inside the walls of a house, it was on a level my grandmother would find familiar.

Given that during the time I was there, the Japanese parliament was suggesting removing the social safety net (social security benefits, in American parlance) for women who chose not to have children, and the issue of young men who expected a stay-at-home wife and young women who wanted to have careers was quite a hot one, I could not then and still do not believe that divide was an accident. The simple fact is that domestic chores take a huge amount of time and energy, and if a woman is occupied doing them, and especially doing them without the machines that speed up the process considerably, means that she rarely has the time to pursue interests and a career. Though for cultural and financial reasons, Japanese houses often house more than one generation, the lack of technology creates so much unnecessary work that most of my neighborhood required both the young mother and grandmother in a household to devote their days to it.

I don't think there's some dastardly man in a high office making Mr. Burns fingers and saying: *EXCELLENT. I have oppressed women for another day! Let us celebrate!* (Except the PMs who wanted to take away benefits for childless women - but not childless men.) This kind of thing is always more subtle than that. People who have imbibed from their culture that men and business are important and women and the home are slightly distasteful and irrelevant spending their time on inventions applicable to one and not the other. Corporate managers approving projects along the same lines. Everyone performs their upbringing in their work in one way or another. Obviously, I don't consider business a male bailiwick and the home the kingdom of woman, but a whole lot of people do, and a goodly number of them have a massive influence on the allocation of R&D funds and the political narrative than I do. Right this very second, here in the US, we are having an actual, serious, if incredibly stupid, conversation about whether or not women should have easy access to birth control. We are having this conversation because significant humans in our government believe women should not have access to it *at all*. I'm super excited about that, because it means it's 1965 and we're gonna go to the moon soon.

And Japan is *hardly* alone. C.f. that entire viciously moronic conversation about the care and feeding of my uterus. I merely noticed it for the first time over there.

The article concerning laundry was fascinating because it is a very high tech response to a domestic issue, which is something I don't come across very often. Most of us are cooking in kitchens quite recognizable from 40 years ago. The Roomba in the corner of my living room is about the only chore-class object in my house that that same grandmother would not have used in cleaning up after my parents.

One of the things that has frustrated me about science fiction is that technology pertaining to the smaller aspects of our lives is often neglected in favor of big giant rockets and exotic weaponry. Birth control seems non-existent and childbirth is still rocking the stirrups. And the home is at best not mentioned much. One of the things that "the future," when we use that word as a metonymy for an idealized world in which machines solve all our problems, is supposed to do for us is give us time. Relieve us from work that is repetitive or unpleasant and allow us the sheer, simple hours in the day to *do more*. And yet, by far the biggest time sink going is the need to clean our habitats, prepare food and clothing, and maintain our environments. For those who have always had the, dare I say, privilege of ignoring that work, you simply cannot imagine how much time it takes to do all that and then turn around and do it again, often multiple times a day if there are offspring at play. Despite the fact that we here in the first world are supposed to have leveled up our gender equality stat, women still perform the majority of this labor, often in addition to a full shift outside the home. Fully automating this activity would free humanity on a scale that even the most awesome BFG can't even begin to contemplate.

And though many enjoy cooking, though food prep has become a source of pride and even a hobby for a lot of people, vanishingly few get excited about what they're going to clean today.

By far the biggest literary offender on this subject, I feel, is steampunk. Because when you're talking about the nineteenth century, the invention that changes everything is not the difference engine, it's not the airship, it's not clockwork robots. It's the washing machine. Nineteenth-century laundry was a brobdingnagian task that took all week, involved caustic chemicals that ruined the body over time, and exhausted both the spirit and the back. Only the ultra-rich could avoid taking part in at least some portion of it. Free women from that and you have a strong feminist movement almost instantly and probably a suffrage movement far earlier, you have a force of political action not broken by lye fumes and the crippling lack of time that hobbles any population attempting to manifest change. And yet we see again and again shiny tech meant to either imitate current "male" sphere toys, military and industrial and computational or to advance that same sphere past nineteenth-century specs, and very little thought at all spared for the half of humanity that spent that century maintaining households at the expense of most other activity.

Even today, that article on self-cleaning clothes was not greeted with near the excitement of the last miniscule change in the specs of a new Apple product or probably uninhabitable planets around a distant star. Yet it is far more likely to figure in the daily lives of each of us than any of that, and represents the first real change in how we do something as basic as cleaning our clothes in human history - soap, solvents, and water may no longer be necessary in the very near future. Even the Romans had dry cleaning - the Urine-Derived Ammonia and Magnesium Oxide Clay Bear didn't have the same cache as the Snuggle Bear, but he got the job done.

Yet it seems silly to get excited about that. It might be cool because the word nanotechnology is involved, but it's not like the camera on the iPhone might be a tiny bit better, am I right? Things culturally associated with women pretty regularly get sniffed at as silly or insignificant or stupid or boring - even if men need clean clothes, too, even if some men somewhere surely do laundry. It's the association that kills the cool, and we are so far from not associating women with housework. If you don't think so, consider why you're laughing the next time you upvote a "get in the kitchen and make me a sandwich" "joke" on Reddit. (It's like a subway. If you missed the last one, don't worry, there'll be another along presently.) Laundry is not essentially feminine. But you'd be forgiven for thinking so, given every detergent commercial ever made, every sitcom scene involving a basket of clothes, and the household chores demographics. And it's a vicious circle, a self-feeding engine, that says women must be especially good at housework because they're the only ones I see on TV or hear talking about it and if there's ever a man doing it in the media he's being comically hopeless at it so housework must be a naturally, centrally, and immutably female activity. Feel free to substitute "child-rearing" "caretaking" or "talking about feelings" for "housework."

The future is not evenly distributed. Not along cultural lines, along language lines, along political, economic, class, or generational lines. And most certainly not along gender lines. A significant portion of the digital world proceeds on the quiet, probably subconscious meme that the future belongs to men and women are just along for the ride. Oh, sure, some women can play with the big boys. If they act right. But not the *girly* ones. They're feminine, therefore: weak and frivolous and shallow and shrill.

They can do the laundry.

Girls? In My Video Games?
It's More Common Than You Think

While battling off my annual Christmas Cold, I decided to do a Round Robin and play an hour or two or three of every game I'd been gifted over the last couple of years and not gotten a chance to play. I mean, really - some of them I got two years ago and have been on tour too often to even crack the plastic seal. Bad gamer.

And lo, in my Lost Weekend of Xbox and Golden Grahams, I did learn something! A universal truth about human life on Planet Earth, true across time and cultures, so important that a game is nigh unto unplayable without stating this truth in the intro. What did I learn, you ask?

Girls are the *worst*.

It was most noticeable in Sonic Generations and Legend of Zelda: Skyward Sword. Girls were merely absent in what I played of Epic Mickey and gender is pretty egalitarian so far in Skyrim and Dungeon Siege III - though the Great Boobs of Fantasy Art are present in force. Portal 2 takes the Metroid route, though it's full of inexplicable fat jokes. It doesn't escape me that of all my weekend games, Sonic and Zelda are the ones aimed at kids. (And holy cats, playing a Sonic game again made me feel like I was smoking *actual* crack. I think I might have discovered the viral source for ADD - we played this game as kids and thus it began, spreading out from us like a contagion.) Who of all of us need to know how terrible girls are as soon as possible, so they don't make the mistake of having anything to do with them.

In the FMV intro to Sonic Generations, everyone is having a picnic to tell Sonic how awesome he is, because he has Protagonist Superpowers and that's what second-tier PCs do with their spare time, I guess. One of Sonic's friends is a girl. We know this because she is pink and because unlike all the other sidekicks who have cool action names like Knuckles and Tails, her name is Amy. (Though honestly, both I and my husband had always read Tails as a girl in the original game - smaller, with a graceful fluffy pair of tails, a vaguely sexually suggestive name and light orange - why not? You take what you can get as far as playable girls. But it's long been explicit in subsequent titles that Tails is a boy. I mean, he isn't pink, so *obviously amirite*.)

Amy is in love with Sonic. Sometimes she tries to kiss him. When she attempts this at the picnic, Sonic *shoves his hand in her face and holds her physically away from him with a look of disgust on his face*. He turns toward Tails and puts an arm around him, all the while crushing Amy's face with his paw.

And of course, Amy continues to be the worst as the game goes on. At one point, Sonic brings her the Red Ring hidden on a level, to which she responds:

"Tee hee! That's not the kind of ring I was hoping for!" She is not playable in this game and Sonic repeatedly expresses his loathing and revulsion of her. Boys rule, girls drool! And they want to get married and stuff! They like pink! So weird and yucky, little kids, don't talk to them! And hit them in the face if they try to kiss you!

Zelda cracked me up hardcore, because I, like many of you, I think, remember the Legend of Zelda animated TV show. In which, at the end of every adventure, Link tried to get Princess Zelda to kiss him and Zelda was so not into it. Not so this time! Girls are miserable harpies now, no one wants to kiss them! Ahahaha, ew.

Link has his revenge in Skyward Sword! Link wakes up on the morning of his coming of age ritual (*again*) and a letter from Zelda arrives (*again*) reminding him that he has to fly his big bird thing in the ritual today, and that he promised to meet her on the roof beforehand. Link makes this *face* like *oh my god you guys, nothing is worse than a princess who wants to hang out with you.*

At which point, he dicks around for awhile before going to the roof and meeting up with Zelda, who is naturally concerned because Link is a lazy shit who hasn't practiced flying his giant bird even though he has a *super special one* and has known he'd have to do this bird flying ritual test for a long time. Zelda tells her father that Link is definitely going to die because he sucks at flying. This is a valid concern! Her father goes on this weird rant about Link's *special bird ZOMG* and how Zelda was so jealous when Link and the bird bonded! LOLZ. He clearly means that Zelda wanted to "bond" with Link, though I prefer to think Zelda was jealous because shitty lazy Link got an *awesome red giant bird* and she was stuck with the magical psychic aviary equivalent of a Dodge Dart.

So Zelda fusses over Link *like a girl* and then kicks him off the roof to sink or swim with his bird and clock some damn sky hours, goddammit, but the special fabulous bird doesn't show to snatch him out of his fall. At which point, Zelda scores fair cool points by zooming down to rescue Link in mid-air and cradles him in her arms while trying to make sure he's ok post-nearly-plummeting-to-his-death.

And Link gives her the Sonic look like: *fuck girls are so gross and weird ew god she's touching me* and immediately jumps up so she won't infect him with her girl cooties.

Okay, so they're not into girls. That's okay, right? Progressive, maybe?

Thing is, I would love to see a gay protagonist in a game. It's high time for a Samus-style switch where you're actually a boy saving a prince at the end of the game. And especially with Sonic, I think it's fairly clear that he and Tails are More Than Just Friends. It's not even coded when the hero is physically shoving a girl away in order to cuddle a boy. Though in my happy world of gay video game heroes, being a gay hero would not give you license to be a towering dick to the half of humanity you're not interested in fucking - and that half would not be reduced to a stereotype and flung at the hero at high speeds so that he could show his awesomeness by crushing her. (Or him.) Wild dreamer, me.

But of course neither Link nor Sonic is canonically gay, and I think the programmers would be horrified at the suggestion. So given that they are mostly marketing these games to young boys and men and the Default Corporate Consumer is usually straight, why do these avatars hate girls so much? Why does Link no longer even want to tolerate the presence of the chick it is The Legend of?

Well, it is because girls are the worst. Their view is supported by Amy and Zelda being all up on the heroes' junk and babbling about rings like disgusting, stupid girls do because they can't kick ass or be awesome like a boy can.

This all came together for me because after my eyeballs and meds could not take Sonic's fever pitch anymore, I watched Patrice O'Neal's last comedy special on Netflix. And wow, it's just nothing but "women are terrible, lolz" from start to finish. With such hits as "men don't want anything but sex from relationships, but women don't even like sex!" and "why can't I harass women in the workplace? I'm a hunter/predator/caveman, it's natural! P.S. You can harass me any time, ladies, as long as you're not an uggo or a fatty because that is gross" and my favorite Chris Rock cover: "allow me to demonstrate the act of physical intimidation I like to perform in lieu of hitting a woman, which I wouldn't do because I am a Nice Guy."

In this case, the act was "mushing," which is grabbing a woman's face and shoving her. And the audience laughed and women cheered when he asked who had had this done to her. At which point O'Neal breaks into a long set about how *all men everywhere fantasize about killing their wives and girlfriends specifically because women are so awful killing them is an act of self defense, and asks people in the audience for their plans on how to murder their spouses.*

Wow.

And all through that stand-up act was the message: *there is no point to a woman except to have sex with her. She is useless unless she is actually having sex right now, willing to have sex in the very near future, or caring for the results of sex. No man would ever want to talk to or engage with a woman unless she is going to have sex with him very soon, and even then she should be careful to not talk or do anything to displease her man or else he might shove her or kill her, but in the end, he's still such a Nice Guy, and she is a Bitch.*

So Sonic was mushing Amy. Fantastic. And since Sonic doesn't want to have sex with Amy, either because he has a boyfriend or because he just isn't interested, she has no purpose and can be mushed with impunity. I'm especially glad that this information is being imparted to young gamers, who are obviously all boys so there's no need to even pretend like a magical supersonic hedgehog could be a girl and accomplish the same retina-searing feats of ring-collecting. Hey kids, girls are unnecessary and gross and whether you're hetero or super into your best slender orange hedgehog buddy but conflicted about what that means for your identity, you should feel totally free to ignore, belittle, and assault them for showing the smallest affection or interest toward you. Now run out and play!

The sheer screaming balls-out hatred of women and displays of female affection shown in these games baffle me. I thought men were supposed to want sex from women? That's what Patrice told me! But even worse is the straw-cartoon-man set up by showing any female NPC or PC as marriage-obsessed, pink, weak, and irritating. See? *They totes deserve it.*

When I was a kid, I remember being so happy that I could play the Princess in Mario Bros 2 - and she wasn't really lesser than the other PCs - sure, she didn't have much upper vegetable-hauling body strength, but she could *fly*. And she wasn't shown as punishably useless or constantly throwing herself at Mario, even if she was pink. If I get into how Princess Peach is currently portrayed this post will never end, but the point is I was a little girl gamer. I am an adult female gamer. And when I see this regressive, ugly gender war crap laid out in the very latest games, I don't understand how the world of late 80s gaming could have let me be a Princess who could fight, a girl who could wear the Metroid suit with no one the wiser, could let me believe Tails was like me, when the kid games of 2012 make damn sure that their audience knows being a girl is a sad, regrettable, even villainous thing, and if a male is even vaguely irritated with one, he should treat her as a low-level enemy and stomp on her face.

Grumble, grumble, as the Moblins say.

Confessions of a Fat Girl

I used to be beautiful.

When I was in high school I had cheekbones that could cut paper, waist-length red hair, and I was about 110 pounds soaking wet. I dressed like a hippie lunatic by way of a nineteenth-century orphanage - barefoot, with flowers in my hair and long flowing skirts with waistcoats and bustles stuck on my jeans. People used to stare at me. I was in theatre and I played the pretty parts: I could be the princess, the ingenue, Juliet, Anne.

In my head, I'm still that girl.

But the fact is, I'm not. Because I'm fat. I'm dieting now because I'm sick of being fat, sick of feeling like I want to show people pictures of the person I used to be because she's better, she's so pretty, you could love her, you could believe she was worthy of love. I'm tired of being careful of which pictures of me end up online, tired of being afraid to be videotaped or even meet people because I feel such shame about my body. But I know, of course, that in all likelihood I will fail at this in some fashion, gain anything I lose back or give up somehow - I've lost significant amounts of weight before, I know how it goes. It's a lifelong struggle, especially in this culture. I'll certainly never be that buck-ten girl with those cheekbones again. Still, I have to try, because I can't stand how much psychic real estate is taken up with feeling like shit about how I look (but I don't *really* look that way, see, because I'm *really* that 17 year old gamine, on the inside, if you squint), comparing myself to other bodies, deciding preemptively that I'm beneath normal people's notice.

And yet it is an inescapable truth that your words, your stories, are more likely to be listened to if you are beautiful. You have more value. I'm not saying that writers are successful because they are physically attractive, but it's insane not to think it's a factor. There are certain SFF authors people absolutely drool over, and you know, they do pretty well, and their heart-throb status sure doesn't hurt. It won't do the work of a good book for you, but if your attractiveness can be used in publicity it will be, and this goes quadruple for women writers. In our culture, beautiful people have stories worth listening to, and if you're not beautiful you're supposed to fake it as best you can, or at least hide it. I used to be so careful about the photos I used - until Facebook and photo tagging made that an irrelevant effort. It's tough not to know I'm fat these days. On the other hand, I still have a certain amount of "pretty privilege" - I have symmetrical features, long shiny hair, clear skin, a lot of other markers of beauty in our culture. I am firmly in the "she has such a pretty face, too bad she's so fat" camp. I am intensely aware of that in-between space I occupy, how that shit you're born with or you're not affects so much of social interactions, romantic interactions, professional interactions. Beauty is the devil's lubricant - it makes thing move more smoothly, but it's laced with cayenne and cyanide, yo. And god, the push back I get when I dress like I have any right to display my body - I cannot even tell you how many times my love of low-cut shirts has been commented on for no reason whatsoever, in condescending and prudish tones *on panels*, as though at a science fiction convention where people are dressed as tentacle monsters I have seriously transgressed by showing the tops of my breasts.

I mean, I perform with some of the most beautiful women I've ever seen. And I go to conventions where there's these shiny, sparkly girls who dance and laugh and look amazing in everything they wear, and I just feel like a freaking *were-manatee* around them. Like a literal monster. I am the odd one out, the ugly sister, the dark girl in the shadows who can tell a mean story but you wouldn't want to fuck her. And yet I know that most of the women I know, even the sparkly shiny ones? Feel the same way.

The trick to all the beauty shit is that you can't win. That's the whole point.

Beauty is a terrible, tenuous, volatile, intoxicating, poisonous thing. And my terror of it, my conviction that I don't have it, goes so deep that when dealing with issues of gender performance I can't even consider how I interface my own body, my gender, *because in my heart I'm sure only pretty people get to play with gender and queerness and be embraced for it*. And that is a terrible thing to think - but there is truth in it, too, in marginalized communities. The beautiful elfin androgyne is almost always revered in a way that the butch lumberjack-sized girl is not.)

So what do you do? What do I do? Feel like shit forever, I guess is the answer. Some people can maintain societally acceptable levels of thinness while eating whatever they want. Some people can stop drinking Coke and lose 20 pounds. I'm not one of them. Neither am I in the Fat Acceptance movement, though. Because I can't freaking accept myself. I hate dieting because it just means I'm thinking even more about what a disgusting pig I am, and how I let myself get this far, about how long it will take before I can look at myself in the mirror without shame. More real estate. I want to write that triumphant blog entry where I talk about how I lost the weight and things are awesome now but the fact is I've been dealing with this shit for ten years and I've never written that post. (The last time I found my body acceptable, I wasn't blogging yet.) I'm dead in the middle of it; I haven't come out stronger and wiser and most importantly thinner. But I look at my friends who are on the other side, who've lost weight, and I think *they are better people than me*. I have an ex who lost a lot of weight after we broke up and even though she is one of my least favorite people on Earth, I still think: *she's better than me because she's thinner than me*.

In our culture, fat is a failure condition. I feel that intensely. Like no matter what I've done, it doesn't out-weigh the weigh-in.

And I want to not think that shit. I want to kick it and be better than that shit. I know these thoughts are awful and unworthy. I want to just live in my body and feel strong and be happy. I don't want to think of life as some kind of constant beauty pageant where I am always Miss Failure 20whatever. But I'm not there yet. I can't do it yet. I hate myself too much. Maybe I'll get there. I hope so. I do know that having once been beautiful, I am constantly haunted by this idea of what I'm supposed to look like that will just never happen again. (I mean, I was anemic and malnourished, but I was so pretty! And god, I will never forgive my ex-in-laws for coming down on me like a sack of hammers and making me feel like garbage and parking me in front of Herbalife scammers for years for getting fat, when "getting fat" meant I weighed 140 pounds. What I wouldn't give to be as "fat" now as I was then!) I'm 31. I'm not an ingenue anymore and don't want to be. But in my head that girl is the only part of me that's any good.

And if I don't talk about this ugly crap, then I just stay the fat girl hiding behind a picture of a skinny girl, and I don't want that. It's a mask that wears, well, thin.

What Women Cannot Allow Themselves to Want

A beloved geek celebrity and gay icon was quoted some time back in a small magazine as saying some impressively awful things about women, namely that they do not enjoy sex, not the way men do, if they did, they'd be sneaking around churchyards and heaths looking for a quick hook-up in the fashion of underground gay culture in the bad old days when nothing could be done without secrecy and shame. They followed up that triple flip with a lovely little salchow of expressed pity for straight men, who can only have sex as part of the transaction of monogamy, because all women want is relationships, and they use the sex they don't enjoy as a tool to get it.

Well, people got upset, perhaps more than usual because the celebrity in question is such a beloved figure, and has invested quite a lot in appearing avuncular, intellectual, and reasoned. It's like finding out your favorite uncle hates you. And the anger dealt out by this man in response to criticism of his statements quite blew my hair back.

Apparently it's totes ok to say misogynist things as long as you say it to your mates and you think it's funny? And if one happens to be a gay man, it's especially funny because *that's what gay men talk about*? And though the conversation was apparently "about gay male sexuality," I guess no discussion of men and sex is complete without a dig at female sexuality. I don't really roll with the obnoxious trend of saying racist and sexist things "ironically" around groups of people who you think share your opinions, or at least your demographics. Given that I doubt the celebrity in question or anyone else would think it was ok for women to make homophobic comments to their female friends, just so long as there weren't any actual gays around right that second, this all appears pretty sketchy to me, and the excuse wears paper-thin.

After all, we've heard it before, we humorless feminists. It was just a joke. Don't you get the joke? It's hilarious. The height of comedy, actually. No? Bitches.

What you say in private conversation, when you think you're safe from criticism, says everything about what you really think.

If our Celebrity Commentator is as ignorant of women's sexuality as he claims to be, it seems not to be an option in his mind to simply not discuss it or comment on it. And this particular "canard," as he calls it, is a terrible and damaging one, one that others women and makes them alien, one that fuels hateful rhetoric about what can and cannot be done to women (hello madonna/whore), enforces the separation of spheres and interests, encourages the idea that since women hate sex you have to coerce them into it, and makes freaks of women who do like sex - which is really rather a lot of them. It's really one of the most pernicious ideas out there. He just thought it was funny and awesome when he said it, and since he said it to another gay man and they don't sleep with women anyway, it's no big deal, *even if he knows it's untrue*. But somehow that doesn't change the *hilarious wry wit* of repeating it, within a community that is also marginalized, unjustly maligned, and stereotyped.

Every time I see this one come up, usually in discussions of porn where it's trotted out that women "aren't visual" while straight male sexuality (no matter how exaggerated) is the baseline norm, I think about why I don't go out to bars trolling for sex, and didn't even when I was single, and wonder why the to me very obvious reasons are either unheard or dismissed by men, or not even brought up as everyone nods and talks about how different and confusing and "complex" (read: different and confusing, not like a hard dick, which is plain-spoken, straightforward, a noble steed and true). And since I am really just sad about the whole affair, I'll lay it out here - why I am not crawling around a heath looking for a lay.

The straight men prowling the heath are not usually looking for consenting women.

I am a woman with a high libido. Oh, it's not always at a constant pitch - and *by the way*, if I have learned anything about men in my years of having sex with them, it's that *their libido isn't constant either*. The idea that all men, all the time, are hard, ready, and made utterly irrational by their need for sex is absolutely as damaging as the notion that women are sexless angels with nothing between their legs. I know plenty of low-libido men who suffer under expectations of their performance and at a moment's notice readiness. Anyway. My libido suffers when I'm depressed or when I'm working hard, and in that I suspect I'm no different than any man ever. But in general, I'm up for it as often as men, so why not go down to a bar where obviously sexually desirable men are waiting to be picked out of a lineup like workers waiting for the factory truck to trundle by?

Well, for starters, it's not physically safe for me to do so. Even if I wanted sex, things could get ugly very fast, and I could find myself raped, beaten, or killed with a quickness. The possibility for violence is just so much higher when you are a woman - especially the bad, sex-seeking kind that can be destroyed because good girls don't like sex. This is also a possibility with gay men, but the size differential and the difference in community - a marginalized group seeking mutual satisfaction vs. a patriarchal dynamic where sex must be seized from an unwilling partner, is just so much more dangerous.

Second of all, despite the equally obnoxious myth that women can just walk into any bar, raise their hand in the air, and get any gentleman she likes, men turn out to have agency, preferences, moods, and sometimes they just want a damn drink and to be left alone. And since we live in a material, and more importantly awesomely patriarchal world, a lot of those preferences don't include women who aren't supermodels, and a lot of those men do not feel the need to spend the hours and hours on personal grooming and dress that women are expected to perform just to be decent enough to leave the house. (It has been long established in mainstream culture that dressing well is gay, or at least metrosexual and thus suspect. Women can express sexual desire only by making themselves passively attractive, receptive, not by pursuing in plainclothes, as men have the privilege of doing.

Yes, y'all get shot down. We do too.

That's what happens when humans with equal agency interact sometimes. The anger and resentment with which I've heard men discuss women having the gall to say no to them often shocks me - do they not have the right to decide? I've been rejected by many, many men. I've never hated them for it.)

So the likelihood of me being able to make that connection, to find some I want to fuck - not take long walks on the beach with, not curl up in front of the fire with, just have a good time, and have them be attracted to me, someone beyond the current societal standards of "hot chick" is really quite slim. Even if the guys I like are also non-standard, this culture teaches men that they "deserve" a certain kind of woman, whatever they themselves have to offer. Some men get that message loud and clear and internalize it; some don't. Geek men, by the way, are not immune. Many still dream of the cheerleader they couldn't get in high school and ignore girls they think of as their inferiors, no matter how many dice she owns.

When you are talking about hook-up culture, it is not about everyone's special snowflake soul. It's a meat market, and about how you can compete in it. That's why it's a hook-up, not a life-bond. You interact with everyone's preconceived notions about sex, and most of those come straight from the firehouse of mainstream culture - that's why it's mainstream. It gets into everyone, to greater and lesser degrees.

And even if I were able to navigate that terrain, which is seriously not so easy as my male friends who assure me how simply and instantly I can get laid by the person of my choice and literally refuse to listen to any of my experiences to the contrary, the chances that this man, in our male-orgasm centered world, our rocks-off culture, would be interested or able to give me a good time? Oh, you roll the dice on that one even if you've been dating for awhile, kids. One-night stands are tougher for women on that raw physical level men love to tout as their personal domain, because we are not guaranteed anything like an enjoyable time. The rocks, they do not always get off, and a strong percentage of straight men don't think about much other than the aforementioned rocks. I promise, if it weren't considered "real sex" unless the woman came this would be a very different sexual universe. Thus, the vibrator is almost always the solid, inexpensive, and reliable choice.

There are wonderful straight men out there who aren't like this. I am unlikely to find one for a random one-night stand. The numbers are just against me. My experiences in the lesbian community have never led me to seriously consider the idea that women didn't like sex. But there are very good reasons for women not to behave like an ugly stereotype of men - most of them having to do with how deeply unequal the sexual arena still is. It's not about internal state, it is about societally enforced external behavior. And I live in a pretty liberal, open part of the world. I am saddened and surprised that a gay man would not understand living in fear of expressing one's sexuality, of being harmed physically, ridiculed, or rejected because society regards the very expression of one's honest sexuality as inappropriate at best.

It's a sad, fucked up world sometimes. I wish it weren't. But look. Some women like sex. Some don't. Some men like sex. Some don't. It's actually pretty easy.

The Princess is an Avatar

Deconstruction, whore of Babylon and mother of critical abominations, involves at her most basic level unearthing alternate narratives from beneath the overwhelming weight of the dominant sequences which comprise the known, accepted canon.

Have fun with that sentence? I thought so. Bear with me.

There is a character most everyone in Western geek culture knows. He is Italian. He is a plumber. He has trouble with women.

His name is Mario, pixilated alpha-male extraordinaire.

And at the end of all his troubles, over and over, he comes to the same dark, empty room and its single, solitary, enigmatic inhabitant: Princess Toadstool, later to be re-christened by Nintendo as Princess Peach, a figure who is intriguing, to say the least, as a kind of shorthand for basic gender relations.

It hardly needs to be mentioned that this dark, empty space which is both the goal of Mario's quest and the source of all subsequent quests is a huge, throbbing Freudian womb-symbol. In addition, it clearly codes the Princess as Other to Mario's Self, almost patronizingly stereotypical in her dominion over the Dark Screen, her association with the atavistic and animalistic Dragon, and her implied, but not explicitly offered, sexual availability to the triumphant hero. Samsara is bounded on all sides by the Dark Screen, the Dragon-Guarded Womb, and incarnation depends upon it: lightless, infinite (from the perspective of its inhabitant) and utterly within the power of the feminine. It is often characterized as the Void: an ultimately passive place, simply existing, waiting for the hero's penetration or expulsion, surrounding and influencing but not functioning in any truly meaningful way.

In other words, the womb is an NPC.

Of course this is a ridiculous metaphor, and only has any meaning at all from the point of view of the hero. But the womb is a constantly busy place, full of complicated hydraulics and systems, and ultimately contained within a very alive and complex entity. It does not, in fact, exist only to either service or create the hero. But the hero sees nothing but his own progress, and with his limited knowledge of the world through which he travels, he simply assumes that while he acts, his opposite number, the Princess, Monarch of the Void, is silently and motionlessly positioned at the linear conclusion of his side-scrolling pilgrimage.

The evolving names of the Princess are an interesting liner-note to this assumption of her as simple a set and mute goal for Mario. Both Toadstool and Peach are food names, things which are consumed in order for the body (the Self) to create energy and then expel as waste. The progression from mushroom (a food which in and of itself originates in waste and decay, only to become waste and decay again when it is eaten) to summer fruit which originates high in the air, on the branches of a tree (the Tree of Life?) coincides with the slow evolution of the Princess from this first game into Super Mario Bros. 2 where she is an avatar, and subsequent incarnations as both playable and non-playable characters, all unified by a constant and immutable weakness. The Princess, as all players know, is a universally weak character to play, almost always slower, less physically formidable (in Mario Kart 64, her almost non-existent weight makes her a particularly poor player in the Battle section of the game) and even, in Mario 2, lacking in requisite upper body strength which the male characters, even the comically diminutive Toad (himself arguably descended from the False Princesses of the original game), possess. She will usually have a compensatory skill, such as her short-span flight capability in Mario 2, however, these skills usually have something to do with her status as light, small, feminine, and less physically *present* than the male avatars.

But in her first foray into Mario's narrative, she is not playable at all. However, to assume that because we as players do not control her she is not herself an avatar is to affirm a crucial element in the gender relations of the hero cycle: women, in Kant's terms, are seen inevitably as means to an end (enlightenment, the grail, sex, what have you) rather than ends in themselves. But I am here to tell you, out of the Dark Screen and the Dragon's Lair: brother, it just ain't so.

The Princess is an Avatar.

One of the most basic misogynistic conceits is that women are not On the Path, they are the Path. They are closer to nature, more primitive, more aligned with Mystical Powers, and therefore do not need the *sturm und drang* of the hero's progress, the pilgrim's striving for enlightenment: nature gives them all the enlightenment they need. They do not need rites of passage, because they menstruate. They do not need art, for they create children. They are Other, existing only to unify with the hero so that he can achieve whatever nirvana he requires, and then to wither away to nothing once they have fulfilled their purpose.

If Mario is our (the user's) Avatar, it is perhaps forgivable that we have seen her from the plumber's perspective, that our gaze has turned her to eight-bit stone, immobile in her black chamber, there only for us, our reward. But deconstruction, like Warp Zones, frees us from the linear progression of traditional narrative, and allows us to imagine a possible gameworld in which the Princess is not perpetually and inexplicably prone to capture by the same old shabby Dragon, but a figure who intercepts Mario at only one point in her own progression, her own game, her own pilgrim's progress. Who knows what circumstances led her to be in that room when we, clothed in our workingman's overalls, encounter her? Like Schrödinger's cat, we cannot know if she has always been there, whether she remains after we have gone. To assume that she has been, and will be, is the height of hubris.

It is equally possible that Schrödinger's Princess has been scrolling through her own Eightfold Worlds, and arrived in the Dark Screen only just in time to appear in the hero's vision as the pixilated Grail Maiden. That we do not play her does not mean that she is not an Avatar; that we do not know her mind does not infer its absence.

Perhaps Bowser is her pet, her guardian, her defense against the inane penetrations of an obnoxious Italian pillager of castles. It is, after all, always and forever a matter of perspective.

The hero forever seeks unification with the Other, with the World-Soul, but he proves his unworthiness by his assumption of the passivity of his goal: he rarely stops swilling pasta long enough to consider that the World-Soul might not want to unify with him, that it may be seeking its own Other, its own unification. It may be perfectly happy hanging out with dragons and chatting up hammer-wielding turtles.

You are not necessarily your Other's Other.

The moral of the story is this: as you travel from Sewer World to Water World to Dark World, realize that you are not the only entity in the Mushroom Kingdom, that there are no true NPCs, and that every Princess is also a hero, a seeker, and an avatar.

And she's not impressed by your fireballs.

Indistinguishable from Magic

Fairy Tales, Myth, and the Future

Follow the Yellow-Brick Road: Katabasis and the Female Hero in Alice in Wonderland, The Wizard of Oz and The Nutcracker

> "One thing is for certain, that the white kitten had nothing to do with it - it was the black kitten's fault entirely."
>
> —Lewis Carroll,
> *Through the Looking Glass and What Alice Found There*

The Western corpus is replete with narratives that serve to define and illuminate the male experience. From *Gilgamesh* to *Tom Sawyer*, there is no paucity of stories that mirror the trials of young men, which guide a homogenous intended audience through the ordeals of initiation, friendship, the integration of the self, physical and intellectual challenge, and death. This is the primary social function of the hero cycle - to provide an exemplum, a blueprint of correct living.

Yet there are comparatively few such cycles for young women. While the traditional folktale often incorporates a feminine character or two, her journey is usually quite short, that is, from birth to courtship to marriage, and from thence either into childbirth and death or to vanish summarily and inexplicably from the narrative. Yet all her efforts are aimed towards and circumscribed by men. This, of course, served a patriarchal purpose: to encourage young girls to follow this path, and not attempt to deviate from it into the more dynamic cycle of men and heroes. But in the postmodern world, where the experience of women is no longer limited to hearth and childbed, where can they look for their own exempla, for heroines that perform the heroic cycle in their own right? That cycle is not now, if ever it was, the exclusive purview of men: women, too, must thread their path through the archetypes it presents.

The current research will concentrate on three such cycles: *Through the Looking Glass*, *The Wizard of Oz*, and *The Nutcracker*. Each of these is a peculiar combination of specific cultural paradigms, mythological mirroring, and psychological case study which explore a feminine hero on her journey through one of the classic landscapes of legend: the Underworld. Each narrative follows a female child through her katabasis, her descent and return, which functions as a metaphor for entrè into adult sexuality as well as a literal passage through hell. Each of them is also problematic as a feminist text *per se*, and fails at key points to rehabilitate the image of the passive heroine on her marriage-quest, nevertheless, they provide a folkloric model of feminine action which is not present in the works of Grimm, Andersen, or Perrault. All three tales have also transcended their text, becoming truly folkloric, for there is hardly a child who does not know Clara and her brave Nutcracker, though almost none of them know of E.T.A. Hoffman. Therefore, this paper will deal with three distinct media into which these women have been incarnated: novel, film, and ballet.

Alice, Dorothy and Clara perform a curious pantomime. All three reflect unerringly the attitudes and assumptions of there own cultures: nineteenth-century Britain, early twentieth-century America, and nineteenth-century Germany. However, they simultaneously mimic the gestures of much more primal navigators of the Underworld: those of Inanna and Persephone, Sumerian and Greek katabaseis which describe the change of the seasons through the harrowing journey of a single goddess through the kingdom of the dead. Inanna and Persephone are very similar figures - Inanna may even be viewed as a parallel Persephone, despite the drastic difference in agency between the two - so it is useful to view them as a single archetype with key differences, and interpret our more contemporary heroines in the light of their histories. While neither Oz, Wonderland, nor the Kingdom of Sweets is explicitly the land of the dead, as landscapes of threat and morbidity, they are certainly siblings to the territories of Hades and Ereshkigal, and the lost children who wander through them are echoes and shadows of their divine foremothers.

* * *

Of the three young women contained in this study, Alice is the figure most divorced from the ambitions of her fairy tale sisters. She does not begin her quest for the purpose of rescuing a male, she has no constant male companions to save her, and she does not end her tale as a wife. It is sheer intellectual curiosity that drives her through the Looking-Glass, convinced that there must be a "room you can see through the glass that's just the same as our drawing-room, only the things go the other way." Unlike Dorothy and Clara, she is not taken by force, but enters Wonderland, or the Looking-Glass World, of her own volition, because *she is trying to get there*. This expression of agency trumps even *Alice's Adventures in Wonderland*, wherein her entrance to the Underworld is more explicit - she literally descends beneath the earth - but essentially accidental. Her truly heroic gesture, unambiguous in its intent, is her penetration of the Victorian mirror. In this act, Alice is a textbook hero. As Campbell delineates the initial progress of the champion:

> The hero goes forward in his adventure until he comes to the "threshold guardian" [the mirror] at the entrance to the zone of magnified power... Beyond them is darkness, the unknown, and danger; just as beyond the parental watch is danger to the infant and beyond the protec-

tion of society is danger to the member of the tribe. The usual person is more than content, he is even proud, to remain within the indicated bounds.

She is separated from her ordinary English home and passes through a liminal space, into an Otherworldly landscape which she has no choice but to navigate. In this sense, Bolster's identification of Alice with Persephone is not the whole story, as Persephone was stolen into Hades and forced to remain, while Alice enters it with wonder and purpose. The more appropriate pairing is with the Sumerian goddess Inanna, who descended in order to confront her sister and shadow-self Ereshkigal, Queen of the Underworld.

There can be no doubt that it is the Underworld, albeit a remarkably different one than in classical representations. It is, like Oz and the Kingdom of Sweets, a baroque, surreal, orientalized geography, a feminine space, at least, feminine and oriental according to the sexual and political dualism of the nineteenth century, and it is ruled over by the Red Queen, the symbolism of whose coloring hardly needs commentary.

Alice almost immediately encounters the Ereshkigal of Wonderland: the Red Queen. It is this enigmatic woman that Alice pursues across the chessboard with all the fervor of a knight pursuing a maiden. She is the black kitten to Alice's white kitten, the Jungian shadow-self which must be integrated into the hero in order to create a cohesive whole. No real motivation is given for Alice's fascination with the Red Queen, for the urgency of her pursuit. None is needed. The hero must seek out his shadow, the life-instinct must seek out the death-instinct, and the self must seek out the other. Gawain is drawn to the Green Knight, Odysseus cannot help but challenge Polyphemus, Arthur must eventually fight Mordred - and Alice must reach the Eighth Square where her Queen waits.

In the grand tradition of medieval ladies, the Red Queen is rather callous and cruel. She is a cold, distant figure, the ideal object of courtly love. The famous line Disney gave to their caricatured Queen of Hearts properly belongs to this Queen: "I don't know what you mean by *your* way, said the Queen; all the ways about here belong to *me*."

Alice must prove herself in order to enter the Red Queen's company, and the entirety of the subsequent narrative is taken up with Alice's striving towards this scarlet woman, accomplishing feats in order to become worthy of her.

The number two plays a great role in *Through the Looking Glass*. In fact, nearly all the main characters occur in pairs, most explicitly doubled. There are two Alices (Alice and her reflection, combined in the book's first act of penetration and integration, but not its last), two Queens, two kittens, Tweedledum and Tweedledee, and the Lion and the Unicorn. For the most part, it is Alice who is the fluid creature, the one which can integrate and grow, rather than any of the other sets of doubles. However, for all their binaries (weak/strong, emotional/ stoic, gentle/implacable), the White and Red Queens are clearly in league. When Alice finally arrives in the Eighth Square, she finds both Queens seated on their thrones: "Everything was happening so oddly that she didn't feel a bit surprised at finding the Red Queen sitting close to her, one on each side. She would have liked very much to ask them how they came there, but she feared it would not be quite civil."

Of course, they have always been there. The White Queen, with all her lessons on feminine conduct - she not only instructs Alice to dress her shawl, but tries to hire her as a handmaiden, and orates on the subjects of proper wages, memory, justice, and faith - can be seen as a Neti figure, Ereshkigal's servant who prepares Inanna for her audience with her own dark sister-Queen. Though Neti is male, the function is the same: to lessen the heroine so that when she will be handicapped when she confronts the adversary/object. Alice is never physically threatened, and she does not, as Inanna does, shed her clothes, but what is stripped away over the course of the narrative is her certainty of her own identity, her confidence in the truth of what she knows, to the point where, when she finally does discover the throne-room, she can hardly recall her own name without prompting. The White Queen is integral in this fracturing of Alice, and introduces the difficult notion of deliberately believing the impossible - something that, on the surface, should be second nature to the ingenuous Alice. However, this seed of relative morality is actually quite pernicious. To believe the impossible is to believe the untrue, is to believe a lie, and thus, the White Queen lays the groundwork for the Red Queen's later attempt to reconstruct Alice's personality into a mirror of her own: into Queen Alice.

To go into the Underworld is to die, whether literally or figuratively. Though a magical resurrection will follow, both Inanna and Persephone do - Inanna is murdered by her sister:

> Then Ereshkigal fastened on Inanna the eye of death.
> She spoke against her the word of wrath.
> She uttered against her the cry of guilt.
> She struck her.
> Inanna was turned into a corpse,
> A piece of rotting meat,
> And was hung from a hook on the wall.

Persephone eats the food of the dead, and for all intents and purposes becomes a dead woman, in order to rule the dead.

But real women cannot cheat death. They cannot come back. Alice is not a goddess, and she cannot literally die and still return to her tidy drawing-room.

Nevertheless, she both eats forbidden food and confronts the Queen of the Otherworld. She is a Persephone who narrowly escapes: she is tempted, and very nearly turned into one of the macabre revelers at her final feast, but she threads the needle.

It is the Red Queen who first offers Alice food: a biscuit.

> "I know what *you'd* like!" the Queen said good-naturedly, taking a little box out of her pocket. "Have a biscuit!" Alice thought it would not be civil to say no, though it wasn't at all what she wanted. So she took it, and ate it as well as she could; and it was very dry; and she thought she had never been so nearly choked in all her life."

This is strikingly reminiscent of the description of the food of the dead in later Akkadian version of this Descent, *The Descent of Ishtar*:

> To KUR.NU.GI, land of no return,
> Ishtar, daughter of Sîn, turned her attention,
> the daughter of Sîn turned her attention
> to the dark house, the seat of Irkalla,
> to the house whose entrants do not come out again,
> to the road whose way is without return,
> to the house whose entrants are deprived of light,
> where dust is their nourishment and clay their food.
> They do not see light, they dwell in darkness,
> and they are clothed like birds in a garment of wings;
> dust has settled on the door and the bolt.

The biscuit is a cake of dust, it chokes the living Alice. It is the food of the Queen alone: the food of the dead.

At the climactic feast which concludes Alice's katabasis, food is also a major issue. The litany of courses is truly bizarre, but also strangely evocative of the Babylonian menu:

> *Then fill up the glasses as quick as you can,*
> *And sprinkle the table with buttons and bran:*
> *Put cats in the coffee, and mice in the tea -*
> *And welcome Queen Alice with thirty-times-three!*
>
> *Then fill up the glasses with treacle and ink,*
> *Or anything else that is pleasant to drink:*
> *Mix sand with the cider, and wool with the wine -*

And welcome Queen Alice with ninety-times-nine!

This is all inedible food, food that will choke Alice, food in which the organic and nourishing is befouled with corpses (cats and mice), earth (sand), and shorn hair (wool). The world of the dead inverts the world of the living; that which was sacred and wholesome becomes poisoned and untouchable. Next, Alice is shown a leg of mutton and a pudding, both of which are subjected to a formal introduction by the Red Queen, and then removed. The pudding actually speaks, and while the food vanishes before it can be consumed, there is a suggestion that Alice is being asked to commit a kind of cannibalism, devouring the flesh of a thinking, speaking being. It is a grotesque, macabre meal, and pointedly, Alice eats none of it.

Yet she has performed the heroic reintegration. She has become Queen Alice, accepted into the community of women, feted and praised. She has accomplished her quest, from pawn to Queen, and absorbed her Other - it is this which gives her the power to end her sojourn in Wonderland as purposefully as she began it:

> "And as for *you*," she went on, turning fiercely upon the Red Queen, whom she considered as the cause of all the mischief - but the Queen was no longer at her side - she had suddenly dwindled down to the size of a little doll, and was now on the table, merrily running round and round after her own shawl, which was trailing behind her.
>
> At any other time, Alice would have felt surprised at this, but she was far too much excited to be surprised at anything *now*. "As for *you*," she repeated, catching hold of the little creature in the very act of jumping over a bottle which had just lighted upon the table, "I'll shake you into a kitten that I will!"

Alice here executes a formidable act of magic. She has achieved her object, her Lady, her sister-self, and, the act done, she reduces the woman in question to a homunculus, and then into her familiar cat. Once the grail is achieved, it is no more than a little cup. Once the Lady is conquered by the virile knight, she is lessened in his sight, reduced to a caricature of femininity, forever chasing her shawl.

Indeed, when she returns, or wakes, she is initially quite as imperious as the Red Queen ever was, having absorbed her darker self, her adult persona, her fully realized womanhood. She orders her kittens about with all the authority of Queen Alice.

Of course, in the end it is all a dream, whether Alice is the dreamer or no. In the end, it must be remembered that despite the strength and resonance of the female hero, this is still a narrative constructed by a man, a man who was, to safely understate the matter, over-attached to the real Alice, a child of four. Perhaps it maintains the comfort level between the Victorian genders to pull the rug out from beneath this proto-heroine, and allow her agency only as part of a fantasy. The sour note continues as Carroll implies that the dream may not even have originated with Alice, but with the Red King, a figure hardly memorable in the text:

> "Now, Kitty, let's consider who it was that dreamed it all. This is a serious question, my dear, and you should *not* go on licking your paw like that - as if Dinah hadn't washed you this morning! You see, Kitty, it *must* have been either me or the Red King. He was part of my dream, of course - but then I was part of his dream, too! *Was* it the Red King, Kitty? You were his wife, my dear, so you ought to know - Oh, Kitty, *do* help to settle it! I'm sure your paw can wait!" But the provoking kitten only began on the other paw, and pretended it hadn't heard the question.

Which do *you* think it was?

And so Alice is robbed even of the dubious honor of having dreamed it all - she is merely a figment, and object herself, a fragment of the male psyche, rather than a fragmented psyche of her own, seeking maturity and integration. At least she is spared the usual metaphor for cohesive maturity: Alice does not emerge from Wonderland with a husband.

Despite this unfortunate conclusion, Alice stands as a truly liminal figure - she is the penetrating hero, usurping all the rights of the masculine, to the point of pursuing a female idol through knightly trials, yet she, as Persephone does, falters and - just once - eats the food of the dead. Thus we know Alice is always bound to return to Wonderland, to stand before the dark Queen, be she a playing card or a chess piece, and perform her unique magic, changing them from animate to inanimate and back again, an act befitting the Queen of Heaven.

The Wizard of Oz

> "Come along, Dorothy. You don't want any of *those* apples."
> —The Scarecrow, *The Wizard of Oz*, 1939 (MGM)

While Disney's 1951 animated adaptation *Alice in Wonderland* has certainly become iconic, with its blonde Alice and pink striped Cheshire Cat, it has achieved nowhere near the cultural resonance of MGM's 1939 musical, *The Wizard of Oz*. For Americans. Judy Garland is the definitive Dorothy Gale, and continuing sales of L. Frank Baum's books owe a great deal to the extreme nostalgia and admiration with which the film is viewed. In addition, the era in which the film was made adds a dimension to the story that Baum could not have foreseen: composed in 1900, of the grayness of Kansas is merely a function of a coastal author's impressions of the Plains States. Filmed in 1939, it becomes a chilling commentary on the Depression, and the Technicolor pageantry of Oz a truly Californian paradise. For these reasons, I have chosen to focus some attention on the filmed version of Dorothy's journey, as well as the original novel.

It should be noted that neither the film nor the novel are actually named for the main character - in fact, of the 15 Oz novels, only one contains Dorothy's name in the title, despite her central position in the plot. *The Wizard of Oz* shares this with *The Nutcracker*, which is named for an inanimate object rather than a living girl.

The charlatan wizard who lends his name to the entire countryside appears only at the end of the film, and is no more present in the novel, where he is even less impressive, giving the Scarecrow, Lion, and Tinman what amounts to junk and telling them it is their hearts' desire. Yet this is the namesake of the novel, not the girl who exposes his fraud. Considering the Progressive movements of the early twentieth-century in America, the drive towards Prohibition and women's suffrage (Baum himself was son-in-law to Mathilda Joslyn Gage, a staunch feminist leader, and it was she who encouraged him to write Oz), this emphasis on the fraud rather than the earnest American child who reveals it seems somewhat disingenuous.

Dorothy herself is the most passive heroine encompassed by this study. Her Persephoniac journey happens *to* her, her exploits are unconscious, accidental: her house is swept up by a tornado, she kills the arch Witch of the East without knowledge or intent, and is thus praised as a great sorceress, a title she has neither earned nor deserves. Like Persephone, Dorothy's descent is almost entirely accidental. Persephone, after all, only picked a crocus, and ate a few seeds. Her fate was decided for her, and her descent involuntary. She does not often "save the day," as her male companions, though each are missing a vital organ of emotional experience, repeatedly solve the problems presented to the group themselves, as in the case of the Witch of the West sending her wolves, crows, and bees after them. The Scarecrow hides them from the bees with his straw, the Tin Woodsman slaughters the wolves, and again, the Scarecrow first frightens and then kills the crows. Even her murder of the Wicked Witch of the West is accidental:

> "You are a wicked creature!" cried Dorothy. "You have no right to take my shoe from me."
>
> "I shall keep it, just the same," said the Witch, laughing at her, "and someday I shall get the other one from you, too."

This made Dorothy so very angry that she picked up the bucket of water that stood near and dashed it over the Witch, wetting her from head to foot.

Instantly the wicked woman gave a loud cry of fear, and then, as Dorothy looked at her in wonder, the Witch began to shrink and fall away.

"See what you have done!" she screamed. "In a minute I shall melt away."

"I'm very sorry, indeed," said Dorothy, who was truly frightened to see the Witch actually melting away like brown sugar before her very eyes.

"Didn't you know water would be the end of me?" asked the Witch, in a wailing, despairing voice.

"Of course not," answered Dorothy. "How should I?"

"Well, in a few minutes I shall be all melted, and you will have the castle to yourself. I have been wicked in my day, but I never thought a little girl like you would ever be able to melt me and end my wicked deeds. Look out - here I go!"

Dorothy is only angry - she has no way of knowing that her actions will kill, and therefore bears no moral responsibility for the act. There is none of the symbolism of the Red Queen and Alice here, there is no doubling. The Witch's presence in the tale is erased by the mid-point of the narrative, and Dorothy's goal is always the Wizard, and through him, Kansas. She is forever is pursuit of this mythical Kansas, which is herself, seeking out not union with the shadow but a return to light. The film re-orients the action slightly, making the Wicked Witch a constant presence rather than a vague threat, which we will return to in a moment.

But Dorothy does make active choices, and she does, again, almost immediately upon crossing over into Oz, encounter a powerful female figure, in the form of the Witch of the North. This figure is merged with Glinda, the Witch of the South, in the film, and her key gesture excised.

"You must walk [to the Emerald City]. It is a long journey, through a country that is sometimes pleasant and sometimes dark and terrible. However, I will use all the magic arts I know of to keep you from harm."

"Won't you go with me?" pleaded the girl, who had begun to look upon the little old woman as her only friend.

"No, I cannot do that," she replied, "but I will give you my kiss, and no one will dare injure a person who has been kissed by the Witch of the North."

She came close to Dorothy and kissed her gently on the forehead. Where her lips touched the girl they left a round, shining mark, as Dorothy found out soon after.

This mark remains on Dorothy throughout the rest of her journey through Oz, and it protects her from harm from *any* source, even the Witch of the West. It is an inverted mark of Cain, which earns her safe passage through the wilds of Nod - and yet, the erotic content cannot be entirely glossed over. Whatever power the Wizard holds over Oz, Dorothy's is a journey book-ended by the desires of women: the Witch of the South brands Dorothy with an unmistakable symbol of sexuality, and the Witch of the West keeps her as a slave. Just as Persephone's connection to Demeter protects her from being entirely ravished by Hades, Dorothy's strange kiss from a sorceress prevents her from being killed outright. With this seal of loyalty, Dorothy commences her journey into the Underworld, seeking out the trickster-Hades at its center.

And Dorothy does choose to make the journey, just as she chooses to accept the charge to murder the offending Witch. It is her continuing ability to choose, and choose correctly, is what makes Dorothy a hero. She unerringly takes the magical items that will aid her: the Golden Cap which controls the Winged Monkeys and the Silver Shoes. Her obsession with Kansas, with herself, drives her to accept what is a truly alarming sequence of events. She is not seeking out her double, but seeking only her *nostos*, her homecoming, an Odyssean gesture which is not, when viewed in connection with the Greek epics, as stereotypically feminine as it would appear.

While her Underworld is equally baroque and bizarre, its strangeness seems uniquely American, utilizing the tropes of the circus or county fair (dwarves, false psychics and magicians, straw men, and automata) and presenting an environment which, especially in the film's startling use of the new Technicolor process, explicitly links Oz with the fairyland of the San Joaquin Valley and Hollywood, where the vast exodus of farmers and their families from Kansas and her sister states terminated. Dorothy deliberately rejects the beauty and magic that Oz/California offers her, and reaffirms the message of the virtue of her own farm:

> The Scarecrow listened carefully, and said, "I cannot understand why you should wish to leave this beautiful country and go back to the dry, gray place you call Kansas."
> "That is because you have no brains," answered the girl. "No matter how dreary and gray our homes are, we people of flesh and blood would rather live there than in any other country, be it ever so beautiful. There is no place like home."

Like Persephone, Dorothy is inextricably ties to the land, even if that land is infertile and spent. She will always return to Kansas, and always return to Oz.

She shuttles between the two with all the regularity of the Corn Maiden. Indeed, it is perhaps her attachment to Kansas that marks her out as a hero in the Campbellian sense: "The first problem of the returning hero is to accept as real, after an experience of soul-satisfying vision of fulfillment, the passing joys and sorrows, banalities and noisy obscenities of life. Why re-enter such a world?"

Yet, despite that attachment, and unlike her sister Alice, Dorothy is not at all shy about eating the food of her strange new surroundings, the food, that is to say, of the dead. Once the food from her own house's larder runs out, she happily eats the fruit she finds in roadside orchards - and perhaps this is an underlying cause of Dorothy's continual journeys between the two world. By the time she reaches the field of poppies, she is subsisting on nothing but the food of Oz.

The poppies themselves are reminiscent of the threatening flowers Alice first encounters - both heroines tread on the distant cousins of the asphodels of Hades. However, Dorothy's flowers, as the source of opiates, are an even darker menace. The link between the magical sleep they affect and death is made quite clear: if Dorothy does not wake up, she will die. In the film, this is the work of the Witch, but in the novel, the poppies are simply the natural flora of the area around the Emerald City. Dorothy, unlike Alice, does symbolically die, falling under the spell of the scarlet flowers and waking only after she is dragged from the field by the Tin Woodsman and the Scarecrow, as they do not breathe. Interestingly, Dorothy only wakes once the kingdom of the field mice have been assembled to rescue the still-slumbering lion, so that she loses consciousness surrounded by symbolic asphodel, and wakes overcome by mice, the symbol of the sun-god Apollo, brought back into the land of the living by her allegorical half-brother.

Though the Witch of the West is no Ereshkigal in Baum's construction, the film does try to cast her as such. She is present from the first scenes of Oz and the source of all the danger which besets Dorothy, rather than such peril stemming from the nature of Oz as a particularly beautiful incarnation of hell. She is Dorothy's great nemesis, not merely the price of her return to Kansas.

One might, perhaps, wonder at the relative ease with which this adolescent girl agrees to commit murder. It is a disturbing dynamic: the powerful male pits women against each other, asking a child to destroy a woman she does not know in exchange for a favor he cannot grant. And here a rather Freudian procession occurs: Dorothy, encouraged by the twisted trickster/father-figure of Oz/Hades, goes forth to eradicate her adult self, the archetype of the wicked mother, who forces her to clean and cook, and perform all the menial duties of a daughter like Cinderella or Snow White. And like Snow White's stepmother, the Witch constantly plots to harm Dorothy, and circumvent the charm of the benevolent, good woman's kiss. But Dorothy prevails, not by integrating the adult, sexualized self - in fact, in her obsession with domination, the Witch can be taken to refer to an expression of female sexuality particularly disturbing to the male psyche - but by melting her, by reducing her to the primordial feminine soup which is the source of so much anxiety, the bubbling, churning, swamplike mass of the Witch's very real body. While *Oz* is, as all hero cycles ultimately are, a coming-of-age story, Dorothy embraces not any reflection of her darker nature, but only affirms that such a thing does not exist: Dorothy is the celestial knight, at least in this first novel, clean of all influence but that of her own Kansas (Heaven) presided over by her beloved Auntie Em (Mary). She dreams of Auntie Em with quite the same devotion that Gawain grants to the Mother of Christ on his own Quest to the Green Chapel.

When she does encounter the Hades figure at the center of Oz, Dorothy does not merge with him in any meaningful way. She commits murder for him, and begs for his help, a daughter submitting to her father's wisdom, but in the end, she cannot even climb into the balloon with him, and is left behind by this manic man from Omaha, disappointed, as all children are when paternal omnipotence proves hollow. Once again, Dorothy escapes the fate of the fairy-tale heroine, and does not emerge with a husband, a result we might term the Inanna Outcome, for Inanna emerges of her own volition, only to send her lover back to hell in her place, unconcerned.

Ultimately, Dorothy's presence in Oz is almost catastrophic. Just as the influx of Oklahomans, Texans, and Kansans into California caused a great deal of damage to the economy and environment, and resulted in an intense animosity between Californians and "Okies," Dorothy's pilgrim's progress is anything but benign. She murders two women, and while these women are universally decried as Wicked Witches, a power vacuum is nevertheless created where a full half of the kingdoms of Oz are left without a ruler. She removes Oz himself from the monarchy and crushes large portions of the china village in the South. These vacuums are subsequently filled by Dorothy's friends - each of them becomes the King of some portion of Oz: the Scarecrow over the Emerald City itself, the Lion over the Beasts, and the Tinman over the Winkies, formerly enslaved by the Wicked Witch, wholesome patriarchal rule replacing corrupt feminine power.

Pointedly, Dorothy is not even offered such a position.

Alice passes through Wonderland without leaving much of a mark - she certainly does not kill anyone - but Dorothy cannot do the same. The power structure of the Underworld is permanently changed, and it will require the return of its favorite Persephone a full 14 more times to maintain itself. Once Dorothy completes her katabasis, hell can no longer survive without her.

In the novel, the reality of Oz is unquestionable. When Dorothy returns to Kansas, a new house has been built and she is greeted by Auntie Em:

"My darling child!" she cried, folding the little girl in her arms and

173

covering her face with kisses. "Where in the world did you come from?"
"From the Land of Oz," said Dorothy gravely.

Dorothy's repeated journeys to Oz in the later novels bear witness to the solid realism of Oz, which is not divorced from our own world, simply separated from it by a great desert. Yet, in the film, the audience is given an Alice-ending, and Dorothy is shown to have been merely delirious with fever, dreaming. Perhaps Hollywood was not as forward-thinking as Mathilda Gage's son-in-law, and loathes allowing such an outlandish female fantasy to stand as uncontested fact. Perhaps Baum's Dorothy, even with her crippled agency, was too ensconced in the male hero cycle to be allowed to retain her presence of mind. Instead she utters the famous line, protesting that she is not mad, that she knows herself and her experience: "Oh, but it *wasn't* a dream! It was a place! And you - and you - and you - and you were there. But you couldn't have been, could you?"

In the end, Dorothy submits to her male relatives' interpretation of events, and denies herself in their favor.

This editorial change is perplexing, and repeated in the transition of *The Nutcracker* from text to stage.

The Nutcracker

And Marie is to this day the queen of a realm where all kinds of sparkling Christmas Woods and transparent Marzipan Castles - in short, the most wonderful and beautiful things of every kind - are to be seen.

—E.T.A. Hoffman, *The Nutcracker and the Mouse King*

There are few fairy tales more textually problematic than *The Nutcracker*. Though it is by far and away the most popular ballet ever performed, thanks to ubiquitous Christmas performances, most theatre-goers are not even aware that it is based on a nineteenth-century work of Romantic fiction - or that they are watching a Russian interpretation (by Ivan Alexandrovitch Vsevolojsky and Marius Petipa, with music by Tchaikovsky) of a French adaptation by famed novelist Alexandre Dumas of a German short story by Ernst Theodor Amadeus Hoffman. Indeed, it is hardly common knowledge that there is a textual basis for the ballet at all.

While modern productions have tended to try to restore some of the Hoffman story, the fact remains that it is the adaptations which have shown themselves to possess remarkable cultural resonance and longevity. In truth, the difference between the original story and the ballet are not as vast as critics like Maurice Sendak believe. The ballet excises a long story-within-a-story called *The Story of the Hard Nut*, and shortens the period before the advent of the Kingdom of Sweets. The name of the heroine, Marie Stahlbaum, is changed to Clara, and, perhaps the only truly fundamental change: once again, the psychological arena of the action is shifted from objective reality to the silly dream of an overactive child.

Clara/Marie's quest is a simple one. She is given a doll for Christmas which all the other children think is ugly, but which she loves dearly. Through her love, the doll comes to life, and together they defeat the wicked Mouse King, gaining entrance into the Kingdom of Sweets, where they encounter the Sugar Plum Fairy and all the attendant beauties of the Underworld. And then, depending on the version, she either wakes up or stays to become Queen.

In Hoffman's story, the similarity to Inanna is immediately apparent. Marie is asked to give up seven belongings in order to satiate the Mouse King and heal the Nutcracker, which is to say, in order to enter the Otherworld: two ribbons, a handkerchief, a shoe, her Christmas candy, her sugar-toys, and a magnificent dress of many colors. Were she to hand over all these things, she would be a mirror-image of Inanna:

> When she entered the first gate,
> From her head, the *shugurra*, the crown of the steppe,
> was removed...
> When she entered the second gate,
> From her neck the small lapis beads were removed...
> When she entered the third gate,
> From her breast the double strand of beads was removed..
> When she entered the fourth gate,
> From her chest the breast plate which called
> 'Let him come, let him come!' was removed...
> When she entered the fifth gate,
> From her wrist the gold ring was removed...
> When she entered the sixth gate,
> From her hand the lapis measuring rod and line was removed...
> When she entered the seventh gate,
> From her body the royal robe was removed...

Inanna and Marie stand together at the gates of that strange world, one naked, the other in her dressing-gown, both alone, ritually pure, and ready to enter the darkness.

In the ballet, it is not her shoe that the little girl sacrifices, but a candle. Since her name was altered from Marie to Clara, it is interesting that this is the new object which kills the Mouse King. Clara is Latin for *bright* or *shining*, and so in some sense the child sacrifices herself - her light self, her civilized spirit exemplified by fire tamed, and with it destroys the irrational monster, the Mouse that walks like a man. In theatrical productions it is particularly noticeable that the Mouse King represents aggressive male sexuality - he is dressed in tight, dark velvet, in the costume of a nineteenth-century rake. With the purity of her light, Clara rejects this destructive sensualist, and wins her Nutcracker's life. The name Marie is also significant: Inanna is the Queen of Heaven in Sumerian mythology, and Mary, the root of Marie, is the Christian Queen of Heaven. That the character's name metamorphoses from a specific source of light and goodness to a general one suggests the lessening of her power which will climax with the skewing of the reality of Toyland.

Marie, in contrast to the later Clara, makes a further gesture of sacrifice:

> "I [Marie's mother] don't know whether or not some mouse jumped out and frightened you, though there are no mice around here generally. But you broke a pane of the glass cupboard with your elbow, and cut your arm so badly that Dr. Wendelstern (who has just taken a number of pieces of the glass out of your arm) thinks that if it had been a little higher up you might have lost your arm, or even bled to death."

Marie has shed blood, which can of course be construed as menstrual blood, the loss of which marks her transit from selfish child (as her brother Fritz is) and self-sacrificing womanhood (evinced by her intervention, whether with shoe or candle) in the affair of the Nutcracker and the Mouse King. She has crossed a symbolic boundary from childhood to womanhood which will be further dramatized by the grotesque Candyland of the Nutcracker's Kingdom.

In Maurice Sendak's comments on his adaptation of *The Nutcracker*, he derides these sequences as childish and silly: "Who in the world needed another Nutcracker? The mandatory Christmas tree and Candyland sequences were enough to sink my spirits completely... I didn't want to be suited to the confectionery goings-on of this, I thought, most bland and banal of ballet productions."

It is shocking that Sendak, himself such a brilliant peddler of the macabre, the dreamlike, and the darkly fantastic, fails to see the depth of symbolism in Hoffman's Toyland, and the ballet's Kingdom of Sweets. His solution of making the implicit eroticism of the animated Nutcracker explicit in the form of an eighteenth-century seraglio is a grotesque interpretation that strips Hoffman of all his subtlety. For the "Candyland sequences" are very much present in the original tale, and not, as Sendak claims, merely as "a short, ironical interlude."

For a child, nothing is more tempting, desirable, delightful, forbidden, magical, or frightening as candy. It is the goal of any child's heart at Christmas and Halloween, and yet it can sicken and harm - it is, for the innocent youth, the very apple of Eden. If it were not, it would not be such a favorite building material of witches. Hansel and Gretel's nemesis constructed the perfect lure - is there a child who can resist the Gingerbread House, who can resist Turkish Delight? If fairy tales teach us anything without equivocation, it is that candy is evil. It is a poignant symbol of civilization, of industry: sugar and honey are natural sweets; candy requires factories and workers, artisans and bakers. It is a made thing, it is *techne*. Marie sheds her clothes and enters the Underworld; Clara exchanges the primitive technology of her candle for the sophisticated, decadent, witch-loved technology of "Candyland." There is hardly a more sinister set-dressing of hell imaginable than to drape it in spun sugar and peppermint.

Indeed, the moment she sets foot in this world, toy-prince in hand, witchery abounds. In the story, she crosses three rivers, which correspond roughly to the Styx, the Lethe, and the Acheron: the Orange Brook, the River of Honey, and the River Lemonade. In the ballet, the first creature she meets is a cameo from an entirely different tale-cycle, the Snow Queen. The Snow Queen, slumming in Germany, is a picture-perfect incarnation of Ereshkigal: cold, implacable, beautiful, and ineffably adult set against Clara/Marie's cracking veneer of childhood. Yet, because she *is* little more than a cameo, and because snow and sugar are symbolically so similar, her character can be elided into the true Ereshkigal figure of The Nutcracker: The Sugar Plum Fairy.

Fully half of the final act of the Tchaikovsky ballet is consumed with the enchanting, yet mysterious presence of the Sugar Plum Fairy. The most famous dances of the production are given to this enigmatic figure, and she all but steals the Nutcracker from his young mistress. This is immediately evocative of Inanna's unfaithful lover, Dumuzi, who dressed in colorful robes and celebrated when Inanna was killed. The Sugar Plum Fairy, again, the fully sexualized, adult female, perhaps the most innocuous-seeming shadow-self in literature, seduces the hapless Nutcracker into her beautiful dance, and since the ballet ends with Clara awakening beneath the Tree, it is possible to read the narrative so that the Fairy was successful, leaving Clara only with the hollow doll-shell in her lap. This would correspond to the Inanna myth, since Dumuzi is set below to take Inanna's place so that she can return to the world of the living.

Inanna and Ereshkigal, much as any heroic pairing of protagonist and antagonist, are a binary set: the self and the other, the shadow and the light. It follows, then, that Clara and the Sugar Plum Fairy share the same relationship. Surprisingly, the famous Baryshnikov Nutcracker makes this textual: the roles of the Snow Queen and the Sugar Plum Fairy are cut out entirely, and Clara is given all the dances that previously belonged to the Fairy, even costumed in her trademark sparkling mauve. In the guise of her other self, Clara reaches a kind of erotic maturity in these stolen dances, a completely integrated self.

In Hoffman's tale, there is no such figure. Marie simply tours Toyland, eventually coming to rest in its Metropolis-Capitol and agreeing to marry the Nutcracker. When she awakes, no one will believe what she has seen, but unlike MGM's Dorothy, she does not accept their judgment, and within the hour produces the metamorphosed Nutcracker, to whom she is now betrothed. Marie is the most self-possessed of heroines, and her unerring faith in her own interpretation of events earns her a throne.

Alone of the three girls considered here, Marie chooses to return to the Underworld, eager to become its Queen. She embraces this other universe wholeheartedly, becoming both Inanna and Ereshkigal, Queen of Heaven and Mistress of the Dead. Little is said of the Nutcracker but that he loved his wife, and we are left with the image of a mature Marie, ruling wisely and well. Neither Alice nor Dorothy is allowed to truly grow up, though we are given to understand they have come of age. Marie, ever so subtly, becomes the Sugar Plum Fairy of the later ballet - the Queen of Sugar and Snow. And though Marie, unlike her sisters, and perhaps because her adulthood is encompassed by the narrative, does end her tale with a husband, so too does Persephone, and both are wed to the King of the Underworld.

Yet, once again, the later incarnations rob her of this magical ending. The postmodern world which prides itself on its enlightenment, its political correctness, cannot bear to create versions of Marie and Dorothy as real heroes, only as deluded children. It was safe for the male writers who, it should not be forgotten, created these texts, to fashion a tidy fantasy in which a girl might have her own *aresteia*, her moment of greatness, a heroic journey not less than those of Odysseus, Theseus, Aeneas: the chances that any real little girl would grow up to be other than a wife and mother were terrifically slim. It was safe to call these girls Persephone, the lone Greek goddess who is married, yet childless. It is safe to call them Inanna, and let them hold a vicious shoe, chess piece, or bucket of water. But in this best of all possible worlds, where real women are no longer bound to the hearth, to tell them stories of the astonishing feats of intrepid young girls is to increase the ranks of women in the Underworlds of the office building, Wall Street, and Congress. It is no longer harmless fantasy, it is the seed of actual heroism, actual strength. And so the tales themselves must become harmless fantasy, in order to keep the Kansas homefires safe from those ravening shadows, those hordes of Witches, Fairies, and Queens.

* * *

—and it really *was* a Kitten, after all.

—Lewis Carroll,
Through the Looking Glass And What Alice Found There

Works Cited[4]

- Baum, L. Frank. *The Wizard of Oz*. Tor Books, New York 1993.
- Campbell, Joseph. *The Hero With A Thousand Faces* The. Princeton University Press, New Jersey, 1949.
- Carroll, Lewis. *Through the Looking Glass and What Alice Found There*, Dilithium Press Ltd. New York, 1990.
- Hoffman, E.T.A. *The Nutcracker* in *The Best Tales of Hoffman*, Dover Publications, New York, 1967. pp. 130-182.
- Sandars, N.K. (trans.) "Inanna's Journey Into Hell," *Poems of Heaven and Hell From Ancient Mesopotamia*. Penguin, New York, 1971. Pg. 130-166.
- Sendak, Maurice & E.T.A. Hoffman. *Nutcracker*, Three Rivers Press, New York, 1984.
- Taaffe, Sonya. (trans.) *The Descent of Ishtar.* 2005.
- Wolkstein, Diana/Kramer, Noah. *Inanna: Queen of Heaven and Earth*. Harper Perennial, New York, 1983.

---

4 The author wishes to thank Sonya Taaffe and Mariane Desautels for their immeasurable help in fleshing out the ideas presented in this paper.

Dragon Bad, Sword Pretty

My dear People, My dear Bagginses and Boffins, and my dear Tooks and Brandybucks, and Grubbs, and Chubbs, and Burrowses, and Hornblowers, and Bolgers, Bracegirdles, Goodbodies, Brockhouses and Proudfoots. I hope you are all enjoying yourselves as much as I am. Four days is far too short a time to spend among such excellent and admirable hobbits. It is also, if I may be allowed to refer to ancient history, the anniversary of my arrival by barrel at Esgaroth on the Long Lake, or possibly of my first major novel winning the Mythopoeic Award; though on that occasion I could not be present. I was only 28 then, and geography seemed very important. The banquet was very splendid, however, though I had a bad cold at the time, I remember, and could only rest at home, saying: "thag you very buch." I now repeat it more correctly: Thank you very much for inviting me to your party. And more, for allowing me to keep you, well, moderately long, with a few after dinner thoughts.

As a child, I did my very best impression of Persephone - I spent summers with my mother in California, and winters with my father in Seattle. Maybe it's because of that split in my world that I've always conceived of my heart as a set of two: northwest/southwest, mother/father - well that's the easy stuff. It never really stopped, though. There has always been a slash through my identity: novelist/poet, science fiction/fantasy, monster/minstrel, classicist/medievalist (which is a lot like the whole virgin/whore thing, but with a lot more reading).

Oh yes, once upon a time, before any of my novels had gotten up the courage to be a twinkle in my eye, I was an academic. When I first saw the theme for this year's Mythcon, my dusty little scholarly heart did a doubletake and clapped its hands - because monsters are my great literary obsession, and long ago, in a department far far away, I was a medievalist. Most people don't know that the very fine graduate program I valiantly dropped out of was in medieval studies. I didn't mean to drop out, but life happens - I didn't mean to fall sideways out of Classics, either, and in fact I was very snobbish about Carolingean Latin for quite some time. I came to the medieval world as an overenthusiastic devourer of difficult languages, but also as a fantasy reader, one who had loved not only Tolkien but most of his imitators, a girl who had grown up at Renaissance Fairs, who had been writing Arthurian plays with Greek choruses since middle school. And what I found was so much more than what my elf-laden interior world had prepared me for - not just the world of vague pleasant villages and princesses in towers, but of The Dream of the Rood and Ancrene Wisse, of Carmina Burana and assorted gorgeous heresies which I, having been raised in a rather peculiar branch of the protestant tree, never dreamed of. Yet I still felt that divide, that doubled identity, that two-headed beast - one girl in the classical ocean, one girl in the medieval wood. I was Morgan le Fay, lamenting to her chorus of Furies.

I must say to you very venerable hobbits that I am not an academic now. That's hard for me to say. I'm not here to present research or read to you from my long put-off new translation of Antigone. It's what I always thought I would be, but you might say I was waylaid in the woods by a certain wolf, and wandered off the path. I never made it to grandmother's house. I have all the training and none of the letters behind my name. But it turns out that a couple of years in those particular mines will serve you quite well as a fantasy novelist. Because the fantasy genre just can't let go of medievalism. That's where it lives, it's the blood that moves it. Steampunk is a blip, a coppery inkspill on the vast page of the fantasy of the village, the castle, the knight and the maiden. Dragon bad; sword pretty.

Why is this? Why do we keep going back to this particular well and hauling on the rope, whether or not the bucket comes up full of water or full of mud? What is it about the Not Very Dark Dark Ages that sits on the fantasy genre like a hoard of gold? This is the question I thought I might try to answer tonight - no pressure, I thought. It's only the nut at the core of my genre's whole identity. Should be able to manage that in 30 minutes.

The easy answer is that it's Tolkien's fault. It's all the rage these days to blame old Uncle John for any sin of fantasy, but that *is* an easy answer, and a thoughtless one. Yes, Tolkien imitators glutted up the scene for a good long time, but the movement of the genre is one of reacting away these days, if Tolkien is addressed at all in the very dark and serious halls of the New Weird and her various runaway punk children. It's a 1.0 answer, and I don't find it satisfying.

The 1.5 answer is that the medieval world provides us a relatively technology-free space in which to employ magic without worrying that someone will come along with a refrigerator instead of a frostfire spell. It's a workaday answer, serviceable I suppose, but it doesn't really hold up - the classical world is also blessedly refrigerator-free, and though the loss of classical knowledge and political structure is certainly a thing that happened, the ancient world offers no lack of kings and vassals and witches - in fact, when I first began writing fantasy it had to be explained to me that my book about magic and talking animals and curses and sorceresses and sentient mazes was not, strictly speaking, realism. In Classics, we just call that Tuesday. And of course the idea that the medieval world lacked all technological progress is more an invention of industrial souls looking for an idealized pastoral utopia than an accurate picture of the mills, nautical advancements, mechanical clocks, gunpowder, and later, the printing press, not to mention the bustling Islamic Golden Age and the highly developed Chinese empire. A simpler time which was never simple at all. Dragon bad; sword pretty.

It's attractive to sum up fantasy as being about the past while science fiction is about the future, about the unreal and the magical as opposed to the plausibly real and the technological. But the past is a country vast and strange, and technology is more than simply that which whirrs and beeps. Sometimes it creaks and groans.

Let's make it personal for a moment - why do I do it? Of my ten novels, two take place during WWII, one in the present day, three in an early medieval period and four in a late medieval period - six if you count The Orphan's Tales as they were meant to be, as four discreet novels.

Well, I do it because of fairy tales. While not all of my fiction deals in folklore and fairy tales, a significant majority shows up for work with three wishes in its pocket and a dizzying array of peculiar shoes. Fairy tales are certainly not confined to the medieval era, and folklore knows no chronological confinement, but thanks to the Grimm boys and a few other perpetrators (not to absolve Disney from this), the Western imagination "knows" that Cinderella isn't a Chinese girl with bound and therefore perfect feet, she's a French or German lass with a peasant skirt and a castle in her cards. There is a sweet spot there - there's always a reason that incorrect ideas about the past stick. Go back too far and many of these stories become religious or at least epic. Little Red Riding Hood trades in her scones for pomegranates, Clever Jack takes 20 years to get home from the war. Too far forward and they cease to be about any kind of belief and become rather naked political and cultural tools. All the mothers become stepmothers, because you just can't talk that way about good, honest German maternity. You can't tell innocent children that the mermaid dies at the end.

Folklore develops most rapidly and with the most diversity among populations of the powerless. Given a lack of ability to affect the world around us and a lack of information about causation, humans tend to kick into high explanatory gear, propitiating unseen forces, insisting that wearing this color will bring bad fortune, this color good, seeking to order a disordered universe. This is part of why fairy tales are considered to be for children - children are engines of folklore, throwing any explanation for a baffling universe over which they have no influence at all at the wall to see what sticks. Fairy tales tell them how to grow up and survive, what the psychological rules are - but that's never enough. Kids make their own. So do other powerless populations both extreme and quotidian: victims of totalitarian regimes and natural disasters, runaways, the rural and urban poor, medical students have endless bizarre rituals, and of course writers participate in their own versions of sacrifice, bargaining with unfeeling gods, and sympathetic magic. The relative powerlessness of the medieval person - not the protagonists, the Black Princes and Joans and Aquinases, but the actual man or even monk on the ground, did create an extraordinarily rich narrative patchwork of Christian, pagan, folk magic, science, half-forgotten philosophy, and political determinism that starkly and strongly informs what we now recognize as the object known as a fairy tale. Something about those stories goes straight to the deep narrative brain, and because we modern and very civilized kittens conceive of the medieval era as somewhat vague and eventless on a macro level if not the micro, a broad grassy plain of peasants in ruddy health, noble kings, women who'd never heard the word feminism, with the dark wood just beyond to provide story and threat and the scintillating thrill of the Other, placing fairy tales there makes them feel somewhat non-specific, and therefore universal.

But I still don't think that's it. After all, while epic fantasy is based on the fairy tale of the just war, that's not one you'll find in Grimm or Disney, and most will never recognize the shape of it. I think the fantasy genre pitches its tent in the medieval campground for the very reason that we even bother to write stories about things that never happened in the first place: because it says something subtle and true about our own world, something it is difficult to say straight out, with a straight face. Something you need tools to say, you need cheat codes for the human brain - a candy princess or a sugar-coated unicorn to wash down the sour taste of how bad things can really get.

See, I think our culture has a slash running through the middle of it, too. Past/Future, Conservative/Liberal, Online/Offline. Virgin/Whore. And yes: Classical/Medieval. I think we're torn between the Classical Narrative of Self and the Medieval Narrative of Self, between the choice of Achilles and Keep Calm and Carry On.

The Classical internal monologue goes like this: do anything, anything, only don't be forgotten. Yes, this one sacrificed his daughter on a slab at Aulis, that one married his mother and tore out his eyes, and oh that guy ate his kids in a pie. But you remember their names, don't you? So it's all good in the end. Give a Greek soul a choice between a short life full of glory and a name echoing down the halls of time and a long, gentle life full of children and a quiet sort of virtue, and he'll always go down in flames. That's what the *Iliad* is all about, and the *Odyssey* too. When you get to Hades, you gotta have a story to tell, because the rest of eternity is just forgetting and hoping some mortal shows up on a quest and lets you drink blood from a bowl so you can remember who you were for one hour.

And every bit of cultural narrative in America says that we are all Odysseus, we are all Agamemnon, all Atreus, all Achilles. That we as a nation made that choice and chose glory and personal valor, and woe betide any inconvenient "other people" who get in our way. We tell the tales around the campfire of men who came from nothing to run dotcom empires, of a million dollars made over-night, of an actress marrying a prince from Monaco, of athletes and stars and artists and cowboys and gangsters and bootleggers and talk show hosts who hitched up their bootstraps and bent the world to their will. Whose names you all know. And we say: that can be each and every one of us and if it isn't, it's your fault. You didn't have the excellence for it. You didn't work hard enough. The story wasn't about you, and the only good stories are the kind that have big, unignorable, undeniable heroes.

But it's a lie. It's a lie most of this country believes, even as they forget that Bill Gates is William Gates III, even as they ignore the difference between a million dollars and the terrifying power of genuine wealth. We think we live in a Classical world, and it just ain't so. For those of us monks on the ground, the world looks much more medieval than the fairy tales say. Technologically we move forward, socially we move back - the middle class dwindles as most of us work all our lives as itinerant laborers, or in thrall to a company that has just enough health insurance to keep us on the estate, the gap between rich and poor becomes a Looney Tunes chasm in which all us poor coyotes fall, signs up, bones broken. Technology itself is unevenly available, religion and the wild, ever-growing tales of Rapture and Revelation it weaves has come again to dominate our government. Industry is no longer even an option for most Americans - factories represent, bizarrely, a safe haven, a good job with union backing, and a time long past when such safety was possible. Corporations prefer to find their way to the cruelest common denomination, turning whole regions and other nations into literal serfdoms.

But here? Here, we have retreated into cottage industries. Many people in this room have an Etsy store where they create unique, unreplicable artifacts or useful items to be sold on a small scale, in a common marketplace where their friends meet and barter. I and many of my friends own more than one spinning wheel. We grow our food again. We make pickles and jams on private, individual scales, when many of our mothers forgot those skills if they ever knew them. We come to conventions, we create small communities of support and distributed skills - when one of us needs help, our village steps in. It's only that our village is no longer physical, but connected by DSL instead of roads. But look at how we organize our tribes - bloggers preside over large estates, kings and queens whose spouses' virtues are oft-lauded but whose faces are rarely seen. They have moderators to protect them, to be their knights, a nobility of active commenters and big name fans, a peasantry of regular readers, and vandals starting the occasional flame war just to watch the fields burn. Other villages are more commune-like, sharing out resources on forums or aggregate sites, providing wise women to be consulted, rabbis or priests to explain the world, makers and smiths to fashion magical objects. Groups of performers, acrobats and actors and singers of songs are traveling the roads once more, entertaining for a brief evening in a living room or a wheatfield, known by word of mouth and secret signal. Separate from official government, we create our own hierarchies, laws, and mores, as well as our own folklore and secret history. Even my own guilt about having failed as an academic is quite the crisis of filial piety - you see, my mother is a professor. I have not carried on the family trade.

We dwell within a system so large and widespread, so disorganized and unconcerned for anyone but its most privileged and luxurious members, that our powerlessness, when we can summon up the courage to actually face it, is staggering. So we do not face it. We tell ourselves we are Achilles when we have much more in common with the cathedral-worker, laboring anonymously so that the next generation can see some incremental progress. We lack, of course, a Great Work to point to and say: *my grandmother made that window; I worked upon the door*. Though, I would submit that perhaps the Internet, as an object, as an aggregate entity, is the cathedral we build word by word and image by image, window by window and portal by portal, to stand taller for our children, if only by a little, than it does for us. For most of us are Lancelots, not Galahads. We may see the Grail of a good Classical life, but never touch it. That is for our sons, or their daughters, or further off.

And if our villages are online, the real world becomes that dark wood on the edge of civilization, a place of danger and experience, of magic and blood, a place to make one's name or find death by bear. And here, there be monsters.

Let me tell you, I am a mouthy, aggressive, ambitious woman. I have been a known monster for quite some time. And to be a woman is to be monstrous, to be queer is to be monstrous, to have a body that is not white, that is sick or broken, that is even the littlest bit out of compliance with an increasingly unreal eidolon is monstrous. To be poor, to be other than Christian, to be old - we're the ones who live in the frightening forest, waiting to prey on everyone else. It's not really a metaphor - culture treats all of us as though our souls are catching, as though we must be contained and punished and shown to be wicked, made to dance in iron shoes, so that no further good folk will step out of line. After all, a gay teacher will make his students gay. A single mother will ruin her sons. A career woman will steal treasure from noble knights. As social powerlessness grows, scapegoats must be found. Strong, pale men with might on their side must be dispatched to triumph. Dragon bad; sword pretty.

To study literature is to seek to discover where we come from. You can never escape where you come from - every farm boy who ever became king could tell you that. And we didn't come from Greece - truly, the Hellenic world is not a Western one. Only seen through the eyes of Rome does it become familiar, and to see ourselves there we must look at Rome through medieval glasses - to see it as idealized, perfected world that we somehow lost. A world gone into the West, to which we no longer have claim. It's nonsense, of course, Rome knew from brutality, but no one speaks ill of the dead. Rome was mighty, Hellas great, but the terrible beauty and unspeakable agonies of those Dark Ages are still moving and shaping us - those Dark Ages illuminated by such strange and unfathomable lights. The fantasy genre is doing the great good work of sorting out our Oedipal relationship with the past, longing to wed the Classical world and murder the medieval, giving us these endless visions of powerful humans vanishing and taking their knowledge and technology with them, leaving us to make do in the mud, looking toward the castle lights on the hill. Fantasy like no other mode of being wields metaphor - not a thing to be scoffed at or shrugged off. We are not like Lancelot. We *are* Lancelot, hands outstretched to a cup the color of history. Fantasy tells us not what we are like, but who we are, and though that is a terrible responsibility, we need it - we will always need it. We live in a medieval world. We require a living, vibrant medieval literature.

That's not going to change any time soon. There's too much still to be done. So much that hasn't yet been touched by the anemic medieval analogues that are easy and common but never have the bite of truth.

But I'll tell you what's changing. The monsters are driving the cart. We're telling our own stories. We are no longer voiceless, but a tribe of Spencerian Errours, dancing amid riot of books and papers. If I have ever wished to say anything with my novel, it has been to speak to the possibility, the beautiful, daring possibility of a fellowship, not of the ring, but of the monsters, to stand shoulder to shoulder against the unfeeling and uncomprehending world, to determine our own identities and our own places in the story, to find just enough power in being the beast in the dark to defeat those boorish, righteous heroes who come barging into our pleasant Saturdays, and then to turn to each other and see what we are: yes, we are old and queer and female and geeks, yes, we are Grendel's mother, and Scylla and Charybdis, Circe and Melisande and the Cyclops, Baba Yaga and the Green Knight and Lilith and the witch with the candy hut. We are all of those things because we're drawn that way and the stories are always written by the guy with the best armor. But we are also magnificent, and we are strong. Dragon pretty; sword bad.

At the end of *Sir Gawain and the Green Knight*, Lord Bertilak explains that Morgan le Fay enchanted him to look frightening and fey, and it was all a trick to show up Camelot as a bag full of fools (and let's be honest, she has a point). And the Green Knight says: *but it's all ok now. All the cards are on the table. No one's been hurt and it's a beautiful Christmas afternoon. We were speaking truth to power, that's all. Can't blame us for trying. Come inside, boy. Morgan's put the kettle on. Sit with us and break our bread.*

Gawain declines. He must - he is a Company Man, Camelot's boy to the bone. He is the Self, and not the Other. He is the knight, and not the monster. He is the patriarchy and privilege and power, and he cannot give them up for even a moment. The establishment cannot sit down with the disenfranchised. The castle cannot break bread with the wood.

But I have hope that one day, after all these centuries of setting a table for the souls on the other side of that slash I keep talking about, after enough ink spilled on stories where the Other speaks for herself, stands her ground, refuses the narrative given to her, shows her troth and keeps it, that Gawain will take the Green Knight's hand and step into Morgan's house, and their table will groan with feasting.

Confessions of a Fairy Tale Addict

A long while ago, someone emailed me to tell me that, as much as they wanted to like my work, they just couldn't read another goddamned fairy tale. It was too much, they said. Everyone's doing it. There's no *there* there. It's tired and trite and they just couldn't be part of it anymore. Look at your life, look at your choices. That sort of thing.

Everyone has a right to cry uncle on a genre every once in awhile. I've done it myself. Sometimes you just can't bear another gear or pair of wings or vampire teeth. You go on a fast and sometimes you come back and sometimes you don't. I get that on a basic level. And there is less than zero chance that folks are going to stop retelling fairy tales any time soon. But I'll never forget that moment. Not because of the sting of it - though of course it stung - but because I was still in the flush of fairy tale love, so sure everyone else found them as thorny and interesting and worthy as I did. Not everyone does. Which meant it was my responsibility to bring the awesome when I showed up on doorsteps with a retelling in tow. And not just the blue light special fair trade organic 2% milkfat awesome. The real stuff, the mountain to the prophet love it like you stole it cut-the-cream-off-the-top-of-the-glass-bottle awesome. I took it as a challenge.

And sometimes I fail at that challenge, let's get that out of the way up top. But you gotta try for it. And this is about trying. And fairy tales. And choices.

Because it is a lifestyle choice, to write fairy tale books. Make no mistake. I mean, in our culture, the phrase "fairy tale" practically means: trite, lightweight, and fluffy.

You know, girl stuff.

Because Tam Lin help you if you're a woman writing fairy tales. Someone clearly didn't play catch with you enough, because otherwise you'd be writing "kickass" books that utilize the F-bomb and feature people being punched/shot/ hit in the face with fists of fire/a clockwork ray gun/a sudden realization of the weight of their sins. Men can get away with it to some extent, but for a lot of readers, a fairy tale retelling is just a nonstarter. Maybe it's because the writer didn't invent the core tale, so there's a whiff of fanfic about it. Maybe it's because we've all been trained to associate fairy tales with Disney and therefore with toothless storytelling. Maybe it's something uglier and deeper, that shrunken, deformed thing that lies beneath all separations of stories into boy stories and girl stories, black stories and white stories, gay stories and straight stories.

Funny thing about Disney. They're postmodern fairy tale retellers, too. No less than I or any other mythpunk kid scribbling stanzas in the dark. They take an old story and change it - sometimes radically, as in *The Little Mermaid* and *Tangled* - to conform to their own sensibilities, what they think it is important to teach children, to reflect the world they think they live in. Sometimes this goes poorly, because the world of Disney is not often the world the rest of us live in, and girls need to learn virtues other than vague spunk, and boys need to learn a role other than privileged rogue. But they are astonishingly good at it. So good that their images of Snow White and Alice in Wonderland have almost completely erased the originals in the American mind, so good that they have essentially bought the idea of a fairy tale from our collective consciousness and made the idea of Disney indistinguishable from the idea of the fairy tale.

That's a pretty good trick.

But I'm not Disney. My Snow White will never replace that girl in yellow. I'm just a working stiff who wants to tell stories. Just about every science whiz can tell you how he or she took apart the TV or the radio when they were kids, just to see how it worked. To see what the world was made of. Well, when I was a kid, I took apart fairy tales to see how they worked. To see what the world was made of. Because those stories represent the purest distillation of what it means to be human. They have been revised for thousands of years by every generation and every culture, boiled down to the core images that move hearts and shape minds, the images that haul up the reptile brain and make it pay attention.

No matter what you write, you actually can't help retelling a fairy tale somewhere along the way. Take the fairy part out. Stop thinking of it as fairy dust and gossamer wings. Think of it as blood and mirrors and death and mothers and fathers and food and fire and resurrection. If these stories had no power, they would have been forgotten. It's far easier to forget than to remember, and I can't think of a book or a movie that isn't retelling some old tale. In fact, the more bald and bold the original moves in its new skin, the more we like it, because we feel a familiarity. We thrill to the newness, but we know the answer to that riddle. I have a friend who doesn't read retellings because he never read fairy tales as a child. And I've always wondered: *why wouldn't you read them now?* They're like the cheat codes to the narrative brain. Play that old game on the nodes and watch the mind dance.

The Girl Who Circumnavigated Fairyland in a Ship of Her Own Making is not a retelling of any particular fairy tale. But it is a retelling - it cannot help but retell. The core narrative is so old, it's got tenure: a girl escapes her life into a magical and dangerous land where she must become something greater than she was. Half the stories in the world go like that. The other half go: "a boy escapes his life." It's growing up, coming of age - that's what almost all portal fantasies are about. Adulthood looks like a fairyland to a child: arbitrary rules, beautiful and reckless and cruel people, dark secrets to do with violence and forgiveness, incomprehensible stirrings of sexuality and an incomplete but growing understanding of wealth and power, the ability to simply reach out and take whatever you want. Of course, those of us who live here know it's not like that. You can't have whatever you want. But to a child who must ask permission for every single thing, adulthood looks like a constant parade of every desire's satisfaction. It is a heady and terrifying place. It is the Otherworld. It is Fairyland. In fantasy, we make this literal. In realism, it becomes metaphorical. Even stories of middle-aged literature professors having affairs are actually portal fantasies - a man escapes his life into a land of desire. It is the biggest tent in the circus of fairy tales. Everyone tells this story - even people who've never written books. *One day I will make a million dollars and escape my life into a land of plenty. One day I will move to Paris and escape my life into a land of magic.*

It is The Story.

And so even though *Fairyland* is not a retelling in the same way that The Orphan's Tales or *Deathless* is - it is not married to any one tale or culture, it is not looking for that sweet spot, that place where you can turn a tale around and show the back of it to the reader, the dark shadow-tale they didn't know they were reading - it is still telling an old tale. And on top of that, the tropes of folktales, fairy tales, and myth abound in Fairyland. It is a place where anything goes, a prism through which the light of folklore is split into many beams. And where those beams fall, you find witches cooking the future, queens wicked and tragic, baths to wash your courage and your wishes, blue-skinned time-traveling water genies, and a little girl who doesn't dream of going home, but of knowing and of loving and of experience. Fairyland is a place where stories go to play. Everything we've wanted so much we were afraid of it. Because that's where fairy tales live, on the border of desire and fear, just to the left of pedagogy and to the right of raw survival.

That's not girl stuff. That's everybody stuff.

And it's why I'll be writing goddamned fairy tales until I'm blue in the face. So to speak.

I Am the Walrus

You never know what a school visit will be like. If the kids will have read your book or not, if they will be engaged and interested or bored and distant. If they will open up to you or shy away, since you are a stranger and an adult and that oh-so-mysterious thing, a writer.

And then sometimes they spin you right around and show you the slice of the universe they carry around in their backpacks.

After my talk in South Portland a couple of weeks ago, the kids were milling around the library and two kids started playing an odd game with a long row of identical powder blue books. Each book was about an individual animal, with that animal's name and a photograph emblazoned on the front in bright colors and large print. The boys stood on chairs behind the shelf so they could pull out books without looking at them.

One, who wore glasses, looked up and yelled "Miss Cat! Come over here! We're playing a game!"

I did, and the boy in glasses told me to stand still and they would pick for me. With a little theatrical flourish, he closed his eyes and pulled one of the books at random.

"This is what he is," he said, gesturing at the other boy, who had blond spiky hair. He turned the book around and held it straight out with both arms. On the cover was a crocodile.

The blond boy yanked out another one. "Oh yeah?" he said to the boy in glasses. "Well, this is what *you* are." He flipped the book to reveal a toucan.

"And this is what you are!" the boy in glasses turned back to me triumphantly, and selected another book.

On the cover was a moose. I laughed. "I can be a moose," I said. "They're big and strong and stubborn and they make funny noises, just like me."

This went on for awhile, grabbing books with closed eyes and trumpeting: *this is what he is, this is what you are, oh yeah, well you're both of these put together, I'm gonna pick three and all of them are Miss Cat. Well, if I were a mad scientist I would make one animal out of these ones and it would be a monster and that would be you.*

I was, variously, a moose, a wolf, a muskox, a flamingo, a grizzly bear, and a walrus. The blond boy was a butterfly, a shark, a mountain lion, a mosquito, a swan, and a kangaroo. The boy in glasses was a dolphin, a hummingbird, a lion, a zebra, a whale, and a rabbit. I was also a whaleantelopebee, and they were an elephantfrogmanatee and a peacocktigerkoala.

And I couldn't help but marvel at them, the very primal and human moment when these children learned how to make metaphors. Not *I am like a swan, you are like a wolf,* but *I am a swan. You are a wolf. He is a shark. I am a rabbit.*

And it's more than metaphors - it's divination. It's folklore. *If I close my eyes and reach out into this collection of randomly-ordered images, whatever my fingers find will say something essential about me, or my friend who wears glasses, or the lady with black hair and the red book who came to talk to our class today. It will not say what they're like, it will say what they are, deep down inside. So If I choose a worm for myself, I will be sad, because it means I am a worm and I have this whole set of ideas about what worms are. If I choose a tiger, I will be happy, because I also have ideas about what tigers are and in the world I live in it's better to be a tiger than a worm. What animal I am tells a story about what kind of person I am, and what my life will be like when I grow up.*

It's this incredibly basic thing, somewhere between magic and storytelling, and you can see exactly where fairy tales come from in these boys grabbing blue books like Tarot cards, like runes. Where totems come from, and fetishes, and half the shamanic toolbox - *oh, no Miss Cat, we'll draw for you. If you draw your own, it doesn't count. Those are the rules.*

No one taught them to do it. No one taught them those rules - though certainly there are cultural narratives at play in their reactions to drawing The Rhinoceros versus The Kitten. Though I found it wonderful that with the exception of the flamingo, all of my animals were the sort usually masculinized - big and strong and somewhat dangerous - and they didn't question it at all. The draw has spoken. Nor did they express particular dismay at being butterflies or swans. It wasn't about what kind of animals they liked. It was a deeper magic, as a certain lion would say.

What they were doing was very real. Paleolithic human wizardry. We still do it as adults, of course, as a million usernames and pagan names and Halloween costumes and D&D characters and cosplayers attest. The marriage of image and soul fuels story and our conceptions of self, all the more so in the world of the Internet where we can use images that are not our actual selves to represent that self - macros and userpics and icons. We are always making ourselves into metaphors. We are deciding with endless online quizzes what animals or fairies or vampires we "are" - in hopes, I have always thought, of borrowing some of the power of those characters and images for ourselves and our actual non-fairy lives. We want those images to mean more, to say something fundamental, and once we decide they do, they do - that's how some kinds of magic work.

In play, we show our best selves, the people we dream to be, long to be. And we pantomime acts and narratives that once upon a time were seen as holy, as the very keystones of faith - because they are instinct, they are beautiful, and they are true often enough.

I spent an afternoon with two small shamans and they told me I was a moose. I was a wolf. A muskox, a flamingo, a bear and a walrus. We did a good trade.

I Am the Walrus

I brought my magic to them in the form of a red book, and they brought theirs to me in blue books. We wizards know a bargain when we see it.

We shook hands when it was over. That's how colleagues say good-bye.

The Singularity

There is a thing and it sits in the future like a big fat egg we spend the present hatching and it's called the Singularity. For those who do not live on the Internet, the singularity refers to the technological revolution beyond which we cannot really imagine the state of our anything: daily life, rate of change, social patterns. Usually this means functional AI, and the resulting technologies: nanotech, FTL, etc. In short, it is the point at which "now" becomes that nebulous *the future*.

I don't have all that much to say about the tech singularity, because by definition we can't really extrapolate - sure, we can talk about what the singularity might be, but to imagine life beyond it you need SF lit, and even there, one is always cautioned to Remember Leningrad - in *Star Trek IV*, Starfleet headquarters reports the loss of power and plummeting temperatures in Leningrad as a result of the whalesongs (*OMG spoilers*). Of course, Leningrad was re-re-named St. Petersburg just a few years later, and is thus a nice shorthand for how the things which seem today like they will safely last forever can be gone by the next sequel.

So Vernor Vinge's Singularity - he coined the term - will most likely occur. The singularity does not actually have to take the form of AI, much as we, raised on Data and HAL, might like to think it must. Our world as it exists today would be unimaginable to even someone from 300 years or so ago. Computers themselves comprised a singularity, as did flight and electricity. As did the breakup of the Soviet Union. There is no one singularity, and I believe that if AI doesn't wake up one day and rub its cyber-eyes and ask for coffee, humankind will still manage new and to-us-unfathomable technologies if we don't blow ourselves to shit first. I'm not really worried about it.

I've started thinking about the word "singularity" and what that has come to mean. The thing is, I'm living in my own personal singularity, a point beyond which I, even right now, cannot imagine. I am in my second marriage, post-publication, post-Navy, post-Ohio, post New York Times Bestseller list and Hugo nominations, post-post. I don't know how to live my life right now, I'm past the edges of my own maps.

Until I was already in it, I did not have any tools with which to build a mental model of a life which did not include being married to my first husband, which did not involve being moved around by the Navy, or returning to graduate school. I could not model a world in which I wrote novels for my bread and board, lived in a rather unorthodox domestic situation in the American Midwest before moving to an island in Maine. All these things were well beyond the threshold of imagining for my 23-year old self, which was not all that long ago.

The Singularity

I think everyone has these personal singularities. When you're a kid, it's that nebulous state of being *grown up*, at which point everything will be more or less awesome and make sense, and you will not have to deal with the issues you have to deal with being eight and grounded. Marriage is another one - we are taught that everything will somehow evolve into kids and a house and grandparent-hood after that, though the process is vague and involves a lot of handwaving. Some of us are still struggling to live in that singularity of adulthood in their twenties, thirties, forties. Probably in their fifties, too, but to my spring-chicken mind, that age is as unimaginable as driving used to be, or being able to buy any toy I wanted, so I can't testify. I realize, oh post-50 friends of mine, that that makes me suck. I accept this.

When you grow up, they often have to do with work: the site launch, the book, the promotion, tenure, going into business for oneself. Or children, the biggest singularity for most people.

But the real nature of singularities is that they can't even be predicted. In some sense, AI is such an easy answer to what the singularity will be. In actual-ity, it will probably be some advance we can't even think about right now, as incomprehensible as the Internet to a potato farmer in seventeenth-century Ireland. He would not even have the tools to begin to understand what it was, let alone, and maybe more importantly, *what use anyone could have for it, and why anyone would care*. There are potatoes to pull, goddammit, leave me alone with that shit.

And it's like that in fleshy, messy singularities, too. In 2002, when I stood in front of a minister and had a ring put on my hand, I fully expected that by 2007, I'd be living in Greece, still married, still in the Navy. Maybe pregnant. If I was very lucky, I could almost imagine the slim possibility of having a book pub-lished by a very, very small press. Maybe self-published. And maybe in 2009, I could go back to grad school. I was comfortable with that timeline, I knew it very well. It was Life, and maybe I didn't like it so much, but you can't really change it, right?

Didn't happen. The books were the first singularity, Ohio was the second. Divorced before 30; remarried soon after. I'm happy in my singularity, happier than in the analog, pre-quantum theory universe I inhabited before. But it does mean that I can't even project what my life will be next month. I have no maps here. Part of my late depression and existential crises are the growing pains, I think, of trying to form an accurate model of my life trajectory, and jettisoning the old one. That process is no joke, not for the weak of heart. Remember Leningrad.

The word singularity is a lie, both in SF and in life. There is no one singular-ity. You keep pushing through them, and it's fucking terrifying, and fucking amazing. You wake up and one day the USSR is gone and the tech boom crashed and you're divorced and you sell tires instead of playing professional soccer and your toaster wants to talk to you about pork futures and the size of your penis and your sofa wants to have a serious conversation about the works of Vernor Vinge. You wake up and you're making independent movies instead of selling tires and Europe up and got themselves a common currency and you had twin girls when you thought your birth control was top notch and the Supreme Court threw an election and gay marriage is so old-fashioned when there are four sexes and flights to Saturn leave daily.

You just keep moving. And in the middle of the night the blue glow of your intelligent sofa tells you it'll be okay, eventually. Singularities exist to be lived in, to be lived beyond. Embrace them. Embrace love in the midwest. Embrace AI. Embrace Vernor Vinge. Face down the new world - and don't flinch first.

My Dinner With Persephone

All writers have their obsessions. That stuff they can't let go, that they return to again and again. Sometimes it's a man with roughly bitten-down fingernails. Sometimes it's a girl/boy/AI hired by a shadowy oligarch seeking some crazy thing across the known world. Sometimes it's the end of childhood. There's always something you straight up just can't quit, and usually a lot of things.

I have a lot of things. Bad parents, abandoned kids, broken girls getting whole, poorly socialized psyches incapable of understanding social systems. I have a lot.

But in the end, I just can't stop writing about Persephone.

I feel bad about it in a way. There's this process by which anything girls love becomes disdainful, cliched, sad, in a way that the things boys love never do. Boys can love pulp SF and westerns and comic books, and they become greater, they become epics and serious films and graphic novels. But for every girl who ever loved Sylvia Plath in high school, for every one who watched that crocus of a girl slipping away into the earth and saw herself, there is a invisible choir of derisive laughter, there is an instant satire of that love - *just another one of those sad, dirty girls, another goth girl who thinks she's special, how can anyone bear that emo poetry, how can anyone take a girl seriously who loves Morgan le Fay and Persephone and ankh-wearing Death, just like all the other girls?*

And I read slush. I know. Basically no one can stop writing about Persephone. (Or did you think *Twilight* was about something else?) There's a reason the greatest Mysteries of the ancient world were about her. Crack open any fantasy-accepting slushpile and you will find Persephone in a hundred stories, maybe one of which adds anything new at all. It's not an obsession that has geek cred. Too much love means you can turn up your geek nose about it.

And so when I go back to that well, that well which to me is so deep and giving, I feel guilt. What if they see that I'm still that girl wearing black in the hallway of some eternal school? What if they see that what obsesses me doesn't make the cover of *Wired* like post-scarcity economics or reputation-based currency system? I feel I should not be That Girl. I should give equal time to others. But I can't help it, I can't help how the symbols of the story crackle in my head, I can't help how I see my life in that story, how few stories we have that are about a girl's journey, and part of the reason this one hits so hard is that there is a rape at the center of it, and we all have to decide how we deal with that elephant in the Sicilian field, whether we say she loved the darkness too, whether we give her all the power, whether we say she was stolen, whether we say she was happy underground, whether we say she was miserable and her mother saved her. We decide if we see our own rapes and our own violations, the men (and women) who have put us in a cage in the dark, who have taken without asking, who have said that because they thought we were beautiful, they had the right to own us. We decide if we see the ways in which we flipped those scripts, and came out swinging into the light. And of course, it's her mother's story too, Hades is basically a motive force that acts once and never again. The rest is the story of women.

And for me, who grew up with parents who hated each other, who spent the all the seasons but one in piney grey Seattle, and summers in California, so hot it felt like hell, felt like being underground, who spent her young life being a punchline to a sad, horrible joke her parents kept telling each other over and over, who married a man who would bury her, who would take her away from the world, to Japan, to a place where no one could ever find her, where no one could break the hold he had on her, who chose to eat those seeds, who chose that man and that marriage, and then had to claw up out of the underworld only to find herself in the rust belt with a dead lake on one side, who saw it was only underworlds all the way down and up too, and you either decide to be a black-eyed queen or you decide to be that broken kid getting dragged away into the night, well, the story just never stopped showing its relevance to me. Never stopped being about me, just like it's about a lot of us.

I don't know if I'll ever be past writing about Persephone. If it will ever stop being the myth of my life. I don't really want to - the thing about katabasis (fancy Greek word for descending to the underworld and returning - it's such an important thing it gets it own word, and my name is Cat, and it's short for everything) is that it never stops. It's a process. And if you don't hit that black stair every year or so things wither up. The whole idea of that story is how a person is a world, and the cycle keeps moving, and it's never, ever over. You have to go into the earth, you have to come back up again.

So I repeat myself. I keep writing this story. Because the world has a stutter, and she keeps picking the crocus. Because for a this girl, a Sylvia girl, a Morgan girl, a Death girl, a pomegranate girl, it's the story that keeps telling me.

A Far Green Country

I'm a fantasy writer, and more particularly, a folklorist and historian. It is literally my job to find value in old things, to show people versions of themselves in ancient stories. Nobody asks me what I think about the future.

It's not that I don't have a dog in this race. I am, I know you'll be surprised to hear, a human living in the early twenty-first century with a vested interest in continuing at least one of those states (human or living in the twenty-first century - I'm not super picky which). And having just written a time-sprawling posthuman AI novella, it's fairly clear I have thoughts on the subject. It's just that, to belabor a metaphor, your dog is a SuperLabrador with paw-rockets, a tail that can hack wirelessly into the holorabbit whipping around the track, and an honest, loving, loyal cyborg heart. Mine is an old herd-dog, shaggy, dark, beautiful and uncanny, primeval and enormous - and every once in awhile, even though her heart is blood and muscle, she wins as if by magic.

A friend of mine said the other day that he'd surprised himself by starting to write a fantasy novel rather than his beloved SF. He felt it was a story he needed to tell, but also confined by what he saw as the limitations of fantasy: that it is essentially about the past and therefore not concerned with *possibility* in the same way - in fact, by definition a genre of the impossible. A genre of might-have-been instead of could-someday-be.

Now I've written before about what I see as the hierarchy of realism, where in terms of literary respect SF must come out on top of fantasy but below mimetic fiction, because SF presents a future which might come to pass, and could therefore be merely prescient, not fanciful. We know there are no dragons in the world, but there may be artificial intelligence, thus the latter is more worthy of serious thought than the former, which is merely escapism. I don't think very much of that hierarchy, but you don't get to choose your paradigms. (Much.)

When I told my friend it was silly to think that fantasy must be a medieval *Risk*-analogue, he asked what, then, was the difference between fantasy and science fiction. I didn't have a satisfying answer, and maybe I still don't. But I have an answer.

There's only a difference where you want one to be.

The famous defense of science fiction is that while taking place in the future or one imaginable future, it is profoundly concerned with the present, taking current trends and understandings of the world and extrapolating forward to a greater or lesser degree. SF always speaks to the time in which it is written.

I have never understood why fantasy is exempt from this. Why is the opposite not taken as equally and unavoidably true? While taking place in the past[5] or one imaginable past, it is profoundly concerned with the present, taking currents trends and understandings of the world and exaggerating to a greater or lesser degree. Why do I never hear this applied to fantasy? It's not even interesting at this point to say *The Lord of the Rings* has a great deal to say about WWI. I don't think it's an accident that *A Song of Ice and Fire* was first published in the aftermath of the Cold War, during a particularly ugly internecine period of struggle in the Balkans, but achieved its greatest popularity in the political climate of post 9/11 America, when fighting a whole bunch of wars all over the world became a reality for many people. Likewise, I suspect the popularity of Lev Grossman's *The Magicians* series has something to do with the generation of college students graduating into a dark world they believed was good and bright, saddled with debt and joblessness. And you know, it's noticeable that steampunk came into its own during a period when life is starting to look damned Dickensian again, when the split between rich and poor has widened drastically, when the aristocrats with the pretty clothes have moved the child-devouring factories to other continents so that no one has to see them at all. Magical realism tends to spring up in totalitarian regimes - when actual life has become a trickster play, when the government is run by magical thinking and words no longer mean what they say books start appearing in which the other-world is encroaching on reality rather than taking place in another reality entirely.

Fantasy is almost always strongly addressing the present and the future.

And while I'm rarely asked about my thoughts on transhumanism, when I write about immortal pre-scarcity beings who structure their whole world around the avoidance of boredom and the cultivation of psychologies which will stand the test of longevity, I'm not just thinking about the world of 1164 - or honestly thinking about it much at all. When I write about a sexually-transmitted city, it's not just because it's a cool elevator pitch, but because I live in such a fully networked world, one in which we all go to this third place where we can be ourselves when the work day is over. When I break the fourth wall to address the reader, it's to tell them what I think I know about real life here on Earth. It has never once occurred to me that in writing fantasy I am not writing directly and profoundly about actual life in the present day - and where that present day might lead us. That I am not translating fairy tales about *then* into fairy tales about *now*. Folklore is how humans explain the world to themselves. Fairy tales are a vital part how a culture promulgates itself and instructs the young (and old). They have always been about how to behave and survive right here and

---

5 Obviously, I don't buy the canard that SF is about the future and fantasy is about the past. I think both are about the Other, how we engage with it, refuse to engage, are assimilated or rejected by it. These things don't play for a particular temporal team.

now. Magic, like technology, merely foregrounds the stranger processes at work.

And if you think we're beyond believing in magic, you've got another thing coming. I can't count the number of times during the 08 crash I heard someone give my unemployed husband and friends the following advice: "Write down the job you want ten /seven/three times on a piece of paper, fold it up and carry it with you/against your skin/with a dollar bill in your left pocket/right pocket all the time." That is a magic spell by any measure. Apple uses the word "magical" to sell the iPad because they know it works, it appeals to us on that folkloric level.

It goes both ways, too. When I read SF, I am always delighted by the old, old magic in it. And the Singularity is such a glittering, magical thing. When I listen to discussions about the Singularity, when I read stories about it, I hear: *one day we will all wake up and turn into fairies. One day we'll all go to Fairyland together. White shores and beyond, a far green country under a swift sunrise.* I hear visions of a world whose technology accomplishes the exact actions that magic strove to: transmutation, transmigration, immortality, altering the body, the granting of wishes, the reading of minds. Something out of nothing, lead into gold. A world whose folk dwell in so much plenty and ease that they might as well be fairies, their countries Fairyland. I hear the same longing for these things that I hear when fantasy authors write about dragons and potions and magic from before the dawn of time.

That, and I hear the ghost of Cotton Mather.

Cotton Mather, for those of you who don't know, was a deeply unhappy man who lived in Boston in the late seventeenth century. I've heard him referred to as New England's first horror writer, and I think that's about right. He was a pastor and an author obsessed with the Rapture to a level that would surprise even Tim LaHaye and his ilk. Both he and his father predicted it would come just about every five years until he died - and in dying he was still waiting for it, bitterly, bitterly disappointed that it had not come in his lifetime. He sparked a Millennialist fever in New England and, rather more famously, was deeply involved in the Salem Witch Trials.

A year or two ago, I came across a dialogue between Cotton and his father Increase in which they discussed what parts of the body they would be able to shed after the Rapture, and which they would keep. The genitals could go no problem, of course, and the digestive tract, since eating would be unnecessary. Possibly the liver as well, since what toxins could survive in Paradise? The heart and the brain posed a problem, however - would we need those organs to think and feel or would we become pure persons, identities intact without bodies?

I said aloud: *What you mean is when you upload, Cotton, buddy. Will you need to maintain a connection to your physical body or will you be able to upload completely?*

The tone of the conversation was exactly the same as the one I hear now - it's not really a joke at all when we call it the Rapture of the Nerds. The same hatred of the body echoed in Cotton and Increase's urgent debate, the same longing to leave all the troublesome processes of physical existence behind, to enter a world where they and their particular abilities would make them saints and kings, and those who mocked them would be useless devils or worse. (Don't think this isn't the very urge behind planning for the zombie apocalypse.) The same assumption that in Paradise, they would be able to affect reality as one would in a VR world, that their highest and purest desires would become manifest. The same desire to witness the end of the world by whatever definition, the same desperation not to miss it, to be the generation that achieved ascension.

Not only New England's first horror writer, but her first science fiction writer.

And to me, it's all one. Not in a flippant way, but deep, primal, unifying. The herd-dog is an uplifted mind. The SuperLab has old, old bones. I do genuinely believe that stories save us. Over and over, narrative tells us how to get through and get beyond, how to be human and how to be inhuman, too, when it comes time to grow. We are, at our cores, narrative beings. And most especially, science fiction and fantasy save us. They tell us who we are, who we can be, who we want to be and who we don't, what we could be and what we can reject if we are strong enough. It says all these things more boldly and yet more secretly than mimetic fiction, which does not often try to speak to the dreams and terrors of a species on the verge.

Ask me about the future and I'll tell you a fairy tale. Ask me about the past and I'll tell you about uploading. We are always writing about ourselves - we can't help it. The difference between a post-human and a fairy, between a dragon and a lobster, is only in the name.

How SF Prepared Me for the Future

I was listening to the radio the other day, and they were very sternly reporting on drug violations at the Olympics, and how the Russian world-record holder in short-distance running might have to return her medal for using performance-enhancing drugs.

My reaction? *Go team cyborg!*

This is my reaction to a lot of things. As a child of science fiction, hungrily devouring every story about what humans *could be*, I don't worry too much about a lot of the things that seem to get the world all het up. I was prepared for the Internet long before it showed up in my dad's house because I read William Gibson and Vernor Vinge and I knew what to do with a Worldnet when I got one: jump into it with love, devotion, and both feet. And, you know, use it to watch porn.

SF raised me, and I think it did a damn fine job. It at least removed a lot of potential sources of anxiety.

I think all athletes should be able to take drugs if they want to, and also have cybernetic enhancements. They should be able to change and use their body however they like, to whatever extreme - let's mod this fucker and see what it can *really* do!

I don't worry too much about bio-proteins grown in vats. Yes, it will taste like crap. Everything in the future tastes like crap! It's how you know you're *in* the future! If it's not grey and amorphous and vaguely morally alarming, it doesn't belong in your face.

I don't worry about stem-cell research. Yes, the government will try to stop it. They will fail. Yes, we will end up a race of mutants who have forgotten what it's like to be human. It's gonna be *awesome*! I'm gonna get a tail, and regenerating limbs, and gills. And all kinds of vibrating attachments so I can finally obey my spam and *give her what she wants*. I can't wait!

I don't worry that machines will replace man - they totally will. I for one... you know the drill. We are going to be living down and dirty and close with garage-level AI and it is going to be so fabulous I can't even tell you. Yes, they will probably imprison us and use us for fuel/fodder/whatever. They'll get over it. Kids are like that. What did you do in the backyard when no one was looking when *you* were a kid? You just wait, we're gonna be playing doctor with the robots in no time.

I don't worry too much about the growing dystopian fascism, either. Yes, the government does listen to everything. Of course they do! I mean, come on. It's kind of funny. It's as if our government read all the dystopian SF *ever* and said to themselves: "These are *fantastic* ideas! Who can we get to implement these?"

But! *I've read the same books*. Therefore, I know that dystopia is survivable and temporary, especially if run by a repressive religious nut, that there is always an underground, that Shakespeare can save me, that the human soul is essentially untouchable, and that if you can say one thing for oppressive dystopias, it's that they usually have some pretty bitchin' drugs.

I don't worry about drugs. Hack your body, kids. Just learn to recognize malware.

I don't worry about global warming. Yes, we will probably be forced to live underground and slowly forget that there ever was a surface world. We will be nameless cogs in a post-industrial nightmare. But the point is I'm ready for that. I have an awesome dog, after all. And free love in the bowels of the earth will probably make up lack of vitamin D, and the architecture down there is worth the trip alone. We'll come out again, we always do.

Because really, what SF taught me was that *we will always survive*. There is nothing which is not survivable, nothing to which I, twenty-first-century human female, cannot adapt. There is nothing in which I cannot find beauty, joy, rapture. The world will always change. I will always change. *It's ok*.

Science fiction will save us.

Life on Earth

An Amateur's Guide

Tell Me a Story

American culture has had a long affair with eschatology. I am often struck by the fervor of those inclined to love the end of the world, those who prepare for both the zombies and the Rapture, the naked need just below the (often) belligerent surface.

I think about the same thing every time I watch football.

I think the urge behind the two, and many more things besides, is essentially the same. Because of course eschatology (fun with the end of the world) is fascinating and not unique to Christianity, but the utter conviction with which some portion of almost every generation since Christ himself said *Dude, be less harsh* has declared the end of the world to be well and truly nigh is astonishing. The eagerness to see the world burn - a sort of fascination with that fascination is a big part of what fuels the cultural interest in fundamentalism in general. But how different is that from geeks looking forward to the singularity with terrible enthusiasm, to the zombies devouring everyone and moaning for more, so ready to see this world pass away, for the veil to be lifted.

And all I can see is how desperately people long to be part of a *story*.

Not just a workaday story either. Something extraordinary, something with high drama and high stakes. Everyone wants it, even craves it. When parents tell stories to their kids, they so often begin: "Once there was a child just like you..." We all turn towards story like sunflowers. And sometimes those stories are full of elves, sometimes they are full of computers, and sometimes they are full of gods, and everything gets so blurry and confusing.

No one wants to be the quiet faithful waiting in relative peace and security for the Great Event - which will occur long after one's grandchildren are dead. That's not *fun*. And while rivers of fire and the moon as red as blood and famine and sackcloth being the new look for spring doesn't sound fun on the surface, it is deeply fun to know that your choices are being made on a universal, gorgeous stage where every step is either prophesied or utterly necessary for the correct dispensation of the world - to know you matter, to know you're real. No one wants to miss out. On the End Times, on the Singlarity. On Peak Oil, which I see certain folk talking about in the same eager terms, looking forward to it in some bizarre subconscious way, disappointed every day civilization does not fall. No one wants to be the generation that *just missed* being part of the greatest story ever told.

So people try to make the story happen now, so they can be a part of it. So it can be a story about them. So they can be Tribulation saints and road warriors and code ninjas. It's the same reason, I think, people get so into sports teams - you get to be part of their story, and there are colors to let you know who your enemies are, and your identity is theirs by this magical proxy, and you are personally invested in the very war-like actions of the team, the tribal activity that answers something very deep in us. Triumph and defeat - it elevates the every day to feel you are part of a greater story.

Don't think this isn't why *The Secret* and other self-help books are so popular - they tell a story wherein you, yes you, are a wizard of extraordinary power and strength who can literally shape the world around to your whim. That, of course, is usually the villain's part, but why dwell on that? What's a villain but a hero in black?

And of course, there are stories happening every day in the real world, birth and death and marriage and betrayal and love and all of it. But it's so much harder to feel those stories, to see the narrative shape of them. Would you rather have a pleasant life in the suburbs or an action packed thriller where you are persecuted, and there are explosions and gods and heroes and villains? We're trained to understand those stories, to think the decisions in them are easier and more obvious. That's why the Tea Partiers are so full of passion and fervor right now - they're part of a story, and they've convinced themselves that the story in their head is the same as the story in the world, and the choices are as easy as picking the side with the white hats. And no one thinks their hats could look black in the right light.

Ultimately, I look at passionate eschatologists and I see cosplayers at a con, dressed up in Biblical drag, wishing so hard that it was all happening just the way it does in their favorite books, quoting the best lines, acting out the most exciting parts, arguing over bits of trivia. I'm not belittling them - I don't look down on cosplayers and I don't sneer at conventioneers. It's an impulse, a terribly human one. And I see in both such desire for extraordinary experience, to stand at a precipice, the way heroes always have. I see the same impulse in the constant handwringing over the death of the American novel, which has been going on since Americans first started writing novels, and the death of traditional publishing - we all want to live at the tipping point, to preside over something amazing. And destruction is so much easier than creation. So much easier to position yourself at the end rather than in the eternal middle, keeping on trucking, doing the work.

We want it so badly. And who can blame us - we start reading and internalizing story, narrative, almost as soon as we can talk. We want everything to go that way, the way it does in stories, where the book, the movie, is always about the most exciting moment, where the protagonist is never one generation too early - and obviously *we* are protagonists. We must be. Aren't we alive, aren't we living in the best and worst of all possible worlds? If we weren't protagonists, we'd be bit players, offscreen, messengers, fools. Most of us, especially those in the West who had also taken in the narrative of manifest destiny with our mother's milk, would prefer to be protagonists. Would prefer to be part of something. In the Great Events, we rarely cast ourselves as part of the inevitable Mass of the Dead. We are rogues and saints and prophets. Because it's a better story. And if the end of the world came, if the resource apocalypse came, if the singularity came - at least we'd feel like we knew what to do, what our parts were. We'd feel like we'd been prepared on some level for the world to call on us that way. Then, we would know that paleolithic primate thrill of having survived something harrowing, having been marked as *special* by dint of survival, marked as *the fittest*, and for the privileged classes who go about praying for the end of all, that thrill, that sense of being vitally, intensely *real* is hard to come by.

But every day it doesn't happen, and the water bill has to be paid, and the rent still goes up, and no one has a flying car, and we can't even see the magic of our handheld, world-networked devices because if we were living in the future *it would be a better story*, and no one would feel lost the way we do, and no one would be confused as to where they stood, and no one would be unsatisfied, or afflicted with ennui, and everyone would be a hero.

And if we were the final generation, cradled in the hands of an angry God, no one could ever say we were ordinary.

O Human Child

I am something of a baby-magnet.

They come up to me, mostly little girls, in the cafes where I work and stand right next to me. Then they smile. And they stand there smiling, not asking for anything, just wanting to be there. It happens at least once a day. The other night we went out to dinner. We were sitting at our table talking about the movie we intended to see when a little boy bundled up for snow appeared, standing beside us, staring at me. Then he smiled.

I'm the oldest of five kids, I'm no stranger to little ones. I have no idea what it is they like about me - maybe it's the Disney Princess hair. Maybe it's that I am used to them, and so don't have the Childless Grown-Up Panic-Stiffening that a lot of people do when a wee one strolls up. Most adults find me brusque and standoffish - I've been told I have an aura that says: *don't touch me* no matter what my mouth says. But kids don't seem to see that aura *at all*. To them, my aura says: *I am full of secret and wonderful things that can be unlocked with a smile.*

I'd say the kids have it right, honestly.

They seem to me like little bear-cubs. Totally wild and unpredictable, small rogue AIs, in no way in control of their impulses, easily spooked, but terribly sweet at heart. Bad little fairies.

Which brings me to the story I wanted to tell. A couple I met at a convention had two beautiful daughters. The kind of kids you just know are totally loved: affectionate, outgoing, well-mannered sweethearts who say things far cleverer than their years with fair frequency.

The younger girl, I'd guess about three years old, was a particularly fey thing. She was more shy and reticent than her sister, spoke more quietly, and had a little cut on her cheek, which made her seem all the more ursine. But from the moment I met her, she wanted to talk and to touch the grown-ups around her. She put her head on my shoulder while we were all sitting in the lobby, played with my hair, poked and tickled my belly, bashfully pulled my midriff-baring shirt down since surely I was cold like that. In short, totally adorable and heart-melting.

And as we were saying our goodbyes, we all shared the last elevator of the con, and this girl looked up at me with enormous blue eyes and held out her little hand.

"I want to touch you again," she said.

"Ok, sweetie," I replied, and held her hand through 12 floors.

We hugged and waved and drove home, but that moment just completely arrested me. I've been thinking about it ever since.

I want to touch you again.

What an amazingly *clear* thing to say. What a nakedly *human* thing. I am terribly impressed with such a small child's ability to state so clearly what she wants - in my family the more common tactic was just to misbehave until someone starting paying attention to you. It's astonishing and a little scary to be able, fearlessly, unabashedly, to ask for human contact, monkey contact, little monkey to big monkey. I would never have been able to do that as a child. I was so afraid most of the time. I've heard people say I was not an affectionate kid, but it wasn't that, I just learned really early on that embraces were a scarce commodity, and one that could turn on you in a moment.

I don't think I am that plain-spoken and fearless an adult, really. I don't have that clarity.

The thing is, we all want to touch and be touched, and we forget how we once had no filters to that, no weird sexual nervousness or social anxiety. I think I probably still misbehave until someone starts paying attention to me and touching me - it's the tactic I learned very young, and its a credit to that girl's parents that she's learned other methods. And that's the funny thing - nothing ever really changes. The previous night the usual con butt-slapping and sexy dancing and casual physicality of big monkeys when they have had scotch occurred, and walking out of the hotel in the morning I thought: *god, wasn't that the same thing?* Bereft of that naked, bare ability to ask for simple contact without background radiation of adult weirdness, weren't we really just holding our arms out to each other and plaintively whispering: *I want to touch you again?*

I think it's the most human thing anyone has ever said to me. I was utterly slain by it.

And I think I should try to be that nakedly human. In my thirties, I should learn how to be more like a small bear and show my vulnerable belly instead of roaring and spilling honey everywhere. I think I should grow until I can say something like that, with that terrible, beautiful clarity. I don't think it's impossible. I don't think being a grown-up is an essentially damage-accruing activity. I think I can still be that real and alive and rooted in the world. I think I can be that clear, that bright, that clean, like glass.

So if a woman with very long hair turns to you someday and says she wants to touch you, know that she is trying hard to be very brave and very human, very exact and very naked.

And hold her hand.

That Ladder of Success is Looking Like a Chain

Sometime before Christmas, we went to an office party that happened to be held at the home of the parents of one of the other employees. It was a huge and beautiful Maine house, nestled at the fork of two burbling rivers, full of light and a huge kitchen and gleaming floors.

I've seen a lot of houses like this. They're usually owned by the parents of people I know.

I was born into a certain class and that class is middle. Meaning - there is some wealth, mostly on my father's side, and the wealth is mostly my grandfather's and mostly new, but not nearly enough for anyone to get any ideas about being oligarchs, though just enough to make folks apprehensive about backsliding. On my mother's side, you've got working class all the way, military and police and odd jobbers, and my mother who is awesome and tenacious and clawed her way into a PhD and a tenured department head position. Mix this and you get a middle that is middle enough that there were Expectations of Performance, but really, I didn't even live with my father's side of the family long enough to get the idea that living near water was a right, not a privilege, if you follow me.

And I look around at the other people I know who were born into that sort of milieu, and I look at our parents' houses. And they are so huge, and so beautiful, and so clean, and I feel like we don't even have a chance at that kind of life now.

Because if you talk to people who have those houses, you'll find that a large number of them got them quite some time ago for fairly cheap. I used to look at the mansions on the backshore of the island I live on and not comprehend how people could ever afford them. Until I started going to the knitting group that meets in them and found out that most of those families got their homes for less than $50,000, some less than $30,000, when no one cared about living on Peaks, and land and homes were cheap. My grandfather bought the land his huge house is on back when no one cared about living in Seattle, and built the house for what would be considered nothing these days.

If we want to ever buy a house that isn't literally coming apart on this island, it'll start out at $250k, and go up sharply from there. It's a distant dream. I mean, I guess this is what the first generation to not do as well as their parents looks like. As a household we make more than my father did at our age, but could never afford to buy the house he bought in his baby 30s. The narrative we know is *kids have it so easy these days*. But shit, it used to be so much easier back in the day! When factories *existed* in this country and unions would keep you employed all your life at a solid salary, when you stayed in one job and one city your whole life, when putting down roots was a viable option. Most people I know, even those born into the upper middle class, are just struggling to find *work*. They're struggling to make absurd rents and health insurance that will still probably leave them bankrupt if serious illness alights. They will never get that house. We actually make fairly decent money when both of us are working, and we'll never get that house.

And yet if you listen to the news, we're all just a bunch of lazy fucks for not living up to our parents' lifestyle. That was built on cheap and easy credit offered at rates that would make a girl weep these days.

And that doesn't even get into how fucking clean our parents (and especially grandparents) seem to be able to keep those homes, clean in a way I just can't even begin to comprehend, where there is no dust anywhere and everything shines and all the dishes are clean *at the same time*. It's like there was a secret knowledge of the ancients that got lost between generations. I'm not even sure it's just that one partner used to spend most of her time cleaning - because they obviously had kids and pets and kids and pets are expert mess-makers. My stepmother had four kids, and yet day to day her house was cleaner than mine has ever been. Like, I am not an idiot. I have an education. And yet that perfectly clean home I remember from my childhood might as well be the holy fucking grail for all the chance of my achieving it is anything like realistic.

There is this myth of upward mobility in American culture. Each child is supposed to bring their parents up. But I feel like our parents really got it all while the getting was good, and now the avenues for something so simple as buying a home that isn't in the middle of economically depressed nowhere and/or falling apart are so few and slim. You need windfalls to make that kind of thing happen. You need to be willing to live in northern Idaho - where of course there will not be any jobs to pay for that house, or that car, or that life.

I'm not trying to be a classist brat or complain because I don't have enough stuff, or that my privilege isn't pulling its weight. I'm actually very lucky, to have had success at a profession that is also much more difficult to break into and stay in than it once was, to be married to someone with a marketable skill. Neither of us are sick, knock on wood. Neither of us have felonies. We are highly educated and we work hard. We benefit from the feminist movement, both of us, and we are that fabled DINK - Double Income, No Kids. And yet. All that work and luck and my mother's ambition in my heart doesn't buy what it bought back then - and it's not like the 70s and 80s were an awesome time of awesome. But there were expectations then that are just so many genie dreams now. But expectations have a horrible kind of sticking power. I think of how my family lives and I think I will never be able to live that way, with kids or without. And on top of that my generation still gets to hear from these very people who were perhaps the luckiest generation in the history of the world how lazy and spoiled we are, how we don't even know hardship, and we just smile and say nothing, because what can you say? The awful secret of the American myth of that ladder of success is that many rungs are missing, and William Gates III was never your average college dropout, and even startups these days come from people who have family money, family histories, pedigrees and legacy seats at Ivy Leagues. It all calcifies, and the gap grows, and your parents ask you when you're going to buy that house, have those kids, get that shitty old car replaced, support them in their old age, come on, chop chop! They did it when they were your age, what's the problem?

It's a life that was sold to us by advertising and was accessible to even just one generation back, but is largely unavailable to their children. Even the chance at it is so incredibly difficult to grasp. That life which was *not even considered to be particularly well off* 30 years ago, simply comfortable and middling, now looks like impossible riches. A house at the meeting point of two rivers, full of light, as clean as a perfect credit report.

Team Fat Buddha

The following is very bad Buddhism. I am not a Buddhist, but I am into that whole knowledge thing and I know it's bad Buddhism and that a) the Buddhas in question are not called that and b) the whole point of the two Buddha weight-classes is to indicate different phases of his life and point out that the middle road is best. This is a metaphor, it is not a religious koan. Also, this has nothing to do with literal skinniness or fatness. In our house, we run the gamut of body types.

The point is, I'm about to repeat a conversation that occurred while we'd all had quite a bit of vodka and roast meat and pie, and therefore it is not a logically thought out philosophy, it's a fireside common room talk.

We began discussing the lifestyles of the geek and famous - high-end programmers, geniuses at the top of their game. Generally speaking, they're ascetic about programming. They don't seem to read much fiction or dick around with knitting and Netflix instant, they read programming books and have apartments that would make monk's cells look lavish and concentrate solely on programming with possibly a little gaming thrown in, though always with an eye to how to code a game themselves. And that's part of why they're so good at it. My husband, a programmer himself, said he didn't know any high level programmers who did not basically come home from work and program more, who did not devote everything to it. I objected to his use of the word ascetic, because it's a positive word to me, indicating the rejection of one kind of life for a better one. Medievalist girl here, I view asceticism as a good thing, but also an intentional thing - you're not ascetic if you don't live the way you do intentionally, so as to be more holy/awesome. If you just forget to eat, you're not fasting, you know?

So not ascetic. Perhaps, then, it's more accurate to say they're Skinny Buddhas. We all have Buddha nature, and these are people who care so much about their one devotion that the rest sort of falls away, whether they mean it to or not.

I am a Gigantic Fat Buddha, then.

Not being a Skinny Buddha comes factory direct with a certain amount of guilt. It's hard not to feel that you'll never be at the top of your field if you don't sacrifice everything else, and yet some of us can't bring ourselves to sacrifice everything else. Because we can't decide which to be, we always feel guilt for not being the other. Fat Buddhas are people who just want everything, who have lots of hobbies and obsessions and interests, even if that means they don't concentrate enough to be a high-functioning perfection machine when it comes to any of them. People who have jobs but find as much or more fulfillment in being foodies and knitters and gamers and social hubs and bloggers and beermakers and glassblowers and decorators and travelers. One is not superior to the other. They're just different ways of interacting with the world. Devoting everything to the pursuit of a goal until you are glowing with ability and achievement, but possibly you live in a grey apartment with nothing on the walls and eat mac and cheese every night, but that's ok because of how amazing you are at your profession.

Or you see your friends most nights and make your own jam/wine/clothes/pastry and watch a lot of stupid movies and play Rock Band all the time and maybe you're not as far along as you'd like to be, maybe you're not at the top of your game or making the kind of money you want to but it's ok because of all the other stuff you do. Stuff that might seem trivial and silly to a lot of people, but that make you happy, make you feel like you're being fed. Maybe you collect books and games and even if you never get to play them all or read them all, it's still a dragon hoard and you sit on it and feel full and fat and sly.

It's really pretty hard to do both, because time is finite. Once you're past a certain age, you have to make choices about how you spend your hours, and re-watching *The X-Files* is maybe not as important as learning Ruby.

Or maybe it is.

Maybe stories and shows and ceramics and D&D are important to you, like they are to me. It's pretty hard - though not impossible - to have a healthy personal life and lots of hobbies and be extraordinary at your job. Something often gives. I did point out that many Skinny Buddhas have children, who take up much more time than any hobby, and fill a lot of those empty spaces in life. And of course, people can get totally Skinny Buddha *about* their kids, and practice the yoga of raising them with hardcore focus and sacrifice.

Being a Fat Buddha is important to me. But it's not easy, it's not a default. I have to work at it. I have a strong instinct toward Skinniness, toward driving myself so hard that the rest of my life withers up and keels over. But I want to experience as much as I can while I'm here. So I work out my Fat Buddha Belly. I watch a lot of movies and I knit constantly and I read - even books that aren't any good - and I cook and I still want to do more. Still, it's pretty easy to slip into total focus on my job, and because my job happens to be manufacturing entertainment, it encompasses a lot of what I talk about, too. People are interested in it, and want to hear about publishing, when what I do for a living comes up. And obviously I've spent a lot of time on it, more than anything else. A few years ago, I felt way too Skinny Buddha about it and knew I needed hobbies that didn't involve staring at a computer screen. It took effort to find some, to get good at them, and I'm a happier person now.

Though I said this was not about actual weight, I did muse that I had come to the realization lately that I could never be trusted not to eat delicious food, and so clearly needed to just exercise a lot, so that I could keep eating home-made fabulousness. Because I like all the little bits of the world that are connected to the body, to physical experience, to all the things that are not work - though I love my work, and it is good work and there's nothing else I really want to do. But if I do nothing else I go crazy, and it's a bit different for writers anyway, because if all you do is write, then your writing sucks because it has nothing else to draw on but itself, and all your protagonists are suddenly writers and the meta, it folds in on itself and that's how black holes are created.

But it's hard to escape the niggling feeling that the Skinny Buddha is the *right path*. The nobler path. Certainly the path to greater pride and status and salary. And maybe it is, though I think there's no better or worse, just different. I think that life is more than a job - and maybe that means I'll never be the very best at my job. I like being a Fat Buddha. Though I have to remind myself sometimes, to stretch out on the porch and enjoy the world, the body, and not kill myself with work until my soul is living on one grain of rice a day. My work takes up a lot of psychic room, but if I get too Skinny, I'm miserable. However, people's souls vary, and some are very fed by the practice of their work. Wherever you find fulfillment, there you are.

Rules for Anchorites

I have this obsession. It's been going on for awhile - since early graduate school, when instead of taking the easy route and getting the damn English Literature degree, my brain took a hard left at Medieval Studies. So it's been about six years now (which seems obscene! - it was yesterday I was that dewy just-married thing poking about in Old French books and cuddling up to a life of compromise and loneliness). It's an obsession that fueled the title of this blog, the icon to your left, and is but one of the reasons I own a pair of manacles.

I'm talking about anchorites, baby. Nuns. *Super*nuns.

People tend to get these perplexed looks on their faces when I light up and tell them I think of myself as a nun. I get so excited I can hardly explain it, and that seems strange of course, after all, I'm neither Catholic nor celibate, with no intention of becoming either. But it's like explaining to someone how you know what your totem is - impossible, but necessary for the understand of this driven, jittery girl. Allow me to explain.

An anchorite (or anchoress, take your pick - I prefer the non-gendered term) is a nun, but not really. A nun becomes a bride of Christ; she is married to God in her initiatory ritual, and lives her life in a commune, a cloister, intimately connected to her sisters and the world, for whom she works and toils.

And anchorite is straight up punk rock. Her initiatory ritual is a funeral. She dies to the world. She is closed up, alone, in a small cell attached to a church, called an anchorhold. Often she is initially buried there, and exhorted each day to dig up the soil of her grave with her fingernails. Sometimes she is manacled, bound to her duty. A priest tends to her, but more often, the folk of the village come to her, bringing bread, milk, honey, beer, fish, listening to her wisdom. She meditates, she fasts, she flagellates, she spends her life in contemplation and deprivation, and often, as in the case of Julian of Norwich, writing books. She is directly connected to God - her spirit goes into the ether, and brings back visions to her village. She is an oracle, an academic, a hermit in the midst of life.

Except there's this little document called *Ancrene Wisse. Rules for Anchorites.* On the theory that there wouldn't be rules about things that people weren't doing, the lives of anchorites seem to have been not entirely hair shirts and flagellation. You may not have overnight male guests (so they should definitely leave before midnight), large banquets, more than two handmaidens. It's not all merriness - there is a lot of talk about rotting in one's cell and how one should "love your windows as little as you can" and never let a man touch you through the window *unless he can provide excellent reason he should be allowed to.* One must also pray less in order to read more, for "reading is good prayer." *The Song of Solomon* is used to illustrate how Christ feels about anchorites, and we all know how that little ditty goes.

The accompanying document to *Ancrene Wisse* is *Hali Meidhad, A Letter to Maidens*, which explains to three young girls that life in the medieval world plainly sucks, and to be married to a man who will make you clean and cook for him, fuck you until you bleed with no care for whether you enjoy it, only to die in childbirth, is pretty much a drag. Being an anchorite, on the other hand, is awesome. It was *freedom*. It was surcease.

I'm fascinated, always and utterly, by the idea of such a woman. Removed from the world yet deeply in it, privy to all the secrets of her town, cared for by folk while she reads and writes, while she watches wheels of fire spinning in the heavens. To be chained, to be disciplined to a lifelong task, to be a wild thing clapped up in darkness for *such* a purpose. You can see why this might appeal to someone like me. It brings strange tears to my eyes to read *Ancrene Wisse*, which is separated into the Inner Rule and the Outer Rule for governing one's life, and is obsessed with animal symbolism and endless classification, as I am, as I am.

And there were many of them, a network of women in holes, a network of light across wild fields and dark barns, women in ecstatic activity, touching the edges of the world.

Secretly, though I do not believe in a Christian God, this is what I want to be. I want to be a cyber-anchorite, chained to her computer, which is the church of the modern world, lifting her pelican-heart to heaven and bringing down such mad, beautiful, impossible books as live among the clouds. Manacled hands on a keyboard of light. A movable anchorhold, an *izbushka*. Tended to by a stern priestly-wicked thing who loves and fears and blesses. Receiving all who need her, trading words for bread. Conscious of death, racing against it. Closed up safe in her own little house, just big enough to contain her. I want, silly as it sounds, to sit at the edge of the Internet, which is my village, and seethe as mad-women do, take a man's name, shed my clothes and utter terrible, marvelous verses. To be so full of *purpose* that I shine. I am at my best when I am an ancho-rite. I am at my worst when I have forgotten how to go to ground.

And to put out my hand through my beloved window, from time to time, to clasp another's skin and kiss their fingers.

> "The wilderness is the solitary life of the anchoress's dwelling, for just as in the wilderness there are all the wild beasts, and they will not endure men coming near but flee when they hear them, so should anchorites, above all other women, be wild in this way..."
>
> —Ancrene Wisse

The Single Male Programmer Type Apartment

You guys, we need to talk.

Believe me: what I am about to say, I say out of love, a kind of all-encompassing, gentle, Kwan-Yin-type of love, out of wanting the best for you, wanting you to succeed in life. I'm not trying to be condescending, but when I see a problem played out over and over again, I feel compelled to try to help, I feel like I have a piece of information you don't, and I'm not a selfish girl; I want to share.

I'm talking to all my single male friends, especially if you are single, male, in your late twenties or early thirties, and a programmer, as that seems to be the direst demographic, the one most in need of a buxom, non-threatening, Kwan-Yin-type of love-intervention.

Please do not assume this is about you personally: every example I am about to give I have personally witnessed over a wide variety of circumstances and years. It's been bugging me forever, and I can no longer just stand by and do nothing.

So, you know, um... huddle up.

It's about your apartments.

Most of the single men I know want to have sex. I feel I have worded that as generally as I possibly can. Most of you would like to get laid sometime in this decade, by a real live human, no less. And you're hamstringing yourselves, and you don't even know it.

If you go on a date with a girl - and I'm gonna be heteronormative here, in part because it's not as much of an issue with young single gay men or young single women, and in part because I am rarely asked back to young single gay men's apartments at night. If you go on a date with a girl - a date *you both know* is a date, with a clear romantic goal - with a girl and she agrees to come back to your apartment, it's pretty safe to say that she has at least thought about some sort of sexual contact with you and decided that it's not a completely revolting concept. *That does not mean you deserve or have a right to sex if she does agree to go back to your place.* But it means you're doing well enough - congratulations! - that she has decided that not only are you not a horrendous, asexual gaptoothed troll, but someone with whom she feels safe enough to be alone. That ain't nothing, kids.

But this is a delicate moment for you, Single Male Programmer Type! It could turn into something wonderful, if you handle it right. And yet, so many of you stab yourselves in the head long before she can kindly turn you down and send you into a downward self-esteem spiral for days.

Imagine: a girl decides that this boy seems nice and funny and he definitely won't accost her, and maybe, just maybe... so she goes back to your apartment with you. And what does she see?

A lonely futon, a computer, clothes on the floor, empty walls, a console system with cords tangled all over the floor, a forlorn Settlers of Catan box sitting on an otherwise empty bookshelf. A bathroom covered in little bits of hair left behind by an electric shaver, an unscrubbed bathtub, and no towel to dry her hands on. Oh god, it's so *sad*. It's like he's not even alive, just treading water until...what? His mother visits? A girl shows up who looks a lot like his mother? Is Settlers of Catan the sole thing he cares enough about to own and display? *Settlers* of fucking *Catan*?

I'm not saying she's going to run screaming. Probably. But if this sounds like your apartment? Your "game" is missing some vital pieces. You've undone all the work you did being charming and funny over dinner in one fell swoop, the minute you open your apartment door. If you were *very* charming and funny, the attack might not be fatal (think of it like a points system: you have just so many charisma points, and your +6 Apartment of Anti-Sex Funk isn't doing you any favors), but that's a big chance to take. It's like Mousetrap - no matter how cool the game is when you play it, the fact is that once you've lost the plastic diver-man, you're not going to be playing any time soon, and maybe never again.

These apartments break my heart. It's not about materialism - I don't care where the apartment is or what it says about your financial situation. I care about what it says about your soul. There is no reason, by your late twenties, you should be living like a dorm-room prisoner. You are a grown fucking man. It's not some kind of noble rejection of the material world to live in a cell with no indication of your personality or implication that you've lived there for longer than five minutes, or plan to be living there for another five. Your apartment speaks volumes about you, whether you like it or not, so stop hollering: *I'm just waiting around for a woman to teach me hot to live! That's hot, right? Right?*

No, it's not. We do not want to be your mothers, to pick up after you and teach you how to make things pretty, or even just other-than-empty. It is not our jobs, and one of the sexiest things in the world is a guy who doesn't need to be taught. The two guys who were most successful with women in my college got together, rented an apartment, talked to all of their friends about what looks nice, and decorated their place *impeccably*. It was like a freaking conveyor belt of girls going in and out of that house. Girls looked around and thought: *fucking in here is going to* awesome.

Because when a girl thinks about a hot one-night stand, she doesn't fantasize about clearing your socks off the bed before slapping your ass and calling you pony-boy. She doesn't get off to thinking about staring at your depressing, empty gray walls while you sweat on top of her to the dulcet tones of Rush. It's not hot, it's just sad, and sad is the *worst*. After college, girls aren't looking to randomly fuck in some dingy-ass sad-sack flat and slink home because it smells too bad to stay over and the bathroom makes her die a little inside. You have got to do better than this, guys. I see it way too much, and the *sameness* of these pitiful dwellings kind of scares me. How do you do it? Is there a conference every year about how to furnish your apartment to repel all women?

Living well does not have to be gendered. Every guy I've ever lived with has been substantially happier living with me than alone, because I make a pretty house that is comfortable and sexy, and they don't know how to do that on their own. Which sucks, because it means all the work falls in my lap. But it doesn't have to be so.

So let's keep in mind a few simple rules, SMPTs.

1. Your apartment is a metaphor for your sexual style.

I'm reasonably sure that if a guy can't even manage to put up a comic strip or two on his walls and spends his days staring at the cottage-cheese ceiling surrounded by old tube socks, I'm not going to have some kind of *amazing sexual dynamo* on my hands once he gets his clothes off. It's going to be vaguely sad and kind of uncomfortable, and afterward I'm going to wish I hadn't and need to wash my hands. Outward environment reflects inner states, and guys: empty is not hot.

I'm not saying you have to be an interior design mastermind, but get some goddamn pictures up on your walls (framed - it's easy and cheap and makes things look *intentional*), pick up the crap off the floor (especially if you know there's a good chance you'll have a girl at your house that night - who brings a girl home knowing there's old coffee filters and random pants lying about? What kind of romantic strategy is this?), get a nice bedspread in a neutral color if you can't get the whole color wheel thing down, organize your good quality books. (Commensurate with the kind of girl you want to attract - like geek girls? Make sure your SF novels are spine-out. It's always nice to have a few female writers in there. Like athletes? Make sure your workout books are nicely organized. I'm not saying buy books to impress, but if you have them, showcase them - for most thinking girls, books are like peacock feathers. They're a mating display.)

Buy all your towels in the same (dark) color - that way you don't have to worry about them matching anything, and they don't stain as easily. Being able to make a mean cup of coffee or tea for a girl is a vital survival trait. The more you can show a girl that you would be a net positive in her world, the hotter you become. Showing her that you were a complete person before she came along is nothing but glorious, and makes you look smooth and happy - whether you're looking for a girlfriend or a one-night stand. It is fully 300% hotter to fuck a guy in a beautiful, urbane apartment and never see him again than to do it in a dreary post-collegiate hovel.

2. The bathroom is a metaphor for your penis.

I avoid going into guys' bathrooms. It's usually a horrorshow. I want to believe they're nice guys, and that is easier if I don't see their bathrooms.

The fact is, if you can't practice basic personal hygiene in your living space, I will have no expectation that you can practice it with your person. If there are shaving bits and clumps of hair all over the bathroom, a toilet that looks like it's never been cleaned, and a moldy shower curtain, it is highly unlikely that once your jeans have leapt excitedly onto your filthy floor, you will reveal a beautiful, clean, muck-free cock with well-trimmed hair and a friendly countenance. Not impossible, but unlikely.

Clean. the fucking. bathroom.

If you know you're having a girl over, take an hour to give a crap how your place is going to look to her. Run a sponge over the surfaces, dump some CLR into the toilet, wait 30 seconds and flush, and throw a .59 air freshener in there. Total investment: 15 minutes. Value of a girl not thinking you are a barely-domesticated breed of exotic pig: priceless.

Level Two activities include a mat on the floor, an opaque shower curtain free of mold around the edges, even a picture or two on the walls of the bathroom (I fully admit the pictures thing matters to me personally more than most: I find completely empty walls a shuddersome situation). Level Three, only for the advanced, includes all of the above plus a few items that indicate you don't think taking care of your body is "girly." Lotion, a nice shampoo (especially if these things are visible in your normal bathroom set up), even a dedicated face-wash, not just, you know, a sticky lump of old Dial. My ex-husband let his feet get so dry they cracked to the muscle rather than use "girly" lotions. This, my friends, is very diverse idiocy.

I don't want this to be gendered. I really don't. But I have never once seen a single woman's apartment look like this. Guys, we're living in the twenty-first century. You do not have to live in your high school bedroom until you're 35 and some girl heaves a sigh and does it for you. I cannot express how much that sucks, and how much it makes you look like an unnecessary second job for an already busy, productive girl. You gotta ante-up.

Want girls? Making yourself attractive, inside and out, is a good start. It doesn't take the biggest penis, the best job, the best body. It just takes a little thought about what the world you construct for yourself says about you.

And clean the fucking bathroom.

3. It doesn't have to be perfect, it just has to look like you're not planning to kill yourself.

People planning suicide often give away all their belongings. Every time I walk into an SMPT's apartment, I worry for them. This is not the path to a rich, sensual life full of willing women, fabulous dinners, and evenings you'll tell friends about years down the line. It's a path to a life that looks a lot like that apartment. Look around: are you satisfied with that?

It's a vicious circle: your apartment looks like Lonely Larry's Despair Emporium, so every time a girl looks at it, a slow, cold wind blows through her mind - she might sleep with you anyway, but the key word there is *anyway*. And so you're lonely, and so your apartment looks like an advertisement for a suicide hotline. Inner and outer are related, they cannot help but be.

I know a lot of men think they shouldn't have to do anything to get sex, especially geeks. Women should accept you as you are, right? You were rejected in school, so you arrange your life to avoid rejection as an adult. And women, no matter how personally revolting they find you, should see through, magically, to the gooey core of sweet, genteel adorableness inside. Of course, you don't go on dates naked or bite your toenails at the table, so you are willing to change a little to impress. The question is how much.

Well, give her a hand, why don't you? Let your apartment say something about that core of sweetness. That's what pictures on the walls and pillows on the couch are: outward expressions of internal passions. I have antique calligraphy and paintings of sphinxes on my walls - they indicate things about me, what I love, what I have experienced, they start conversations, they are a museum of me.

Do you want your museum to consist of a bucket and a "Please Excuse Our Mess" sign?

Things do not have to match perfectly, your curtains don't need to pick up the violet in your napkins or any of that nonsense. Shop at Wal-Mart, I don't give a shit. Hardly anything really has to match these days, but if you want a quick studio-apartment color primer: buy a bedspread, doesn't matter what color, but something at least vaguely not neon. Pick other decor based around that color. Make sure all your particle board is the same finish. It'll look put together and nice, no matter what that color is. You may have to fake caring about this shit for awhile, but after awhile you'll notice: *you feel better when you operate from a place of power*, and your apartment can be a place like that.

Bruce Wayne does not live in an apartment with a broken futon and a dusty TV, guys. None of the greats do. This is your lair. Treat it with respect.

And keep it clean. That's all. You will get laid more, because you will appear to be a real, interesting human that dwells in the sensual world, lives his life beautifully, and thinks about things other than code and D&D. How hot is that? *Very*.

I feel so strongly about this. I've seen too many friends go 'to the Dark Side, and then they complain to me that they haven't had a girlfriend in two years. And I think: *Jesus, I wouldn't fuck you in this Patented Programmer Pen either.* And I want better for the boys in my life. I want you to allow yourself to feel attractive, no matter what twenty or thirty years of living in our toxic culture that says men are not beautiful, they shouldn't care about how anything looks, they are incapable of a whole sphere of living. It just isn't so. I want women to swoon for you, guys, and for you to feel strong and lovely and powerful and competent. As such, this has been a public service announcement, towards helping you towards a better life.

The More You Know.

A Generation of Leaves

> *A generation of men is like a generation of leaves;*
> *the wind scatters some leaves upon the ground,*
> *while others the burgeoning wood brings forth -*
> *and the season of spring comes on.*
>
> —Homer, *The Iliad*

What is my generation? Am I X or Y this week? Or some other geometric determination of my identity - Z or X2 or Triangle ABD, perhaps? In what sleek, A-line, postmodern fashion can I declare myself disaffected, disconnected, and dismissed? Is there a T-shirt I can buy? A brand of eyeliner named for my particular age group - Carter Kid Charcoal? Chernobyl Chartreuse? Is there a lapel pin I can wear which will mark me as one of the inner demographic circle? What defines my generation is the extent to which I can say I am not a part of it, I am above it, or better still, below it - sub-cultural, subverting the dominant paradigm, subtracted from the whole. Yet to be subducted this way, driven under the tectonic action of *kultur* to the point that I phrasify in German rather than downhome, patriotic English, is to be quintessentially part of my generation, a generation of outsiders, glorifying the edge because we cannot bear to be part of the center.

I was born in 1979, the year the reactor at Three-Mile Island foreshadowed Chernobyl, the year the Soviets invaded Afghanistan, the year the Seattle Supersonics won the championship. One year before Lennon was shot, before Reagan was elected, seven years before the Challenger explosion, twelve years before the fall of the USSR. And generational discussions usually boil down to this - locating my place in the world via listing of major events communally remembered. Oh, yes, we all love the 80s, don't we? Pong and Rubix Cubes and Hungry Hungry Hippos. It's so much easier to line up artifacts from all our childhoods than to recall a six-year-old girl cowering in her room with a World Book encyclopedia open to H for *Hiroshima*, M for *Mutually Assured Destruction*, N for *Nuclear Winter* and a neat little diagram of a bomb, terrified that tomorrow or the next day, the world would end. Yet that always seemed to me to be the thick red line that divided my generation from the one that came behind us - we remember, I remember, when Russia was a swear word, when I prayed that we would be at the center of the blast, so that my little brothers wouldn't have to suffer.

Conventional wisdom would have me call myself Generation X - 1960-1981. But it's not so - a 21 year old can have a child, and a person twenty years older than I simply does not have the same cultural backround, the same memories, the same generational self. Yet I can't full call myself a Millennial, either. I am part of a cadre of something different, something less disaffected, but more earnest. Something that falls between.

It seems likely that we will now be remembered as the 9/11 generation. This is our cataclysm, our "where were you when." It is, as we are told by every news channel, the communal event which will color the rest of our lives - though it seems to paint only in shades of fear and xenophobia.

But we have always lived in fear. My generation feared the Soviet menace and nuclear annihilation with the pure terror that only children can summon up. We were helpless - we were just kids. We did not experience it the way the adult world did, even the nascent adults who came of age during those days. We were not a part of the world, we only watched it. We could receive the mandate to hate communism, but to us, there were no mediating details. Lenin meant nothing; *glasnost* was no more a word we could define than Jabberwock. The command was as simple and unadulterated as a stop sign: red means danger. We experienced that world without filter, and without attachment. The benchmarks that the then-unnamed Generation X clung to were dazzling and out of reach for us. We watched Ferris Bueller and wanted to be that assured and careless, that capable of escape. We watched Molly Ringwold and thought we would never grow up to be that beautiful; we listened to Madonna with the blissful non-comprehension of little Dalai Lamas. We just wanted to be old enough to save ourselves.

Look at us now in our slinky, low-slung clothes and see boys and girls who never dreamed of being astronauts because we watched Christa McAuliffe detonate into the sky over our orange juice and eggs. Look at us and see boys and girls who were raised to be afraid, who were raised to distrust, who were painstakingly taught that nothing ever lasts. If there were a textbook on how to rear a nihilist, it could not have delineated a bleaker *paideia* than ours.

It was not MTV that deadened us. It was the repetition, the numb recitation of events with no more creativity than kindergarten paint-by-numbers, reproduced time after time by clumsy and untrained hands. Shall we color in the borders of Iraq or Panama, Islamic minarets or the spires of the Kremlin? From the day we were born, we were told to fear everything around us, to look in the corners and shadows for spies, for Vandals out to sack the beloved Republic. 9/11 is nothing more than a Renaissance for us, a return to old familiar ways of understanding, a return to ducking and covering under our wooden desks for protection. It is a communal event, but for us it does not mark the beginning of a new world order, but a revival of the old one.

Look at us. We are not Lost, we are not the Greatest, we are not Boomers, we are not X, we are not Y. We are not Pepsi's generation, we are not Microsoft's. We fall between the cracks of the brand-naming of age groups. If any symbol must be applied to us, we would prefer it be no symbol at all: ~~Generation~~. For we are not a generation; we are leaves scattered on the ground. We are defined by our separateness. We take a long step back, my generation and I, and ask not to be a part of the machine that so loves to label and collate itself.

Look at us; look at the twenty-somethings with hands shoved into our pockets, grunting noncommittally at a world we still cannot affect. We are grown up, we have come of age, and nothing has changed. We do not make eye contact; we do not form ties that bind. We are overeducated, we are overburdened, we are overdosed. We are incapable of refraining from living as though there is no tomorrow, because part of us never believed we would make it this far. We are not shocked, we are never appalled. We believed as many as six impossible disasters before breakfast - what is another, and another, and another? We pride ourselves on our disillusion because we own nothing else we have earned so completely. We navel-gaze because our navels have never shown us horrors, and we mock everything with sardonic gesticulations practiced in front of the mirror each evening. We stand apart, because apart is all we know, all we trust. If we stand apart, we cannot be implicated, we cannot be hunted, we cannot be found. We are a generation that refuses to define ourselves. We do not want to commit to the system of definition - we are still six, still huddled behind the bedposts reading about Ragnarok in an encyclopedia.

It walks like apathy, but it doesn't wear the right clothes. It is knowledge, and it is fear. We are still certain we are never going to grow up, not because we are Lost Children in Neverland, but because Neverland has gone up in a cloud of smoke and fire, and the fallout is still floating down from the sky.

A Parliament of Valentines

I have never understood the desire to stomp all over Valentine's Day and snuff it out. Every year it's a litany of: "This is a fake Hallmark holiday and no one should celebrate it!" and "I hate this day, who's with me?" and my personal favorite guilt trip: "If you *really* loved your partner, you'd treat them specially every day."

I don't get it. I don't understand the fervor to destroy a holiday. To force others to see it through the same black glasses. To shame anyone who celebrates the 14th with anything other than bile, vitriol, and the occasional superior sneer.

I know that most of us were shunned on Valentine's Day in school. Believe me, my little cubby was empty, just like yours, and I yearned for a construction paper heart from boy after boy - and never got them. I understand that there is a history of trauma, and the standard geek reaction to past trauma is to organize the world so that there is no chance of that trauma re-occurring. Thus, Valentine's Day must be killed.

But here's the thing. This world is a beautiful place, but it is also often dark, and cold, and unfeeling, and life slips by, not because it is short, but because it is so difficult to hold onto. Holidays, rituals, *these things demarcate the time*. They remind us of the sharpness of pleasure and the nearness of death. They tell us when the sun leaves, and when it comes back. They tell us to dance and they tell us to sleep. They tell us who we are, who we have been since we lived on the savannah and hoped to taste cheetah before we died. I know we're all punk rock rebels, but the paleolithic joy of fucking in the fields and dancing around a fire doesn't go away just because certain of us would like to think we're beyond that. This world needs *more* holidays, not less. More ritual, the gorgeous, flexible, non-dogmatic kind that isn't about religion but about ecstasy in the sheer *humanness* of our bodies and souls. More chances to reach out, to sing, to love, to bedeck ourselves in ritual colors and become splendid as the year turns around.

And no, I'm sorry. It doesn't work to say "make every day special." First of all, most of you know damn well that you don't shower your partner with gifts and adoration and that most precious of things: dedicated, mindful *time* every day of the year. Even the best relationship is not a 24/7 orgiastic festival of plenty and perfect moments. No human can sustain it. If every day is special, none of them are. If every day is special, specialness becomes monotony. What makes days special is the time between, the anticipation of a the day, the planning, the surprises, coming together, cooking, playing, reveling in sheer *time*, watching the dedicated colors and rituals that wire our brain for pleasure spring up in the world to remind us that we live in it. The entire purpose of holidays

228

is that they are a kind of otherworld we step into, full of special symbols, that informs and shapes everyday life - and some of life, no matter how some bloggers would like to deny it in their Grinchitude, is always everyday.

We celebrate the harvest. We celebrate the spring. We celebrate birthdays and death-days and the beginning of the year and the end of the year. We celebrate our parents and labor and Presidents. What in the world is so terribly wrong with celebrating love? I know not all of us have partners, but it is a rare soul who is without love of any kind. What kind of shrunken, sour heart does it take to insist that everyone else stop delighting in ritual and love? So few of us post about the magic of holidays - I think they're ashamed to. It's not cool to take unabashed pleasure in the silly and the soft-hearted.

As for the commercialism of it - well. It is commercial. So is every holiday, yet somehow we don't stomp all over Easter the way we tar and feather Valentine's Day. Valentine's Day is no more a fake holiday than any other. If I hear someone call it a Hallmark holiday, I'm actually going to scream. I'm only going to say this once. Valentine's Day, boys and girls, entered the Western mind in Chaucer's *Parlement of Foules*, fully-realized as a day to celebrate love via an obscure saint, with red hearts and everything. Yes, celebrated in an allegorical bird-nation, but guess what? *That makes it even more awesome.* I will take a holiday my buddy Geoff invented over almost any other. If I had my way, we'd start exchanging bird-themed gifts and ditch Cupid.

This is a *great* holiday. It's pure physical, sensual pleasure, divorced from any dogma at this point. Saint whatever. Pass the sex and food.

And as a medieval holiday, it has quite a long pedigree, thank you very much, even if you don't count in the Lupercalia (which you really shouldn't, unless wolf skins play a large part in your personal celebrations. If so, more power to you). The fact is, some human made up *every single holiday there is*. They're *all* fake. No one is more real or authentic than any other. At least this one was invented by a broke poet instead of a bunch of sex-starved priests. We live in a postmodern world - everything is what we make it. If Hallmark wants to force mainstream kids to buy jewelry they can't afford, they're more than welcome. I don't have to care about that, or take part in it. But I also don't have to get up on a soapbox and crush their joy in it. I know better. I know this day is an act of literature made flesh. But their world is not less valid for being Geoff-less.

And more than Geoff - think about it for a second. In the midst of winter, we are encouraged to come together and have sex (let's not be coy.) To escape the snow and ice in each others' bodies. The colors are red and rose and white - the colors of fire in the winter, of blood, of survival even in the barren times. We exchange *hearts*, the very vital core of our bodies. It is the last holiday before spring, to remind us that the fertile world will come again, with flowers and sweetness and love. Even surrounded by death, by blood on the snow, be it St.

Valentine's blood or your own, life will win out. The traditional food is chocolate - which can be preserved through the winter and does not rot, full of sugar and fat which keep our bodies going through lean times. This holiday is as old as time: *o world, even in the freezing storm, come together, make love, make children, feast, smile, and know the sun is coming soon.*

Seriously, you have to stop trying to take that away. If you remove ritual from the world, you leave it greyer, and sadder, and all you have in its place is the triumph of having ruined something another person loved, which is a shallow and bitter triumph indeed. Get down off the soapbox, have a little chocolate, look out at the melting snow, and say something kind to someone you love. To be human is to take part in ritual, to demarcate the time with feasting and song and vestments and ecstasy. Life slips by, so very fast. Spend it in the practice of joy, not the destruction of it.

Happy Valentine's Day. Geoff bless us. Every one.

The Story

I am going to tell you about something secret.

When I was in fifth grade, I had a teacher named Mr. Danielson. He was a known trickster-imp among the teachers in my school. The kids with behavioral problems didn't often end up in his classes because they wouldn't have been helped by his style, which was to basically let us run wild, while he guided energy that into various useful channels. He was bald with bushy eyebrows and I thought he was just the king of the world.

One day, Mr. Danielson called off classes for a week. He closed the blinds so the room went dark, and he said the seven most magical words in the world: *I'm going to tell you a story.* Interested? Sure we were. Fifth grade is almost too cynical to want to be told stories (like a baby) but not quite there yet. *It's going to take a week to tell it to you,* he said. *You'll come in every day and work on math or spelling for awhile to keep the administration happy and then I'll tell you this story. All day. We'll stop for recess and lunch.*

Here's the catch. You can't ever tell this story to anyone else. Not even your parents. It's a secret. You have to make the promise or, if you don't want to, I'll write you a note and you can sit in with Mr. W's class for a week. This is a pact between me the kids who are in my class. I've told this story to every class for twenty years, and no one has broken their promise yet. You won't break it either. You can talk to kids from my other years about it if you want, but no one who didn't sit in those desks can ever know.

And he told us a story. And it took a week.

I'm not going to tell you the story. I made a promise. The promises you make when you're ten are pretty much fairy-bound and sacrosanct. I'll tell you it was science fiction. I'll tell he was very good at telling it, and it never got boring or esoteric. I'll tell you he had beautiful drawings done up as slides to go with it. I'll tell you it was strange and sad and complicated, and I don't remember all of it now but I remember how good he was at every bit of the spell he was casting, at establishing this magical place where the rules of life were different for a week. Where class wasn't class and The Story was the only thing that mattered and he could insist this thing really happened, the way good storytellers always do, and we believed him.

I can't begin to express to you the effect that week had on me, and the other students, too. We'd shared in something secret that we couldn't even tell our parents, on point of grounding and/or death. We'd stopped the whole world for the sake of a story, and nothing had gone wrong. It was ok. In fact, the world was better because we knew that stories could matter like that, could make you keep a promise, could make the tedium of school stop out of the blue, and turn around and show you something so bright and strange and shimmering that you could hardly look at it. I'm sure many of them forgot that moment in the next year, but I never did.

I don't even know if you could do that kind of thing now, the way public school is set up. Would parents freak, that their kids were being taught to keep secrets by a charismatic teacher? That they weren't being taught the standardized test for a week out of the year? That something was given to the students of one teacher that wasn't given to the others, or that there was no parental approval of the contents of the tale? I suspect all those things. I also suspect that if Mr. Danielson is still teaching, he's still telling the story.

Several years later, one of my brothers was in his class and I finally got to talk to someone about The Story. I don't think the tale-telling aspect affected him as much as it did me, but the secret of it, the precious sacred space, the idea that we suddenly, at age ten, were part of a tradition, and had something that was ours, that no one could take away, hit him, too. How could it not? Can you imagine such a thing landing in your lonely adolescence, all unlooked for?

There's no one moment that made me a writer. But you'd better believe this was a foundational stone. It taught me what one person, telling a story very simply, could do to a person's heart, to their whole life.

We keep talking about publishing and ebooks and ways of communicating, how to get our stories out there, how much we fear losing the few channels we have now. And I'm worried about all that, too. But I also think about Mr. Danielson and how there are hundreds of kids who know his story and keep his secret and how special that is, how fey and lovely, and how it says to me that stories told in the dark will never stop being the very thing that people crave and need and want, stories told as if they were written and performed just for them, so that a lonely little girl could grow up to be a science fiction writer, so that a brother and sister could sit on a porch years later and open up the little secret packages buried in their hearts, and talk about the stars for awhile.

So that Mr. Danielson could create a tribe, in the midst of a difficult public school system and a rural wooded town most of us would never get out of, that is, I suppose, not so rural anymore, so that we could *be* a tribe, we could have that, know what it was like. To be tied together by a story and a promise. Participate in a rite. And know all that at a young enough age that we'd seek it out forever, wherever we went, because that kind of thing is the good stuff, and we get it so rarely in this world. I still seek it out. And if by the ridiculous magic of the Internet someone else is reading this who listened to The Story, well, we can sit for awhile and talk about it, and share that dark classroom again, listening Mr. D, the patron saint of storytellers in my own personal pantheon. Cross-legged on the green carpet, where every breath was held, waiting for the next part to begin.

As a distribution system, it's inefficient, but spectacular.

Two Kinds of Love

I think it's impossible to live with someone for years and not draw lessons from them, about the way they live and interact and express themselves.

Even if those people are dogs.

I have two: a golden retriever named Sage, and a german shepherd named Grimm. I got Sage in Japan when my ex-husband left on his first (nine-month) cruise, in order, basically, to not kill myself from loneliness. If I had to take care of something, I would probably keep going. I drove to West Virginia to get Grimm because her mother's name was Breeze, which is the name of my ex-husband's family dog, who I had known as long as I'd known him, and who had just passed away due to complications with hip dysplasia at the time. Sometimes, Breeze took better care of me than the ex did. It's been hard to have two big dogs and travel and work, but I love them so. They are my monsters, and my goofy girls, and my twin hounds at the gates of dawn.

But they are two very different creatures, and sometimes, like this morning, when I couldn't sleep and so went to curl up in the guest room and Grimm padded quietly in behind me, unwilling to be in a separate room than I, I think about how differently they express love, and what that has taught me about human love.

Sage is practically the perfect dog. She's fluffy and yellow and has no behavioral problems, but is very quirky and hilarious. You can wrestle with her and be rough with her and she will never bite back (though I have taught her literally the greatest trick ever, which is to wrinkle up her muzzle and growl when I throw horns and say: "Be Metal!"). She is patient and loves everyone. She's boisterous with affection and stares lovingly at just about everyone who comes into the house - because Sage is a bit of a free love advocate. God help you if you're male. She has a distinct gender preference. But of course we're special and she especially loves my husband Dmitri, who is like her human OTP. And what's more, everyone loves Sage. People react to her with unerring positivity. She's the All-American Dog, despite being Japanese. They cuddle her and play with her. Everything she does, even bad things, is adorable. There is a line of people waiting for this dog if we ever got it in our heads to move to Ulan Bator and had to give her up.

Grimm is almost twice as big as Sage. She doesn't really know she is, though. She whacks her front or back half on walls she thinks she's safely past, and awkwardly galumphs everywhere. Yet she's so careful and dainty and reserved. She's embarrassed of her size and awkwardness. She doesn't like to be cuddled too long, and she has opinions about her dignity. She has trouble with manners - she barks at everyone as they walk by, not to threaten! She thinks she's being neighborly. But people leap back from her in terror. She's absolutely beautiful - but she looks like a wolf. People are afraid of her, even though she's so sweet and would never bite anyone. People react to her with worry and fear, and no one asks to pet her when we walk her. It pains me that she is so often the ignored one, or avoided, because she's just about the best dog ever. She quietly moves through the house to be wherever I am, and positions herself between me and any door, the better to guard me, and when Dmitri tickles me, she gets worried that I'm hurt, and howls and nips his feet till he stops. When we took her to the ocean, she came into the sea when I led her, but was not impressed, and once she was out was beside herself with anxiety that I was not with her, but was *swimming around in it OMG.*

Sage's love is easy to recognize. It's universal. She's happy and fuzzy and cute. Grimm's is harder. She's wolfish and sometimes aloof and doesn't always know what to do in social situations. People look at her and are sure she's mean. She doesn't do hilarious tricks and you can't wrestle with her, she's too big and GSDs can be fragile - and it just worries her that you want to fight. (She is utterly convinced of my dominance, and doesn't see why we have to have it out again. When she misbehaves she instantly rolls over to show me her throat. This is because the first day I brought both dogs home, I flipped them on their backs and put my teeth on their throat and growled. Later, Rinse, Repeat, Alpha.)

Grimmy is a lot like me. People judge from a distance, think that because I bark loudly I'm mean and angry and by my nature unkind. Because I am awkward and toothy and often weird. I'm not a golden retriever. My love is not very fuzzy, until you get past the wolfish exterior. I've had Sage lovers and Grimm lovers and boy, the Grimm kind is always harder. It's so easy to love a Sage. They return everything you give them instantly, photogenically. They're awesome, and fun, and a balm to someone neurotic like me who is always convinced no one really likes them. Dmitri and Sage get on like houses for a reason, though of course the analogy isn't perfect.

And yet, when I woke up this morning, it was Grimm who was curled up by the guest bed, determined not to spend a single night away from me, quietly, gently, showing her loyalty and love and protection. I knew she was there without even opening my eyes. I stretched out my hand with them still closed, and without any word being spoken, she got up and put her head in my hand.

Then I went and tackled Sage and we wrestled.

The world is not divided into two kinds of love. But sometimes my house is. And both are real and true and whenever I look at Grimm I promise myself to try to see the wolfy love of people I know who do not seem fuzzy and bouncy or boisterous in their affections - because I do not. Because my love is not easy or cute and people miss it, a lot. But in the end, I'll always be there in the morning, putting my head in your hands.

My Country, 'Tis of Thee

I lived in Ohio for several years, and I currently live in Maine. These places have a strange and furtive relationship with themselves: they remember what they used to be, and *they can't let it go*. They look into a mirror and see a booming, industrial paradise where they all had jobs - factory jobs but jobs. The mills and yards, be they textile, steel, or ship, ruled the world. They look out the window and see a wasteland.

I listen to stories of the steel mills in Youngstown, car manufacturing in Detroit and Cleveland, shipping in Portland, textiles in Massachusetts. How it used to be, when unions mattered and whole cities were devoted to single products. Whole cities that were lively, economically viable, and productive (so they tell me). Sure, crime was an issue (it still is) the environmental wreckage was severe (it still is) the big companies who invented these towns to be their personal cattle ranches often despised and exploited workers (sound familiar?) and the work often sucked (it still does), but these cities were built on hope and economic booms, and there was a time when they worked as units in the whole. Many, many Americans believe that time was the best it ever was.

I can't even imagine this America.

It seems like a fairy tale to me. For the entire duration of my life, it's been the Rust Belt, not the Steel Belt. Youngstown has been an abandoned disaster. Cleveland has been struggling to survive, Portland has been a dying waterfront, one of the last that has not been turned into a tourist trap, the cod is gone, the lobster is slowly dwindling, and the haddock is deeply overfished. This is the world I know, the world *as it has always been*, for me. I don't understand any idea of these cities that features whole, inhabited buildings, bustling downtowns, factories, people talking about things other than being out of work.

It's like when older writers bitterly tell me about the collapse of the distribution network, and how things used to be, and how maybe it'll come back someday, and they'll start selling their novels in drug stores checkout lanes again. I nod sympathetically and pretend I commiserate, but really, I'm thinking:

They used to sell *novels* in *drug stores*?

Like, not just Stephen King, *Twilight* and a shelf full of romance? Did they sell unicorns, too?

I just can't even imagine a world where a standard print run was 100k books and bookstores hadn't yet caught on to their draconian returns policy. I can't imagine being able to stay with one editor/publisher for your entire career. I can't be bitter that it's gone, *I never knew the world could be organized like that*. Ever since I transmogrified into a thinking adult, everything has been broken, every system degenerated. Hell, the tech bubble had burst before I was a sophomore in college. The cod was in crisis in Maine, Nova Scotia, Newfoundland, long before I was even born.

The world I live in is full of abandoned houses with broken windows, and towns that long for the steel mills like a lover who has abandoned them, *book-stores that don't even really sell books, work a talismanic thing. If I could only get work. If I could just work.*

But the steel mills aren't coming back. People my age, we sit and listen and nod, but we know the world is never going to look like that again, and we can't feel the tragedy of it, we can't feel the outrage, entitlement, hopelessness, bitterness of it, because we just weren't there when all the machinery worked. We assume we'll be out of work pretty frequently in our lives, that everything we own will be made outside the country, that if we're damn lucky, we'll hop mortgages and jobs and marriages and editors and publishers like beads of water on a skillet until we die. We know we probably aren't getting Social Security no matter what happens.

We grew up expecting to get screwed.

Trouble is, the world still wants us to act like that other universe of productivity and permanence exists. Sign up for this 30-year mortgage! Explain why you've moved so much, clearly that's the sign of a dilettante! Pay into a hundred programs of which you will never see the benefit. Commit to this job with all your heart and soul, make it your whole identity, despite the fact that we'll lay you off in a few years. But don't even think about forming a union, or you'll be fired.

Did you know that the phrases "laid off" and "downsizing" came into wide use only within my lifetime? *They didn't used to even have words for this shit.*

So. Welcome to the New World. Some of us didn't know there was an Old World. But we all have to live in this one. We'll figure it out. We'll create de-centered systems and wide social nets to catch each other and become nimble and versatile enough to hold a dozen and more jobs, a couple of marriages, a heaping pile of rental houses and a couple of home start-up companies in a lifetime and not be depressed about it. But until the people who keep hollering at us that their mythical five minutes in American history is coming back, those precious moments after the robber-barons but before those fucking hippies ruined everything, their pink candy-castle America of contented industrial towns, endless cod, 30-year mortgages, and benevolent steel mills, *just you wait,* until those people die off, the genuine new paradigm of how to live and thrive in this new world is just sitting at the bus station, waiting for a ride.

Descent Into Cleveland

There was a poet who lived in Cleveland once named d.a. levy. He was kind of a local Ginsberg back in the day, where the day equals the ever-present Sixties. He was political, radical, modernist edging on the postmodern, stream of consciousness, fire in the belly. I'm not a huge fan of his work, but I'm compelled by it because so much of it deals with his home city, a place where I lived for several years. Cleveland has had so few home-bred bards. He killed himself, too, which seems to be a thing one always remembers to say about poets, as though the fact of suicide is as important as anything else they ever did. He also went through a court obscenity battle that was moderately well-known - the Big G came out from San Francisco for the trial.

If poets were still local heroes, he'd be one, even many years dead. A friend of his wrote a book with the title *Descent Into Cleveland*, which you had to know I'd pick up in the store, mostly about his own fascination with levy (lowercase is by preference of the poet) and the pair's Milleresque adventures in Cleveland - they were so sure it would become the San Francisco of the heartland, so sure they could make it a Mecca of art and poetry. "I have a city to cover in pages," levy (quasi-) famously said. Quite so.

Now levy is dead and Solomon, who wrote *Descent*, is living in Northern California, and who is the great light of Cleveland now? Who will cover that city in pages?

I learned the city bit by bit when I lived there. I learned what it was before the familiar late twentieth century ghouls of gentrification and public safety descended - both the good and the bad. Coventry is lovely, but from what I have heard it was probably more interesting before. The Flats were horrific tenement - occasionally actual tents - housing and are now trendy bars and lofts. There was almost a war over iron shipping on the Cuyahoga between the east side and the west side of the city, which seems to be carried on by a dogged, good-natured animosity between the two to this day. There is a mall on the west side which has a nineteenth century graveyard in the middle of the parking lot. The river burned here once - the water so polluted it burned for days. There is a city called Chagrin, and I live in it. There is a waterfall there; there are wild strawberries. The restaurants offer fish specials during Lent. And there is Erie, always Erie, and the snow comes blowing in off of the lake.

I was never the poet Cleveland wanted. I was not born there - I could only see it through an outsider's eyes. I could only see it with California tugging at my sleeve. But I thought I could feel it mourning for levy, not because he was the greatest poet who ever lived - he emphatically was not - but because he was the minstrel of the burning river, and this city bore him, bred him, loved him, cursed him, and killed him. He belonged to that place. I read his work and I looked into the dark and the snow and the snaking freeways and tentatively wanted to love this place - oh, I dis love it, I was happy there, but there is a love between human and city which dares not speak its name, and I never quite became intimate with Cleveland. I felt a concrete back turned to the girl from the blue Pacific and the green palms. *You are not serious enough to love me*, she said. *You will break my heart and move on to a flashier place.*

And I suppose I did.

I think of Cleveland as a middle-aged woman with a very aristocratic nose and shakily-applied eyeliner in a thick brown coat with patches at the elbows. Her hair is always in her face. She wears impractical shoes, but she won't give them up. Her skirt is dark, expensive Irish wool, ironed and crisp; her blue shirt is untucked and sweat-stained, a foundry-worker's nametag blazing on the breast. She stumbles sometimes, when she has had a lot to drink, but often she walks in a straight line, her face set and proud, her eyes very blue and clear, bluer and clearer than anyone thought they would be at her age.

levy never left me, she says. *I wouldn't let him.*

She knew better than to think I'd stay, so she would never let me up to see her apartment, she wouldn't let me cover her in pages. That's not her kink any-more, she sniffs. But I tried. I was persistent. And she knew how much I love the snow.

There is a zen to the Midwest. Like any, it requires patience and practice to learn it. Breathe in - the lake frozen white. Breathe out - the fire thrown into the night sky by the oil refinery. Breathe in - a doe at your window. Breathe out - a poet killed himself less than ten miles from where I sit, and he never turned his city into the place he wanted it to be.

Once I told my mother that I was terribly disappointed that Cleveland was just the name of a man. It had seemed so much deeper a word to me.

"Cleave-land. It should mean the cloven land," I protested.

"Or the land you cleave to," she said.

Breathe in - the city. Breathe out - cleave.

Awesome

I have noticed something lately.

That something is the word "awesome."

I just used it three times in one email. I hear it constantly, more than when I was a kid and had a hot pink bathing-suit that said *awesome* across my non-existent boobs. Such and such is made of awesome. So and so is full of awesome. It is my goal to become more awesome. Awesome, awesome, awesome.

At first I was irritated - can I not branch out in my adjective-use? Why am I doing this? What the freaking hell?

But the other night while we and I were brushing our teeth and getting ready for bed, which has become a nice moment of quiet conversation as we switch off sink use, I started babbling about how ubiquitous awesome has become.

And I realized that when I say ubiquitous I mean ubiquitous among the online community, my friends, my colleagues - who are all geeks of one stripe or another. There was a point in my life when I was the nerd among mainstream people, and that time is no more.

And we, geeks and nerds and bloggers, are using it to mean something different than just a synonym for "great." We're using it to mean *arete*.

Yes! The classicist strikes again! But it's true. We have altered the meaning with usage, which is how language rolls.

More awesome. Full of awesome. Made of awesome.

We're using it as a noun, as a word for excellence, for personal excellence exercised in daily life, whatever is our own awesomeness, our own skills, our own passions, even if they are small, housecleaning or debugging or patching jeans. We did it with awesome, and were awesome because of it. We are using the word that means the greatest thing Achilles can achieve for himself for the greatest things we can achieve. And when someone at a con says that she is questing to become more awesome, that's what she means: more perfectly herself, more precisely and intensely involved in everything she does, doing what she does in the best and most fabulous way it can be done, more hardcore, more awesome. We are awesome, you are awesome, they are awesome.

We are using a new word to mean a very old, very beautiful thing, and we use it over and over because it resonates, not that word necessarily, but that *meaning*. That need to be perfectly oneself. *Arete. Aresteia.* We are telling each other how to do it, when we've managed it, how we hope to reach it in days and years to come. We are pointing to things great and small and saying something a Greek thing with an English word, and it has become meaningful, it has become part of the vocabulary of the virtual world.

And that... is *awesome*.

Credits

Publisher / Editor-in-Chief
Lars Pearson

Design Manager / Senior Editor
Christa Dickson

Associate Editor
Joshua Wilson

Designer (Indistinguishable from Magic)
Matt Dirkx

The publisher wishes to thank... Cat, not just for her ability to write books that are lightning in a bottle, but for her repeated habit of birthing blog entries so fully formed, they put most Internet commentators to shame (God, I wish I had half her talent); Seanan McGuire, for providing such an elegant introduction for this collection (God, I wish I had half her talent too); Amy Houser, for the evocative cover; Christa Dickson; Matt Dirkx; Shawne Kleckner; Robert Smith?; and that nice lady who sends me newspaper articles.

1150 46th Street
Des Moines, Iowa 50311
madnorwegian@gmail.com
www.madnorwegian.com
And please join the Mad Norwegian Press group on Facebook!